AT 90.

SKETCHES

OF

BORDER ADVENTURES

IN

THE LIFE AND TIMES

OF

MAJOR MOSES VANCAMPEN.

BY HIS GRANDSON

J. NILES HUBBARD,

AUTHOR OF RED JACKET AND HIS PEOPLE.

EDITION OF 1842.

REVISED AND ENLARGED BY

THE AUTHOR.

EDITED BY

JOHN S. MINARD

New preface by Stephanie R. Zebrowski.
New illustrations by Dennis D. McKibben.

CONCLUDING WITH A

BIOGRAPHICAL SKETCH

OF THE LATE

JUDGE PHILLIP CHURCH.

ILLUSTRATED.

PUBLISHED BY ZEBROWSKI HISTORICAL SERVICES AND PUBLISHING CO.
JERSEY SHORE, PA
1992

Copyright © 1992 by Zebrowski Historical Services and Publishing Company

All rights reserved. Permission to reproduce in any form must be secured in writing from the publisher.

Second edition originally published Fillmore, NY, 1893
Reprinted Jersey Shore, PA, 1992

PLEASE DIRECT ALL CORRESPONDENCE AND BOOK ORDERS TO:
ZEBROWSKI HISTORICAL SERVICES AND PUBLISHING CO.
R.R. 1, BOX 400
JERSEY SHORE, PA 17740

Library of Congress Catalog Number 91-68579
ISBN 1-880-484-03-X

Printed in the United States of America

DEDICATION.

TO THE MEMORY OF

THE BORDER MEN

OF THE

AMERICAN REVOLUTION,

whose Valiant Services contributed so largely
to the success of the Continental Armies,
and resulting independence of

OUR COUNTRY;

and who later, armed with that
"Wondrous Instrument,"
the Axe, opened our
dark and silent forests for the

LIGHT OF CIVILIZATION,

and the

GLORIOUS ARTS OF PEACE.

This story of the strangely eventful life of one of the
bravest of their number, and sketch of one of the

MOST DISTINGUISHED OF PIONEERS,

is respectfully inscribed.

Fillmore, *N. Y.*, March 6, 1893.   J. S. M.

PREFACE TO THE REPRINT EDITION

In the preface to the First Edition of this work, editor J.S. Minard wrote that only "slight notices" had been given those whose names do not figure prominently in the historic annals of the American Revolution. Yet, it was the support, the carrying out of missions of "extreme danger," the fortitude and courage of those who have been described as the ordinary frontier settlers who held the land, who peopled the armies, and scouted the forests and enemy camps. Men of the likes of Moses Van Campen have long been the unsung heros of such events.

It is in recognition of this fact that the trend amongst museum professionals and historians had finally turned toward the recognition of those lesser known because they lacked the social and financial standing formerly believed necessary to number them among the prominent. It is with democratic maturity that they are now receiving their due and our concept of hero is changing.

Moses Van Campen was, by all accounts, a hero among men. His daring, intelligence, fortitude, and bravery in the face of all he endured for his family, his neighbors, and country is the stuff from which legends are made. His grandson and author of this volume, J. Niles Hubbard, grew up a witness to the steady stream of visitors, old foes, and comrades who corraborated his grandfather's stories. Accounts of Moses Van Campen are to be found in the *Pennsylvania Archives* and in numerous histories. And yet, he has not been memorialized as have the more prominent citizens of the Revolution.

That Moses Van Campen is a heroic frontier figure was but one factor in the choice to republish this book. Hubbard framed his accounts of his Grandfather's life with an accurate history of the events surrounding Van Campen's life and times thus putting his Grandfather's life into recognizable perspective.

The Van Campen family, Dutch New Jersey settlers, migrated first to Northampton County, Pennsylvania, " a little above what was called the Water Gap." Soon after young Moses' sixteenth birthday, Van Campen's father and uncle purchased land in the Wyoming Valley, an area known to Pennsylvanians as the "most beautiful land in the world." Cornelius Van Campen soon reconsidered his decision as the land dispute between Connecticut and Pennsylvania intensified. In 1773 he purchased a tract of land eight miles above the junction of Fishing Creek and the Susquehanna River where he and his young son Moses began to clear the land for a new farm. The door to adventure and the annals of history had been opened.

The pages of this volume contain the events of Van Campen's life from his first shot to his foray into battle as a part of Colonel Plunkett's expedition to remove the Connecticut settlers from the Wyoming Valley, his association with Colonel Kelley, the building of Wheeler's Fort, and the capture of a band of Tories masquerading as Indians which nearly cost him his life. Hubbard has also furnished us with a full and accurate account of the Battle of Wyoming and the unusual first-hand account of the escape of Lebbeus Hammond from the Death Circle of Queen Esther. Quartermaster for Sullivan's army, Van Campen also served as Sullivan's handpicked scout and ventured amongst the Indian camps dressed as one of their own. He built McClure's Fort on Fishing Creek and rebuilt Fort Muncy in 1787. Captured by the British in the same year, his account of the British among the Indians is as entertaining as it is historically interesting. The fact that British officers prevented his certain death at the hands of the followers of Chief John Mohawk, by providing guards and spiriting him away to Montreal when it would have benefitted their relations with the Indians to turn him over, is proof of the esteem in which he was held by friend and foe alike.

Van Campen, no doubt like many other frontier settlers had, before the years of hostility, made friends with the Indians, learned to hunt and to understand his forested environment. He respected their civilization, describing them as "considerably removed from barbarism" and partakers of the "order which characterizes more civilized communities." This is perhaps why, for many years after hostilities had ceased, so many of his most ardent foes, Chief John Mohawk and Shongo among them, visited him at his home in Angelica, New York, while his Grandson listened at his knee.

Though this volume contains within its pages one of the great adventure stories of the American Revolution, Van Campen used it as a vehicle to correct inaccuracies he found in the historical accounts given by others. He minces no words, for in most instances he had been an active participant, a witness to the event.

Moses Van Campen was a man of integrity, a practical joker, knowledgeable and intelligent, brave almost beyond belief. He was certainly one of the many "minor officers" who played a major role in the events that civilized the American Frontier.

As you read the Editor's Preface you will note that J.S. Minard credits the illustrations of Van Campen's encounter with Chief John Mohawk and the running of the gauntlet at Caneadea to a Mrs. A.R. Dodd. Not sharing Mr. Minard's polite opinion of the illustrations thusly furnished, I commissioned artist Dennis D. McKibben to provide new illustrations which are historically accurate. The fact that they are more aesthetically pleasing can only contribute to the value of this volume.

STEPHANIE R. ZEBROWSKI
Jersey Shore, PA, 1992

EDITOR'S PREFACE.

Well do I remember, when but a school-boy, along in the forties, the last years of the era of log school houses, my frequent visits to the School District Library to make selection of books for study and recreation.

There, side by side, with Rollin, and Gibbon, and Dick, and other venerable tomes, were found Weem's Franklin, Wirt's Patrick Henry, the adventures of Daniel Boone, the great hunter, Indian fighter, and pioneer of Kentucky, a book devoted to the story of Gen. Francis Marion, and the last to name, but by no means the least sought for, a substantial leather bound book, which showed most conclusive evidence of use : The Life of Major Moses Van Campen. It was not, however, always to be found when sought for; indeed, it was quite generally out.

In course of time a decadence of interest in the old School Libraries followed, owing largely no doubt, to the very general diffusion of literature in the way of papers, magazines and periodicals, and later on, the old book disappeared in some mysterious way, and was rarely, if ever, more seen. The Van Campen book always possessed a peculiar charm for me; mainly perhaps, for the reason that some of the incidents and exploits narrated therein, occurred within the limits of my own county, and also, from the fact that the hero I so much admired, actually lived, and moved, and had his being, right here in "Grand Old Allegany," and was known by, and really had dealings, and personal acquaintance with, our people.

These considerations commended the book to my youthful mind, and invested the story of his life with an interest which no other book in that old library could excite.

Some time since, one of the venerable old treasures came under my observation. Its covers were gone, as were also its first and last leaves. It was soiled, worn, torn, begrimmed and dirty; in a sorry plight indeed. It started, however, a train of thought, reviving most vividly the memory of my boyhood's happy days. I perused its pages (what there were left of them), and the old time interest was awakened, and with this revival of interest came the thought that the old book, I had prized so highly when a boy, was worthy of being reprinted and rounded off with some additional chapters devoted to his later years, and perhaps some incidents not known when the old book was put out, and the more I considered the, matter the more I became convinced that it would be a very proper thing to do.

I consulted with friends, for whose judgment in such things I have great respect, and they were unanimous in opinion as to the propriety of such an enterprise.

Inquiry for the family or decendants of J. N. Hubbard, the grandson, who wrote this book, was at once commenced. My impression was that he was dead. One to whom I directed my questions was negligent in answering; another was sick and could not, and so from various causes my effort in that direction was for a time fruitless.

I had, however, resolved to undertake the work, and carry it to completion, if it should be encouraged by subscriptions sufficient to warrant its publication. So, equipped with the old book referred to, and a picture of Major Van Campen, cut from an old Scribner's Magazine, I made the experiment of a preliminary canvass, and was agreeably surprised at the alacrity with which people subscribed.

Pursuing the canvass, mainly in my own town, I soon had a list of three hundred names, when a friend informed me that Mr. Hubbard was still living, and resided in Tracy, California. Correspondence was opened with him at once, and soon was revealed the fact, that yielding to the importunities of eastern friends, he had devoted a considerable part of the Winter (1891-2) and Spring to a revision of the old book, adding to, and improving it generally, with a view to republication.

The exchange of a few more letters, and the intervention of a "mutual friend," resulted in Mr. Hubbard's abandonment of the enterprise of republication, and the turning over to me of all of his manuscript, as well as original data pertaining to the last years of his grandfather, and so, supplementing his work (which comprises the first twenty chapters), with five chapters, bringing his life down to its close in 1849, I have gone on with the work.

This discovery, correspondence, and resulting arrangement, though it has somewhat delayed the publication, has, it is confidently believed, given to the public a better book, and more general satisfaction.

In making proper acknowledgment for assistance in the prosecution of the enterprise, I desire, first of all, to express my obligation to Mr. Hubbard, to whom I am largely indebted, and who has been so wonderfully favored with a long life of usefulness, drawn out to considerably more than the alloted "threescore years and ten," and enabled, after the lapse of over half a century, to devote himself to the revision of his old book, which is indeed remarkable.

In the matter of illustrations I must thank Mrs. A. R. Dodd, late of Houghton, N. Y., for kindly favoring me with the two designs: "Running the Gauntlet," and "The Encounter with Mohawk," and express my opinion (which I find quite generally shared), that they are historically correct; in other words, that they agree exactly with a strict and literal interpretation of the text.

The Hon. Wm. P. Letchworth kindly furnished the photographs from which were obtained the fine halftones of the "Old Council House," and "The Site of the Old Indian Village of Caneadea," (Gah-ah-yah-de-o).

Moses Burr, Esq., of Angelica, a grandson of Major Van Campen, favored me with the compass, Jacob-staff, rifle, powder horn, etc., from which was obtained the beautiful picture which makes such a pleasant memento of his grandfather.

To Major Richard Church, I wish to express my thanks for the loan of the "Book of Surveys," from which was obtained the *fac simile* of the Major's work in his ninety-first year, regarded by many as, in some respects, the finest illustration in the book; also for the excellent miniature of his father, the late Judge Philip

Church, by the world renowned artist Fagnani. The fine half-tone picture of this historic likeness, accompanies the Biographical Sketch of the Judge, which it is thought is appropriately introduced in this connection, for the reason of his long and intimate relations, and close business associations with Major Van Campen, as well as, for the other reason, of his acknowledged prominence as a pioneer of Western New York. Major Church has rendered much other valuable assistance, and his courteous treatment in kindly allowing access to very valuable manuscripts and papers will ever be pleasantly remembered.

E. D. Barnum, Esq., lately and for several years the owner and occupant of "The Old Van Campen Place," has my thanks for the fine photo from which was obtained the beautiful half-tone of that historic old home.

To Mr. John B. Chnrch, of Geneva, I am under obligations for valuable assistance and timely suggestions.

To George H. Harris, Esq., of Rochcster, N. Y., a kind friend and helpful advisor from the outset, my special obligations should be thankfully acknowledged, for the loan of the photo of the "Historic Hatchet," from which was obtained the full page half-tone engraving of the same, and also for the valued privilege of making excerpts from his forth-coming interesting "Life History of Horatio Jones," which give the history of the hatchet, and throw additional light on an important event in Van Campen's life.

It was the original intention to have devoted the number of pages necessary, for a list of the subscribers to the first 1,000 copies, and was so set forth in one of my circulars, and I have to a few persons so stated. Finding, however, that the book has grown into larger proportions than was at first anticipated or designed, and feeling that the space which it would have been necessary to have devoted to such a list (some sixteen pages at least), has been much better employed, and that all will say so when they see it, I shall beg to be excused from inserting the list.

And so at last, without any claim to literary merit or excellence on my part, with a deep sense of obligation for generous support and encouragement, this little book is launched upon the public, with a hopeful trust that it will revive such an interest in the Life and Adventures of Moses Van Campen, as will keep green for a long time to come the memory of a distinguished historical character, and also impress upon the youth of our land a higher estimate of the services rendered, the struggles, hardships, sufferings and privations, endured by those patriotic and determined frontiersmen of the Revolution, to whom, under God, we are so largely indebted for the rich inheritance of popular and personal liberty we now enjoy.

JNO. S. MINARD.

Fillmore, N. Y., March, 1893.

PREFACE TO THE EDITION OF 1892.

Half a century has passed by since an unpretending little volume, entitled, "Life and Times of Major Moses Van Campen," was presented to the public.

A large edition was printed and sold, but for many years it has been out of the market. The Author at different times has been requested to publish another edition, but various things have hindered until more recently.

When considerable progress had been made in the work of revision, his attention was called to the fact that the book was about to be published by Jno. S. Minard, of Fillmore, N. Y. The length of time that had intervened, and the supposition that the Author was not living, led to the prosecution of the undertaking, until it seemed desirable to carry it forward to completion.

Through the interposition of a friend, who thought the public might be better served by bringing our work together, a satisfactory arrangement has been made to this effect, and the present issue combines the labor of the two persons, J. N. Hubbard of Tracy, California, and Jno. S. Minard of Fillmore, N. Y.

PREFACE TO THE FIRST EDITION.

It may, perhaps, be due to the reader to state some of the reasons why another book should make its appearance in public, to claim a share of the attention which is paid to whatever is new.

The Author will render his excuse in due form, and present also the authority upon which rests most of the facts recorded in this book.

Major Moses Van Campen, the subject of this memoir, has long been known by many in this part of the State, and by many also in the State of Pennsylvania, as one who took an active part in the struggles which gave birth to our National Independence.

Especially is he known for the severe encounters he has had with the Indians, and for the hardships which he has endured in watching for this wary foe, as he made his sudden and fearful incursions upon what were called the border settlements.

The service which he has thus rendered his country as a soldier, entitles his name to some remembrance among a free and grateful people. But this claim is not presented as a reason for making this offering to the public. It is rather in compliance with the wishes of friends, who have been desirous to preserve some record of the events which are here recorded.

Some apology for this work might be gathered too, from considering the fact, that, while the leading events of the Revolution have been recorded in their proper order, and due credit has been given to those whose office gave them a prominent place in the eye of the public, slight notices only have been made of the services rendered by minor officers, who have held posts of extreme danger and have acquitted themselves in such a manner as to impart dignity to American arms. It is but just that these also should receive the honor which is their due, while our countrymen shall hold in sacred remembrance the deeds of those, who, fired with the holy zeal of liberty, have periled their all in the decision of the single question which has resulted in one of the freest and happiest nations that our earth has ever beheld. So far as the following pages may accomplish this design, the Author hopes that it will receive the approbation of the public.

Another reason for submitting these pages to the press arises from the hope that they may give some new interest to the history of our border warfare, and thus prove to be of permanent benefit, by adding one more chapter to those that have already been written, which shall exhibit in a slight degree, a few of the hardships and sufferings which were undergone by those who were engaged in the struggles of the Revolution.

The materials of this memoir have been gathered almost entirely from him who is its subject, and the credibility of those facts which rest entirely upon his own authority, none will question, who are acquainted in the least with his character.

One word in this place about the chapter which has been introduced, giving a brief sketch of the causes which led to the war of the Revolution. Some may think it altogether unnecessary, and others, perhaps, presumptous, that a youth should undertake a task to which the knowledge and experience which belongs to age is only equal. It was written at the suggestion of Major Van Campen, under the impression that many would read this book to whom such a review would be useful. Yet the Author would say in reference to this, and indeed the whole work, that it is given to the public with a feeling of unaffected diffidence, and it is only from the encouragement of those who have examined parts of his manuscript, that he dares submit it to the press.

Dansville, August, 1841.

Strongly surmising that the readers of this book would be pleased to know just a little, if not more, about the man who first brought out the Van Campen book, and has survived for over half a century since, retaining his powers and falculties in so remarkable a degree, the editor on his own motion ventures, right here, the following necessarily brief sketch drawn from data quietly drawn from Mr. Hubbard, during quite an extensive correspondence.

John Niles Hubbard was born in the old Van Campen home at Angelica, N. Y., August 27th, 1815. He fitted for college at the Canandaigua Academy, a school of considerable renown in those days, and entered the Freshman Class at Yale in September, 1835, graduating

PREFACE TO FIRST EDITION. XV

with honor in 1839. Soon after, determining to enter the ministry, he applied himself to the study of theology, and commenced preaching in 1842, his first settlement being at Hannibal, Oswego Co., N. Y.

February 18th, 1845, he was united in marriage with Miss Margaret McDougal, of Sterling, Cayuga Co., N. Y. After serving the congregation of Hannibal for eleven years, he received a call from Dansville, Livingston, Co., N. Y., where he remained four years, when a diseased throat made imperative a rest from public service. This rest from public speaking continued for six months, when his throat having regained its normal healthy condition, he afterwards preached at Belmont and Friendship, Allegany Co., N. Y., until 1861.

He was then re-called to Hannibal, and remained their pastor for six years, when a request to visit California was entertained, and during the last twenty-five years his time has mostly been given to feeble churches in that State, the larger portion of the time having Tracy as a centre.

From his labors in school houses, churches have grown up, new towns have appeared, and the region supplied by his labors, has been marked by changes of a hopeful character.

Scarce any impairment of his ability is discernable in his writing, and judging only from his correspondence, he is good for years yet to come. May those years be spared to him.

J. S. M.

February 20th, 1893.

CONTENTS.

CHAPTER I.

Van Campen's birth—Family connections—Removal to Pennsylvania—Early recollections—Nicholas Depew—School-boy experiences—First trial of a gun—Habits of the people of his time—Shooting a deer—How disposed of. P. 1.

CHAPTER II.

Hunting excursion—Successful shot—Experience in boating—Ancedote of "Old Simon"—Trouble in Wyoming Valley—His acquaintance with Tom Shenap—Col. Plunket's expedition. P. 12.

CHAPTER III.

England's supremacy in America—Stamp Act—Opposed first in Virginia—Resolutions of Patrick Henry—Colonies united in their opposition—Preparations for war—Van Campen enlists in the army—Resolves to defend the frontier settlements. P. 22.

CHAPTER IV.

Van Campen's entrance on the life of a soldier—The Six Nations decide to engage in the war—Settlements guarded by scouting parties— Deficient in supplies—Notice of the campaigns of '77—Adventure at Reid's Fort. P. 30.

CHAPTER V.

Great Indian Confederacy at the West—Meeting of Major Rogers with Pontiak—Pontiak invited to meet Commissions in council—Indian invasion and captures—Great alarm—Indian ambuscade—Indian strategy—Demand to surrender the fort—Refused to comply—Effort to capture—Its failure. P. 40.

CHAPTER VI.

Hostilities in 1778—Van Campen appointed Lieutenant—Ordered to build a fort on Fishing Creek—Indians approach the border settlements—Alarm—Inhabitants gather at Fort Wheeler—Houses burned—Successful defense—Unexpected visit—Van Campen ordered to capture troublesome Tories. P. 47.

CONTENTS. xvii

CHAPTER VII.

Valley of Wyoming—Its invasion anticipated—How discovered—Preparations for defense—Decision to meet the enemy—The Battle—Defeat—Scenes after the battle—Escape of Lebbeus Hammond—Adoption of Samuel Carey. P. 57.

CHAPTER VIII.

Result of the battle of Wyoming—Scattering of forces—Surrender of Fort Forty—Terms—Possession given—Indians lawless—Removal of some of the settlements on the Delaware—Surrender of Fort Wyoming—Van Campen's return to Northumberland—Ordered to Fort Wheeler—Lancaster men act as scouts—Comical experience—Van Campen and Salmon make a trip in disguise—Meet with men on their way—Col. Hartley's expedition. P. 71.

CHAPTER IX.

Gen. Washington's plan of protecting the frontier—Gen. McIntosh ordered to Sandusky—Col. Clark looks after the Indians in Illinois—Surprises Kaskaskia and other Indian towns—Illinois erected into a county—Gov. Hamilton, of Detroit, resolves to capture Col. Clark—Occupies Fort Vincent on the way—Sends parties to annoy settlements—Col. Clark endeavors to reconcile the Indians—Preparations to receive Gov. Hamilton—Information given by a Spanish merchant—Col. Clark's plans changed—Expedition against Fort Vincent—Fort reduced—Gov. Hamilton taken captive—Sent to Virginia—Gen. McIntosh's expedition—Builds Fort Laurens—Indian strategy, P. 85.

CHAPTER X.

Invasion of Indian country—The Six Nations—Gen. Sullivan's campaign—Gathering at Wyoming—March to Tioga Point—Joined by Gen. Clinton—Trouble from Indians—Van Campen sent to the Indian camp—Leads advance guard—Indian ambuscade—Gen. Clinton joins Gen. Sullivan—Great flood without rain—Indians risk an engagement—Battle at New Town Point—Indian visit—Interesting meeting of Van Campen and Shongo at Angelica, long after the war. "*Co-waugh,*" "*I same Indian.*" P. 94.

CHAPTER XI.

Effect of the Battle of New Town—Destruction of Indian villages—Route taken by Sullivan—Catharine's Town—Pass by Seneca Lake—Kanadaseaga—Honeoye—Connissius Lake—Oneida Indians—Taken captive—Brother's address—Comparison—Cruel death of Lieut. Boyd. P. 113.

CONTENTS.

CHAPTER XII.

View of Northumberland—Hopes of its early projectors—Names of historic interest—Boyd's family—Thomas Boyd—His burial—Close of Sullivan's campaign—His return—Spring of 1780—Capture of Bennett and Hammond—Their escape. P. 129.

CHAPTER XIII.

Van Campen taken prisoner by the Indians—His father and brother killed—A fresh cause of alarm—Van Campen's thoughts of escape—Consults with his fellow prisoners—Plans arranged—Success—Encounter with Mohawk—Young Rogers—Capture of Capt. Harper—Van Campen builds a raft—His party sets out for Wyoming—Arrive in safety. P. 140.

CHAPTER XIV.

Van Campen comes to Fort Jenkins—And meets with Col. Kelly—Interview with his mother—Col. Kelly's devotion to the cause of his country—Notice of Capt. Salmon—Chosen Col. of militia—Van Campen chosen major. P. 174.

CHAPTER XV.

Catawissa and Bloomsburg—Dangerous inhabitants—Settlements contrasted—Favorable situation—Testimony—Demonstration against treasonable inhabitants—Capt. Klader to assist—Coming of British and Indians—Attack on Fort Rice—Design to intercept Capt. Klader—Situation at Scotch settlement—Sugar Loaf massacre—Burial of the dead—Capt. Robison sent against Tory settlements—Van Campen and Salmon surprise the inhabitants—Their capture—Taken to Northumberland—Agree to leave the country. P. 182.

CHAPTER XVI.

Opening of the year 1781—Van Campen receives the office of Lieutenant—Builds a fort—Incident—Alarm—Scouting party—Surprise a company of savages—Return of the scout—Care of Hessian prisoners—False alarm—Court-martial. P. 197.

CHAPTER XVII.

Spring of 1782—Lieut. Van Campen goes to Northumberland—With Capt. Robison repairs Fort Muncy—Heads a scouting party—Discovered by Lieut. Nellis' band of Indians—Attack—Defense—Overcome by a superior force—Scene after defeat—Saves the life of one of his men—Critical situation. P. 210.

CONTENTS. xix

CHAPTER XVIII.

Come near an Indian village—*Ga-ah-yah-de-o* (Caneadea)—Running the gauntlet—Exciting scene—Introduced to Capt. Nellis, the father—Dinner party—Indian dances—Van Campen takes a partner—Dispute between young Nellis and Doxtater. P. 230.

CHAPTER XIX.

Continuation of the year 1782—Van Campen is adopted into the family of Col. Butler—The Indians make a discovery—Seek to obtain possession of him—He is sent to Montreal—Scenes in prison—Sent to New York, and returns to his friends on parole. P. 244.

CHAPTER XX.

Van Campen returns to the service of his country in the Spring of 1783—Takes charge of Wilkesbarre Fort—Leads a party to intercept the Indians in pursuit of plunder—Interesting meeting with "Indian Allen"—Retires from the service—Close of the war—Note to the reader. P. 267.

CHAPTER XXI.

December 10, 1783, marries Margaret McClure—Assumes the management of the McClure estate—Removes to the "Briar Creek" neighborhood—Disposes of the "Briar Creek" property—Gift to a religious society—Migrates to what is now Almond, Allegany County, N. Y.—Journey thither—Interesting meeting with John Mohawk at Canisteo—Is employed by Col. Williamson as surveyor—Capt. Church pays him a visit—And secures his services—Exploration of the "Church Tract"—Pleasure trip to Niagara Falls (?)—Selects a site for his home—And erects the first brick house in Allegany—Thrilling incident. P. 271.

CHAPTER XXII.

As surveyor and public official—Sub-division of the "Church Tract"—Estimate of his abilities and work by modern surveyors—Surveys numerous other tracts—And State Roads and highways for towns—The various offices he held—His qualifications. P. 280.

CHAPTER XXIII.

As first citizen—Respect paid to Van Campen in his old age—His relations with Capt. Horatio Jones—Death of Capt. Jones—Van Campen's loneliness—Removal of the remains of Boyd and Parker and their comrades to Rochester—Van Campen called to preside over the exercises at Cuylerville—Geneseo names a new brass field piece in his honor, and use it on this occasion—Interesting remarks of Major Van Campen on surrendering the remains of his comrades in arms. P. 287.

CHAPTER XXIV.

Major Van Campen's relations with the Indians in times of peace—John Mohawk pays him a visit—Visits him again. "*Yankee done it. Yankee done it.—Peace now.*"—Van Campen and Mohawk meet at Hume—Mohawk carves a ladle and presents to a member of Van Campen's family—Burial place of John Mohawk—Relics of Van Campen.   P. 295.

CHAPTER XXV.

Major Van Campen's residence in Dansville—Methodical habits—Is stricken with paralysis—Partial recovery—Removes to Almond—And finally to the "Old Place," at Angelica—His death and funeral—Inscription on his Tomb-stone—Extract from Obituary.   P. 299.

BIOGRAPHICAL SKETCH

OF THE LATE

JUDGE PHILIP CHURCH,

OF BELVIDERE, ALLEGANY CO., N. Y.

By Jno. S. Minard.

CHAPTER I.

Birth and parentage—John B. Church—The family coat of arms—Commissary to the French army during the American Revolution—Loans a large sum of money to Robert Morris—The security—Narrow escape of infant Philip—John B. Church takes up his residence in Paris—Later in England—Philip sent to Eton—His favorite quotation from Goldsmith—Studies law—The family return to America—Philip resumes his law studies—Is admitted to the bar—Acts as second to Philip Hamilton in his duel with E. Eckhard—Appointed to a captaincy in the infantry of the Provisional army—As aide-de-camp to Hamilton, attends the Washington obsequies in Philadelphia—Letter of Gen. Washington. P. 307

CHAPTER II.

Preliminary exploration of the "Church Tract" in 1801—A lonesome night in the forest—Trip to Niagara Falls—Visits Batavia and Geneseo—Site selected for the village of Angelica—Determines to build the Manor house and makes a choice of its location—Builds a saw-mill in 1802—And a grist-mill in 1803 In 1804 builds temporary residence, "The White House"—The Hamilton and Burr duel—The famous duelling pistols—Marries Anna Matilda Stewart—Erection of the stone mansion—Moves into it—Is appointed Judge. P. 318.

CHAPTER III.

Visits England—Is tendered a public dinner at Yarmouth—Visits Mr. Coke—And the Duke of Bedford—Mrs. Church attends the annual festival of the Indians at Caneadea—and is

(xxi)

given a name—The Caneadea Indians offer to guard Mrs. Church's house—Judge Church returns— Introduction of improved cattle and sheep—Queer way of transporting a buck—Becomes interested in internal improvements—Genesee Valley Canal—Erie railroad—Distinguished visitors at Villa Belvidere—The Judge's fondness for athletic sports—A good marksman—His and Van Campen's wonderful shots—Closing years—Last sickness and death—Funeral—Resolutions of respect—The family. P. 327.

ILLUSTRATIONS.

	PAGE
Portrait of Van Campen,	
Van Campen's Encounter with Mohawk,	161
Present Site of Old Indian Village of Caneadea,	221
Running the Gauntlet,	233
The Old Council House,	241
The Van Campen-Mohawk Tomahawk,	248
The Van Campen Place, Angelica, N. Y.,	278
Van Campen Relics,	296
Fac-Simile of Tables,	304
Judge Philip Church,	307

LIFE AND ADVENTURES OF MOSES VAN CAMPEN.

CHAPTER I.

Moses, son of Cornelius Van Campen,* a respectable farmer, was born in Hunterdon County, New Jersey, January 21st, 1757. His paternal ancestors, on coming from Holland to this country settled in New Jersey, where they were known as industrious, worthy citizens. His mother's name was Depew, and her descent was from a family of French Protestants, who fled from the persecutions of the eighteenth century to this land of religious freedom, and found a home in the State of Pennsylvania. Her father was a wealthy farmer, living on the Delaware river, noted for his exemplary religious character, as also for his kindness and liberality to the poor. For a number of years he was Justice of the Peace, and in discharging the duties of this office, seemed much like a father consulting the interests, and settling the difficulties of a large family. He would not allow a

---

*Van Campen is an ancient and distinguished name in the history of Holland.

In its early application it signifies land-men—men of the fields, or camp-men. Van prefixed, was intended as a designation of distinction or eminence which they, in common with other Dutch famílies were supposed to have merited. The name in its early spelling was with "K" and was pronounced "Van-Kompe."—Ed.

suit between any of his neighbors to come to issue before him, without endeavoring to effect a reconciliation between them, and in this was in almost every instance successful.

Of other near relatives in the line of Van Campen's ancestry little is known, since no record has been kept, but that in the old family Bible, and this was swept away by a flood that removed many other things of household value. He had brothers and sisters, but their lives were thrown so widely apart that little is known concerning them. Two brothers, Samuel and Benjamin, very worthy men, settled in the same County, Allegany County, N. Y. Samuel a few miles above the residence of Judge Philip Church, on the Genesee River, and Benjamin in the town of Almond. A sister of his also was married and living, when last heard from in Memphis, Tenn.

Soon after the birth of his son Moses, Mr. Cornelius Van Campen removed to Pennsylvania, and purchased land in Northampton County, on the Delaware river, a little above what was called the Water Gap. Here Moses spent the years of his childhood, and though three-fourths of a century has since intervened, the scenes and impressions of that period still remain, and are readily called to mind.

He speaks of the old farm house with its grave-looking walls, of the barn where he and his brothers used to play "Hide and Seek," and of a thousand things that go to fill up a picture of happy boyhood days.

A beautiful flat spread its broad green apron for miles to the north and south. It may have been under Indian culture years before, for no indications of its ever having been a forest were to be seen. The Delaware river bounded it on the east, as it came gracefully winding its way around the base of the Blue Mountains, that arose in places very abruptly, presenting to the eye varied and beautiful scenery, and it was skirted on the west by a range of hills that rose gently from the plain, marking out an undulating line on the distant horizon.

"Here," said he, "my father lived in the immediate vicinity of my mother's relations, many of whom memory recalls with great pleasure." He remembers particularly Nicholas Depew, Esq., a cousin of his mother, who in his day was extensively known as a man of large estate, and of great capacity for business. " I love to recall his name," says he "for the happy influence he threw around my boyhood. I never entered his house without receiving a smile, and I seem to see it yet whenever I think of the man ; and the pleasant tones of his voice, calling me his '*little Moses*,' still linger about me like the floating sounds of distant music. So uniform was his disposition, I never remember seeing him otherwise than in a pleasant mood. Added to this were the still higher graces of the Christian. None ever questioned the reality of his piety. It exerted over him a controlling influence, and whether at home or abroad, he manifested alike his adherence to the principles he professed. He was very systematic in the management of his farm ; the hours of labor, of relaxation, and of rest were so arranged, and so uniformly observed, that any one who understood them, would know what were his engagements at any particular part of the day.

The buildings on his farm were mostly of stone, and were arranged with the same attention to order that characterized whatever he did. His domestics had no occasion to interfere with each other, for each had his appointed labor, and his separate apartment, and things within and without the house went on harmoniously and pleasantly.

His kindness to the poor was a marked characteristic of the man. They came to him in their need and found him ever ready to administer to their real necessities. Many who were thus assisted he could easily distinguish by their voice ; and happening one day to be passing by a public house, in his neighborhood, he overheard some of them indulging in boisterons wit, and singing bar-room songs. He was much pained with their conduct, and learning that they were accustomed thus to idle away their time, and spend their earnings for what was worse than useless, he began to question the propriety of giving to such men, whether it did not tend to encourage them in their vicious habits, and whether he was not chargeable with ministering to their depravity, instead of doing them good. He resolved therefore to give them no more. But learning that some who were reached by his bounty were worthy and were made to suffer from their connection with these dissolute persons, and condemned their conduct, while unable to prevent it, he receded somewhat from his purpose, resolving not to withhold his assistance, so long as it was reaching the really deserving. Such was the character of this excellent man, and I can but feel in reviewing it that "the memory of the just is blessed."

The early history of Van Campen we gather from his

own lips, and events that were impressed deeply on his own mind, would very naturally assume a more prominent place than others, and these might not be alike interesting to all. Yet there are influences common to all, gathered around the firesides of our homes, whose tendency is not to be mistaken, and so far as they have exerted a permanent effect on the character, deserve more than a passing notice. Of this kind were the influences thrown around Van Campen's early years, by a tender and affectionate mother. These influences though at the time they may have been considered slight, have no doubt been effective in giving direction to his whole after life. She was a woman of more than ordinary force of character, yet this did not embrace anything not appropriate to her sex. Affectionate but at the same time decided, she was admirably fitted to mould the youthful mind, and give to it touches that would retain their impress, even amid the distracting tumults of life.

A better illustration of this could not be given, than in the fact that from her he received his earliest impressions of religion ; and though these impressions may seem to have been lost amid the rough scenes through which he passed, yet the experience of after years gave ample proof of the power they retained over his mind. She early instilled into his mind the first principles of truth, and taught him to acknowledge and revere the overruling presence and power of the Supreme Being. The first nine years of his life were under her care and tuition. He was then sent to a neighboring school, where after learning the first rudiments of education he was permitted to enter upon the study of surveying. He also gained some knowledge of navigation, in hope of some day sailing on the water ; a hope never realized.

The boys at the school had a play called *Throwing at Buck*, which interested him much. A stick ending in three prongs was placed so as to stand upright. The point in the play was to see who by throwing at the top of this could knock it over the greatest number of times. The boys of the school were nearly equally divided between those who came from up the river, called the *Upper School*, and those who came from down the river, called the *Lower School*. The game was usually played by dividing between Upper and Lower schools. In these games the upper school party to which Moses belonged, were more often victorious, which unfortunately gave rise to many unpleasant feelings between the two parties. One side claimed a superiority which was not acknowledged by the other, and their disputes at length arose so high it was decided to try the question of comparative strength by a regular fight.

The day of battle was appointed, and when it came the boys naturally loitered around the school-house, until the teacher was out of sight, and then came up in battle array to commence their scuffle. Moses led his party and advanced with his men, determined on gaining the victory. The reception was warm and the scuffle continued for some time doubtful, but finally the upper school began to gain the ascendency, and soon their antagonists fled and left them in possession of the ground.

The experience of Moses' school-boy days differs little perhaps from that of others attending a public school. There are the same strifes and jealousies, defeats and victories, animosities and friendships, common to all, which relieve these days of monotony, and impart to them the novelty of adventure. But the time of his boyhood was not wholly given to the school-room, and his physical energies were not impaired by the protracted labor and confinement often given to an extended course of study. His bodily strength was improved by surroundings demanding of him constant activity, and it seemed prophetic of the active life that awaited him.

He speaks thus of himself: "When about twelve years old my father and mother went to meeting on a Sabbath morning in September, and left me at home to watch a field of wheat. My business was to watch this field and drive off the pigeons, which came down upon it in such multitudes as to cover the ground, and threaten to pick up the grain before it had time to sprout. I obeyed the orders given me, and drove off the pigeons till I became tired. For as often as I started them up from one side of the field, they would fly a little way and light down again, and go at picking up the grain. In my perplexity and trouble I thought of my father's gun, a famous old fowling piece brought from Holland, five or six feet long, which hung up in the house, in a place where it was always to be found when not in use. With childlike eagerness I ran to the house climbed up by a chair, and made out to reach the gun, already loaded with a good round charge of powder and pigeon shot; shouldered it and hurried back to put my new plan on trial. As I came near where the birds were all at work filling their crops and having no thought of danger; I crept carefully up to the fence, and putting the trusty old piece between the rails, I fired away at them bravely. The gun kicked me over. I never had fired a gun before, and had as little thought of being served that way, as the poor pigeons I shot at. I had seen my father taking sight when he shot, and trying to do as he did, I put my face down close to the piece just back of the lock, and when I fired, it flew back, knocked me over and raked my nose from end to end. I made havoc however among the birds, killing according to my best recollection about twenty of them. I felt at first highly gratified; I thought I had performed a great exploit. But this feeling did not last long. I soon began to be troubled, for I knew my father would not approve of what I had done. I had taken his gun without liberty and fired it, and a flogging began to haunt my imagination. I carried my game to the house and deposited it in the cellar, and wished I might in some way escape detection. But I wished in vain, my poor nose betrayed me.

My mother in the tenderness of her heart would have passed it by, because I was generally obedient, and because she knew when her husband resorted to the rod he did not use it lightly. But my sadly scraped nose and the empty gun were two witnesses that could neither be bribed nor put to silence. The result was a thorough dressing and a charge to take care what I did in the future."

From this time forward, until he was sixteen, the habits of young Van Campen were those of early rising and of hardy industry. Not being accustomed to effeminacies of any kind he grew up with a vigor of constitution that could brave the inclemencies of the weather without any great inconvenience from the exposure.

In the fall when the people usually plowed the flats for wheat, he was accustomed to be up, have his horses harnessed and be ready to start the plow as soon as it was light enough to trace a furrow. This was the fashion among the thriving farmers in that part of the country, and all the lads of his age grew up fresh and strong, fitted for any kind of labor and resolute to carry it on. The flat land along the Delaware river was generally reserved for grain, while the hills bordering on the west afforded abundant pasturage for cattle. The country was new and deer were often seen sporting or cropping in the woods, or leaping up the hills, or crossing the cattle-paths with which the forest abounded. When Van Campen was between fifteen and sixteen years of age, his father allowed him to carry his loaded rifle when he went to drive up the cows.

"It was a new thing for me," he says, "I was very anxious to handle a gun and try it on a deer. As I went along I watched with a great deal of solicitude for an opportunity to get a shot, and as I was pursuing my way through the woods, what should meet my eye but a fine large buck! He was passing along not far away, and when he came opposite to where I was, stood perfectly still, and looked toward me, with his broad side exposed to my view. I rested my piece across a log and fired. The deer darted away furiously and in a moment was out of sight behind the bushes. I was so much of a novice in hunting I did not know whether I had hit him or not, and made no stop to look after my game, but went right on with the cows toward home.

My father had heard the report of the rifle and as soon as he saw me inquired:

'What did you shoot at, my son?'

I answered, a deer, but did not know whether I had killed him, or even hurt him at all.

'How did he act?' said he.

He jumped into the air, said I, kicked, switched his tail, and was out of sight in a moment.

'You must have hit him,' said my father,' can you take me to the place?'

I said I could, and went with him to the place, and found a tuft of hair lying on the ground.

'You have hit him,' said my father.'

A few steps further and we saw blood, and we tracked him by the blood, and very soon came to where we saw the noble animal lying, stretched out on the ground before us.

It was the first deer I had ever killed, the first indeed I had ever shot at. I felt myself a man at once, and nothing would do but I must carry a quarter to our neighbor, Mr. Shoemaker, a connection of my mother by marriage. As soon as it was dressed I shouldered it and marched off, carrying it with a light and joyous heart to his house, happy in being the bearer of the important present myself. I arrived quickly at his door, when he accosted me very abruptly.—

'What have you there on your shoulder?'

A leg of a deer, sir, said I.

'Why!' said he, 'You will be prosecuted and sent to jail. Squire Depew is in the house, and if he gets his eye on you, you will be brought up and tried for killing a deer contrary to law. Run with it into the kitchen, and don't let him see you on any account'

My high thoughts dropped in an instant. I felt cheap enough. The idea of being sent to jail for breaking the law alarmed me greatly, and I hastened home as fast as possible. The fact was I had shot my buck at the time of the year when the law did not allow deer to be killed. The law authorized the hunting of deer only between the first of July and the first of January. I had killed mine in June, and was therefore liable to prosecution.

My alarm however died away very soon, and I began to feel myself a man again, and of sufficient importance to have a rifle of my own. I had fired but two shots at any kind of game, and in both instances had done execution. One of my shots however, I did not speak of very often. I had grown to be nearly a man in size and was able to make such a plea for myself as to induce my father to buy me one."

CHAPTER II.

Van Campen was now sixteen years old, the owner of a rifle, and disposed to use it, when occasion presented. A fall of snow afforded a fine opportunity for tracking deer, and invited him forth to try his skill in hunting. Traversing the woods for a time he discovered three; the leader a doe followed by her two fawns. Aiming at the first he made a wild shot, and hit the last. This part of the story he kept to himself, and carried home his fawn, thinking he would make a fortunute hunter, he had shot but three times, and each time had killed, and a fortunate hunter in his opinion, was quite an important person.

By his frequent trials of the gun and his wanderings through the forest, young Van Campen was making himself familiar with the forest, as well as the use of his rifle. Yet this was not the only training he had at this period of his life. His duties as a farmer imposed on him a life of activity, and toil, and occasionally of real danger.

The farmers living on the Delaware above the Water Gap, were accustomed to send their surplus wheat down the river to Philadelphia, to be sold. They used for this purpose what were called Durham boats. They were large, and capable of carrying ten or twelve tons apiece. Wheat was their staple and much depended on getting it safely into market.

"In one of the late freshets in the spring of 1770," he says, "my father in company with Mr. Shoemaker fitted out a boat, which was manned by myself, young Shoemaker and four others including the pilot. A negro belonging to Mr. Shoemaker's family was one of the number. He had never been down the river, and was attracted by the novelty of a ride upon the water. When everything was ready we pushed off from the shore and were soon moving along at a merry rate down the river. We made very good progress, with little of variety other than a good natured joke, and a hearty laugh from old Simon, the negro, until we came in sight of Trenton Falls. Here our pilot began to express fears about a safe passage, remarking that the river had fallen very much within the past few hours. He said—'Boys keep your eyes out, for we shall have a pretty close rub here.'"

The Trenton Falls were rapids where the main body of the water divided, sweeping off to the right and left, and ran between ledges of rocks, the one called the Outside, the other the Inside Gap. It was quite dangerous to pass over these falls, at high water, extremely dangerous when the water was low.

They watched the boat with great anxiety, as she began to move faster and faster, borne along by the rapid, and every heart beat quick as she entered the Gap. When she had passed about half way through, she struck a rock ;—a plank was knocked in ;—the boat leaked very fast, and they were in danger of losing their whole cargo, if not their lives.

While in the height of their peril, and they were struggling, as in a case of life and death, old Simon called out to young Shoemaker :—" *Young massa, pray ;—we all get drownded ;—you never pray ;—time you begin now ;—if old massa here,—he pray for us.*"

What effect it had on young Shoemaker, is not known; Van Campen was considerably impressed by it, and it may have led them all to realize their dependence on a higher power for success. As it was they worked hard, ran the boat ashore, and were successful in saving most of the wheat, yet their fortunes were not made by the trip.

It will not be expected, neither would it be desirable for us to record every event of Van Campen's early life, yet it will be seen from the incidents already given, and which indeed are common to every newly settled country, that they were adapted to foster a bold and enterprising spirit, and lay the foundation for that physical endurance demanded by the events that were destined soon to come into his life experience.

Not far from this period of Van Campen's life, his father, in company with a brother, was led to purchase land in the valley of Wyoming, intending if circumstances should favor it, to make this his residence. The fame of this valley had been widely circulated among the inhabitants of Pennsylvania. It was called the most beautiful land in the world. In fertility of soil, it was said to surpass all other lands. Hence it was regarded as something very desirable, to obtain possession of so delightful a portion of the earth; and though the title was unsettled, being in dispute between the States of Connecticut and Pennsylvania, Mr. Van Campen ventured to purchase under the title of his own State, and

in the spring of 1769, took his son Moses
cultivate his newly purchased farm. The oth
of the family were left at home, under the i
that it would not be well to bring them into wh
then, and what continued to be for many years, a scene
of conflict.

This valley had been a subject of dispute between those two States ever since the year 1753 when the thought of planting a colony here was first entertained by the people of Connecticut, under the belief that it was included in the grant of James I., in 1620 to the old Plymouth Colony. A company formed with a view to the possession and settlement of this valley by Connecticut, and called the Susquehanna Company, was directly opposed by another formed by the Pennsylvanians, called the Delaware Company, which maintained that the grant from Charles II to William Penn, covered the claim of Connecticut. To strengthen these claims each party bought the land also of the Indians, who were doubtless well pleased with the opportunity of selling the land twice. Still further support was claimed by each, from legal decisions obtained in England.

Those who came from Connecticut to settle here relied, no doubt, on the validity of the title received from their own State. The Pennsylvanians also had full confidence in the title of their State, and as there appeared to be very little hope of coming to an amicable settlement of the matter, each claimant seemed disposed to maintain his possession by force. Angry feelings gave rise to bitter words, and these in turn to blows, until finally there was a resort to arms. One party retained posseson until driven away by the other; and this in turn held its ground, until compelled to yield to the superior numbers, and power, of the opposing Company.

Such being the condition of things here Van Campen the father, thought it unadvisable to bring his family into this region of turmoil and strife, and hence relinquished, for the present, the idea of cultivating the beautiful land of Wyoming, and having disposed of his farm on the Delaware, he removed with his family in 1773 to Northumberland County on the North Branch of the Susquehanna, and purchased a tract of land on Fishing Creek eight miles above its junction with said river.

Moses was now in his seventeenth year, and finding here a territory abounding in a variety of game, he was allured more than ever to the use of his rifle. Wild turkeys and deer abounded in the upland wood bordering on the flats, and no pastime was more inviting than the hours he could spend, when released from the labor of the farm, in wandering over hill and dale, until laden with the spoils of the chase, when he would return to share the booty with others. The exercise was healthful and pleasant; it served to expand and strengthen his frame, and at the same time extended his acquaintance with the region traversed.

In these excursions he often fell in with parties of Indians who came here to hunt. They came here often from their settlements along the waters of the Genesee river, and encamping here would spend several weeks in hunting. In his intercourse with the Indians he became acquainted, among others, with a chief belonging to the

Seneca tribe, named Ton Shenap. He was a very successful hunter, and had the name also of being a great warrior. He had a noble, dignified appearance, and seeming to be courteous, and quite accessible, Moses soon established with him a familiar acquaintance. He was invited to his camp, and often hunted with him during the day, and would stay with him during the night. In these hunts Moses always found him to be his superior; and became anxious to know how it was Shenap excelled him so much in killing deer. He was led to inquire of the old chief one day, how much he would ask to show him how to kill deer. "*I want you to teach me,*" said Moses.

Shenap said,—"*I will tell you how to kill deer for a quart of rum.*"

Moses agreed to give him the quart of rum, and desired him to tell him there and then. But no; he would not do this before he brought the rum. The rum was obtained, and when handed to him, Shenap said,—" *Well, —now I tell you.— You get up early,* VERY EARLY, *in the morning;—you go to the head of little streams;—there deer feed;—walk slow;—look sharp;—bime-by you see him;—then shoot close, and you kill him;—that's all*"

During the two years immediately following the coming of the Van Campens into Northumberland county, the events of special interest to young Van Campen were connected with the chase. These were very numerous and so ardently did he engage in this fascinating sport, that he became quite an expert in the use of the rifle, and familiar with the best grounds for its use. With this preparation he was coming very near the time when hostilities would commence between Great Britain and her American Colonies.

At about this time, 1775, the old feuds existing between the rival Companies interested in the settlement of the Valley of Wyoming, arose to their height. During the few years before this time, several encounters had taken place, in which blood was shed on both sides, notwithstanding which the population had increased largely, while the hostility between the two parties had been growing apace, so that the quarrel seemed likely to assume the character of a civil war between the two States claiming the ground. It was at a time when every arm should have been nerved in defense of the whole country.

The weighty interests involved made it desirable that this strife should cease, and the energies of all be concentrated on the struggle for national independence. One more effort however was made by Pennsylvania to maintain her right to the soil, which she thonght invaded by the people of Connecticut. For this purpose a company was raised to march under the direction of Col. Plunket, and as Mr. Van Campen was one of the proprietors, he was called upon by the other owners to enlist in the enterprise Being young and fond of adventure Moses asked his father if he might not go in his place. His request being granted, he joined the expedition.

A company consisting of seven hundred men commenced its march about the first of December. They were well provided with arms, provisions and military stores, conveyed up the river by a large boat, while the little army marched with it along the shore. Their march was slow; being governed by the progress of the boat, impeded in places by the rapidity of the current, and by the ice that floated in the river.

On the twenty-fourth of December they came to the foot of Nanticoke Falls, a little below the outlet of Wyoming Valley. Here the river was so full of ice it was found impracticable to ascend the falls; Plunket ordered a halt, and directed his men to take in their knapsacks a supply of provisions and march directly for Fort Wyoming

Leaving therefore, a small party to guard the boat, he proceeded with his men up the river. Before advancing far, they came in view of an abrupt point of Shawanese Mountain, which extended down toward the river and presented a rough precipitous front. Approaching this they found it strongly fortified, and as they came near, the settlers rose from behind a rampart and discharged at them a volley of musketry. Though this fire did little harm, it sent a sudden panic through Plunket's troops, and led them to retreat, so as to be out of reach of their guns, and here they held a consultation on what was best to be done in this emergency.

It seemed very clear the colonists had anticipated their coming and were prepared for a gallant defense. To drive them from their fortification would be a hazardous undertaking, and to march into the valley through the defile, under the rampart would expose themselves to a fearful loss. The only course left for them, seemed to be to cross the river and march into the valley on the other side. This they resolved to do, and having a batteau, they conveyed it by land above the falls, and with this expected to gain the other side of the river. Plunket was in the first boat that started across. The settlers had anticipated them here also, for before they reached the opposite shore they were fired upon from an ambuscade and one of their number killed. Plunket directed the boat to be steered down the river, and as many as could, to lie down and thus escape the fire of the enemy. Plunket's men who remained on the western shore saw that the fire proceeded from the bushes on the opposite side, and they fired into them and killed one of the colonists named Bowen.

Plunket's army was again in consultation. It was found that the obstacles they would be obliged to surmount, were greater than they anticipated; what they supposed would be an easy conqnest, they found could be gained only by a severe, protracted and perhaps doubtful struggle. They were not prepared for a long siege, or for a hazardous encounter, and as winter was threatening soon to close up the river, it was thought best to return without further effort to force their way into the valley. In accordance with this determination they commenced their march homeward and found it easier to go down the river than up.

Though in this expedition young Van Campen held no conspicuous place, nor performed any daring exploit, it may have proved of some advantage, as it gave him a knowledge of a few of the dangers and hardships of camp-life ; and as at one time he heard the bullet as it whizzed by him, he could judge whether there was something in it so terrifying, as to lead him ever after to shun the field of battle. Such a decision at this time it was important to make ; for the hour had come, when one voice was whispering in the ears of all, bidding them—

> " Strike,—for their altars and their fires,—
> God,—and their native land."

CHAPTER III.

The year 1763 is memorable for the dawn of English supremacy on this continent. Peace had been concluded with France, the arms of England, by land and sea, had been crowned with signal success;—never before had she risen to a higher pitch of dominion and glory. But her achievements had been gained only at great expense, and added largely to her already heavy indebtedness. Her ministry in looking about for means to replenish her treasury, conceived the idea of taxing the American Colonies, that were supposed to have been profited by her warlike enterprises. With this in view the Stamp Act was passed by Parliament to come in force, "from and after the first day of November 1765."

Notice of the design to tax her American Colonies had been given the year before. It did not come upon them suddenly, there had been time for reflection. When it came it created great opposition.

It is worthy of note that when those differences began, which resulted finally in the separation of the colonies from the parent country, their germinal influences may be traced to the time, when her achievements had made her the leading power of the world. It is likewise a a deeply suggestive thought, that the fathers of our country were not awed into silence, by this overshadowing power ; and were not prevented by it from expressing their earnest and honest convictions. The thought of resisting it, did not terrify, the idea of meeting it in battle, did not overwhelm them with fear.

The first note of opposition to the Stamp Act was raised by Patrick Henry in the house of burgesses in Virginia, in May 1765. The resolutions that voiced his sentiments, were strenuously opposed by some who were afterward foremost, in their support of the Revolution. Yet after a long and heated debate they were passed by a small majority. These resolutions defined the rights of the colonies as British subjects, established by royal charter, and justly entitled to all the immunities and privileges of Englishmen, and denied the right of the British Parliament to impose a tax upon them, asserting that to the colonies alone, belonged the right of taxing themselves. In his bold and impressive speech in support of the closing resolution, Mr. Henry used these significant words :—" Cæsar had his Brutus,—Charles the First his Cromwell, and George the Third,—"Treason!" —cried the speaker,—"treason,—treason,"—echoed from all parts of the house,—without faltering in the least, he assumed a loftier attitude, and in a deeper, more impressive tone, added,—"*may profit by their example! If this be treason, make the most of it!*"*

These resolutions issuing from the heart of Virginia, aroused a kindred spirit in the other colonies, uniting them all, in their opposition. The repeal of the Stamp Act, being followed by measures, alike subversive in their tendency, to the liberty of the colonies, resulted in the call of a Congress, to be composed of delegates from

*Wirt's life of Patrick Henry.

all the colonies. This Congress assembled at Philadelphia, Sept. 5, 1774. Peyton Randolph of Virginia, was chosen its President, and when the assembly was organized for business, a deep silence pervaded the house, that seemed like the solemnity of death. The most distinguished men of the nation were here assembled. Their deliberations would materially affect the condition and prospects of millions of people. Every heart realized the immense interests pending on the occasion. Who would break that silence, more impressive than the power of words to express?

Then it was Patrick Henry, justly styled, *the orator of the Revolution,*—" arose slowly, as if borne down by the weight of the subject. After faltering according to his habit, through the most impressive exordium, in which he merely echoed back the consciousness of every other heart, in deploring his ability to do justice to the occasion, he launched gradually into a recital of colonial wrongs. Rising as he advanced, with the grandeur of his subject, and glowing at length with the majesty and expectation of the occasion, his speech seemed more than that of mortal man. There was no rant,—no rhapsody, no labor of the understanding, no straining of the voice, —no confusion of utterance. His countenance was erect, —his eye steady,—his action noble,—his enunciation clear and firm,—his mind poised on its centre,—his views of his subject comprehensive and great,—and his imagination corruscating with a magnificence and variety, which struck even that assembly with amazement and awe. He sat down amidst murmurs of astonishment and applause."

Such is the admirable portrait drawn by the pen of

Wm Wirt of this wonderful man, as he stood on the floor of this Congress of the colonies ; and the few glittering fragments of his eloquence, on colonial rights and British oppression that have come down to us, clearly evince how largely instrumental were these utterances in nerving the minds of the American people, for the struggle before them. The excitement passed from one colony and neighborhood to another, until the conviction prevailed in every community, that the only escape from the oppressive measures of the British ministry, must be by an appeal to arms.

It was at this stage of the dispute between America and Great Britain, that young Van Campen became fired with the spirit which was carried into the remote settlements, of resisting, to the last breath the oppressive measures of England. He had watched the progress of this discussion, had beheld with an indignant feeling, the oppressive designs of the British Parliament, and was ready when the opportunity came, to cast his feeble might into the scale of opposition.

He was residing at this time with his father on his farm on the waters of Fishing Creek, twenty-eight miles above Northumberland He was considerably removed from what then appeared to be a point of danger, yet should the Indian take part in the conflict, he was where this terrible foe would be likely to come.

As the notes of preparation for the anticipated struggle continued to fall more and more distinctly on the ear, the lines of difference became more and more apparent, and friends were readily distinguished from foes. The night ride of Paul Revere to spread the alarm, and arouse men to defend the military stores at Concord, the firing of the British on the men gathered at Lexington, the hasty assembling of men to punish the British on their return from Concord, firing at them from stone walls, trees, rocks, fence-corners, and whatever other rampart they could find, seemed but to echo back the voice of Henry reverberating through the land," " *We must fight, I repeat it sir, we must fight.*"

Public speakers passed from one settlement to another, setting forth in glaring colors, the imperiled rights of the Americans and infusing the people with the spirit of war.

To prepare more effectually for the crisis at hand the young men of Van Campen's age, living on the north branch of the Susquehannah, chose him as their captain and met once a week, to practice with the rifle and engage in exercises suited to the battle-field. They were already expert in the use of the gun in pursuing game, with which the country abounded. Almost every young man in that region had his gun, and was accustomed to its use. But this skill they deemed insufficient for the struggle in which they were to engage.

Their preparation contemplated two kinds of warfare. They needed to understand the maneuvers of a disciplined army, to meet successfully the soldiers of Great Britain. They needed also to have some acquaintance with the wiles of the Indian, and his methods of fighting.

Their practice was with reference to both kinds of warfare. Besides the regular exercises of the militia service, they engaged in the maneuvers of Indian warfare, in the thicket and in the wood; they threw the tomahawk and drew the knife. Concealing themselves with the adroitness of the savage, they practiced a sort of skulking fire on their enemy, and having killed, they went through the ceremony of taking his scalp.

Sometimes they would draw the figure of an Indian warrior on a board with chalk, representing it as large as life, and then place the board behind rising ground, where, by going a little distance it would be out of sight. Then selecting some part of the figure at which to shoot, they would retreat some distance, and creep up with trailed arms, until they came in sight of the object, when they would rise, fire and retreat. The size of the bullet holes indicated the shot each had made, as the bores of their rifles differed in size. Some other part of the figure might be selected, when the same action would be repeated, and the same examination take place to see who had made the best shot. This practice would be kept up until their Indian warrior was well nigh shot to pieces.

A similar practice was undertaken with the tomahawk. The figure of an Indian would be marked out on a tree, then standing a certain distance away, they would throw the hatchet, aiming at the forehead,—between the eyes, or any other part selected, and they would very seldom miss the mark.

Little did the British imagine when sending their troops across the Atlantic to awe into submission a few "*rebellious subjects*," that the boys of America were trimming the woods with their hatchets, and driving nails with their bullets, that they might cope with the Indian, or take the button of a "*red-coat*" as far as eye could see whenever the soil of freedom should be invaded. A nation of such spirits cannot be subdued. Foreign armies may overrun their territory, its inhabitants be driven from one point to another;—to seek refuge in mountain fastnesses, or bury themselves in their forests, but be subdued, they never will.

In 1776 a regiment was raised in Northumberland County, under Col. Cook, designed for the continental army under Washington then stationed near Boston. Young Van Campen eagerly enrolled his name in the service of his country, was appointed to the office of Ensign, and prepared to march to any place designated for his company.

But the Committee of Safety for the county, through the influence of Mr. James McClure, one of their number, and a man of high respectability and of much influence, dissuaded him from leaving the frontier, telling him he was needed where he was, and could make himself useful there if anywhere,—that it was the residence of his friends,—where his lot was cast, and it appeared natural and proper for him to stay and defend those endeared to him by the intimacies and attachments of home.

He knew that Van Campen had made himself familiar with the Indian modes of warfare, and wanted neither the disposition or skill, to meet them in their own place, and fight them in their own way, and as it was expected they would take part in the war, and join the forces of the British, it became important that the frontier settlements should be guarded; for there the Indians would be likely to come, and there his ravages would be experienced, and the severest injuries inflicted. Mr. Mc-

Clure therefore used all his influence to persuade him to remain where he was, and listening to his sound reasoning and kind persuasions, he resigned his commission, and resolved to remain at home. This decision formed one of the turning points of his life.

CHAPTER IV.

Though Van Campen had been active in preparation for the impending struggle, it was not until the year 1777 that he fairly entered upon the life of a soldier. The war had been begun,—the news from Concord, Lexington and Bunker Hill, came with electric touch, to a thousand patriotic hearts, and multitudes began to move toward the scene of strife ; from Maine to Georgia men stepped forth to meet, as best they could, the arms of the British. Every royal governor in the colonies had been removed, Independance declared, and sustained by the almost unanimous voice of the people.

The Indians had hitherto been persuaded to remain neutral ; but by appeals to their cupidity they were induced to take part in the war. The Six Nations having assembled in council at Oswego, were to'd by the Royal Commissioners,—" that the people of the States were few in number, and could easily be subdued, that because of their disobedience to the King, they justly merited all the punishment it was possible for white men and Indians to inflict upon them ;" stating at the same time " that the King was rich in money and in men ; that his rum was as plenty as the water in Lake Ontario ; his men as numerous as the sands on its shore ; and that the Indians, if they would assist in the war, and persevere in their friendship for the King, should never want for money or goods."

Persuaded by this appeal to an appetite, created and fostered by the vices of England, the Chiefs entered into an agreement with the Commissioners, pledging themselves with their people, to take up arms against the rebels, and continue in his Majesty's service until they were subdued. When the treaty was completed, the Commissioners presented each Indian with a suit of clothes, a brass kettle, a gun and a tomahawk, a scalping knife, a quantity of powder and lead, a piece of gold, and promised a bounty on every scalp they should bring in.*

Indian hostilities were now expected by those living in the settlements that bordered on the Susquehanna. Indeed news had already reached them, of one and another falling at their lonely habitation in the forest, by the hand of the Indian.

This part of the frontier had hitherto been protected by the volunteer scouts, that ranged up and down along the outer settlements; yet notwithstanding their vigilance, the wily Indian had found occasion to rush from his hiding place, and bring sudden and terrible death upon many of the inhabitants scattered along the North, and West branches of the Susquehanna. Some means, it was thought, was necessary to secure more effectually the inhabitants of that region from Indian depredations. To supply them with a regular, instead of a temporary force, acting at intervals, and not sufficient in number to afford effective resistance to the invading foe, the militia was

---
*Mrs. Jemison's Narrative.

brought into the field, and in this Van Campen served as Orderly Sergeant, in a regiment commanded by Col. John Kelly, and in the company of Thomas Gaskins.

The regiment was ordered up the river, to take their station at Reid's Fort, built opposite what was called Big Island, in the Susquehanna river. From this point scouting parties were sent in such directions, as were likely to afford the best opportunity of detecting the approaching foe. Constant vigilance was thus maintained to prevent any sudden attack upon the inhabitants within the region they were enabled to traverse.

The services of the year were mainly of the same character; the greatest inconvenience suffered here, was from an occasional failure in their supply of provisions. Yet even at such times they had relief by resorting to the neighboring fields, where they found potatoes. Many of the inhabitants through fear of the Indians had fled from their farms, taking with them what they could of value, but leaving quantities of potatoes in the ground. These proved of great service, for they were often so destitute, that had it not been for these, they would have been in a condition of actual suffering. A small company was detailed to go after them, and a part would dig with a spade and hoe, while a part would stand on guard. In addition to this simple fare, they were sometimes favored with a few rounds of fresh pork. Many had left their hogs that ran wild in the woods, living on roots and acorns, and thus they obtained, in their need, a supply of meat.

About the only circumstance that seemed to open anything like an opportunity for adventure, while Van Campen was stationed here, was the sending out of a company of men to look after a party of Indians reported as having encamped some thirty miles above, on the river, at a place called Young Woman's Town; from the daughter of a chief, who had once presided there over the remnant of a tribe, occupying this ground.

Van Campen was ordered to go with his company and rout these Indians. A part of two days were occupied in marching to the place appointed, keeping runners ahead, to report anything they might learn about the enemy. No traces could be found, though the search was continued for several days. They returned to camp by different routes, without making further discoveries.

Such was the nature of the service rendered by the regiment of Col. Kelley while stationed at Reid's Fort. Scouting parties ranged the country in every direction, yet very few Indian depredations were committed in this part of the frontier, owing doubtless to the fact that these sons of the forest were largely employed in the warlike enterprises going on at the north. A large number of Indians were in the army commanded by General Burgoyne. This army having obtained possession of Lake Champlain, Crown Point, and Ticonderoga, was pressing its way toward Albany, in pursuance of a design to form a junction with the army then at New York under the command of General Clinton. His army was to move north at the same time, and the two were to come together at or near Albany. The union thus formed would give the British free communication between New York and Canada, and at the same time separate troublesome New England from her sister colonies.

Connected with this was still another scheme, the success of which would result in a still greater concentration of British troops, at a point favorable for the conquest of the rebellion, as represented by the armies of the North.

Captain Brant, the distinguished leader of the Indians, was under engagement to meet Col. St. Leger at Oswego and then, with the forces under their command, they were to go down the valley of the Mohawk together, and bring up finally with the forces that were to assemble at Albany.

Col. St. Leger paused on his way to reduce Fort Stanwix, afterward named Fort Schuyler.

This fort was under the command of Col. Gansvoort and the coming of this army of Indians, British regulars, Hessian auxiliaries, and New York loyalists, had been anticipated by such preparations as they had been able to make and as were greatly needed to withstand a siege.

Col. St. Leger supposing the garrison would readily yield to his superior force, sent in with a flag of truce a very pompous proclamation, lavish with promises in case of a compliance with his wishes, and fearful with threatening in case of refusal, demanding a surrender of the fort.

But there was no thought of surrendering this fort to the enemy. The siege had been anticipated, and officers and men, had determined upon defending it to the last.

As soon as the advance of Col. St. Leger became known, the militia of Tryon County were summoned by Gen. Herkimer, to march to the relief of Fort Schuyler. The news of their coming reached the enemy and to arrest its progress, or defeat its design, Brant, with his Indian warriors, was sent forward to meet them. In accordance with their custom an ambuscade was skillfully planned and arranged, and Gen. Herkimer's men, from their impatience to move forward, were suddenly and unexpectedly drawn into it. The result though disasterous, was saved from defeat by the stubborn bravery of the General, who though severely wounded continued to order the battle, and turned what promised only defeat, into a victory. The Indians were punished so severely as greatly to dishearten them, and render welcome the retreating cry,—"Oonah!" as they saw their numbers greatly diminished, and were ready now to fly in every direction, under a shower of bullets from the surviving Provincials. Very soon the siege. which had hitherto been vigorously prosecuted was broken up, and the enemy disappeared leaving evidences of having departed in great haste.

A trick very adroitly played upon them, served to occasion the belief that General Arnold was coming at the head of a large body of soldiers to break up the siege at Fort Schuyler, and that he was near, and would soon be upon them.

Suddenly, and to the amazement of all, the camp of the besiegers was broken up, and the British and Indians fled in great haste, as when the Syrians were made "*to hear the noise of chariots, and the noise of horses, even the noise of a great host, and fled in the twilight, and left their tents and their horses, even the camp as it was, and fled for their life.*"

So great was their panic, and such the precipitancy of

their flight, they left their tents standing, their provisions, artillery, ammunition, their entire camp equipage, and large quantities of other articles enhancing the value of the booty.*

The campaign of General Burgoyne was equally unfortunate. Constantly beleaguered by the foes he had conquered, with the necessity of obtaining supplies for his army from a distance, which increased as he continued to advance, by roads well nigh impassable, from continued and copious rains, deficient in the number of horses required for this arduous service, and his men wearied and worn by the discomfort and labor attending their march, he began to realize that it was not an easy undertaking after all, "*with ten thousand men to march through the whole rebel country at pleasure*," as he vauntingly declared in the presence of his countrymen, before setting out to grapple with the realities of the undertaking. Difficulties continued to increase, and draw their ever tightening folds around him, until he was led to surrender his army on the 17th of October 1777.

Whlle Van Campen was at Ried's Fort, an incident occurred which serves to illustrate somewhat the customs prevailing at that time, as well as give an idea of his physical strength. He was now twenty* years old, his constitution naturally firm, had never been impaired by sickness or by any injurious habit. "Nurtured," as he is wont to say, "in the school of the rifle and tomahawk," he had acquired great power of endurance, with muscles firm and strong. He was about five feet and ten inches

---

*Col. Stone, Life of Brant, Vol. I. p. 262.

in height, well proportioned, fully developed, standing in the pride and full vigor of youth.

On the west side of the river, nearly opposite where they were located, was a tract of land settled by what were called squatters, men of great muscular strength and activity. Having derived their title to the land from the Indians they were called, Indian-land-men. The men of the fort were called Northumbrians. They were challenged by the others to a wrestling match.

Wrestling was a very common exercise at the time and as there had been some dispute between the two in reference to their comparative strength, the Indian-land-men, having a sufficiently high opinion of their own powers, gave the challenge to the Northumbrians to bring on their best man to match the one they would select, and let it be decided by them, which party had the best right to boast of its strength.

The mode of wrestling then practiced was to stand breast to breast, and each place his hands on the other's hips, clinch his trousers near the waistband and at the word "*ready*," to put forth all their strength, the one to lift the other off his feet, and throw him off his balance if possible, and he who was the quickest and smartest, was the best fellow. Captain Gaskins believing he had men in his company equal to the occasion, accepted the challenge.

Among those considered as likely to prove a sufficient match for the champion selected on the other side Van Campen was chosen. The time and place were appointed, the Indian-land-men attending on one side, and the Northumbrians on the other. The whole party formed a ring large enough to allow all to see the sport, when the antagonists stepped into the center. Gentlemanly arrangements were made so that no unfair advantage should be taken, and requiring that each of the combatants should have an equal chance. Both were to stand perfectly still till the question was put, "*Are you ready ?*" When this was put and answered in the affirmative, the struggle was to commence. and each was at liberty to use his utmost strength to throw the other.

Van Campen's antagonist was a stout muscular man, McCormick by name, and the elder of the two. He was accustomed to such exercises and seemed to be confident of success. The men on his side were all raised to an intensity of feeling that became very manifest, as every movement was anxiously watched, since they no doubt considered their honor was concerned in gaining the victory, after having given the challenge.

As for Van Campen, though young he was full-grown, round built, full chested, large limbed, and to the eye of an observer, apparently clumsy and slow motioned, but in reality he could lay out all his strength in an instant, or throw it into a single twitch. Aware that his Captain, and all of his company were looking on with interest and would feel unpleasantly to have their man defeated, he determined to do his best, and if possible give the first spring.

With this in view he was careful, after they had taken their position to put the question himself,—" *Are you ready ?*" " Yes," said his antagonist,—as quick as a flash, he jerked with all his might, raised him from the ground, took a lock upon him and threw him in the twinkling of an eye, upon his head and shoulders. He rose in a second unhurt, and said, "*Sir you can't do that again.*" Van Campen replied promptly, *We'll try it, sir.*'

They took another hold and the other was then too quick for Van Campen. He attempted to take what at that time was called the "crotch lock;" Van Campen understood his design very well and partly evaded his hold, but he managed to raise him up from the ground on his breast, carry him to the ring and made a great effort to throw him on his back, but failed, for while he was laboring to throw him into a horizontal position, Van Campen slipped his lock, and in the struggle made out to get a firm foot hold on the ground, and as soon as it was felt he in turn took the hip lock upon him, that is threw his hip under him, bent forward with his hand clinched in his trowsers near the waistband, raised him and swung him through the air with his feet extended, and hit a tall militia man six feet high, knocked him down and several others at his side, and left his man in their midst kicking and tumbling in a heap.

This raised a shout of laughter on both sides, and having thrown him twice out of three times, Van Campen was crowned conqueror by the laws of the game, and his Captain and comrades were highly gratified to find that their man had won the day. But as every thing had been conducted fairly, no ill blood was excited, and no unpleasant circumstances followed.

CHAPTER V.

Many of the western tribes also were drawn into the British service. The Miamies, Ottawas, Chippewas, Wyandots, Pottowatomies, Missisagies, Shawanese, Ottagamies, and Winnebagoes, were united in a confederation more extensive and powerful, than any other known to the whites in this country. The Ottawa as the oldest tribe had precedence in the general councils, and Pontiak their chief was recognized as emperor of a wide domain, extending south and west of the Great Lakes, including also the valley of the Mississippi, and its tributaries. His authority was more extensive than that of any other Indian known to the whites in this country.

When Major Rogers after the fall of Quebec, came into this region to fulfil his orders, "*to displace the French ;* Pontiak sent embassadors to say, "Our chief is not far away, and he desires you to halt, until he can see you with his own eyes;—*he is the king of this country.*"

Pontiak soon met the English officer, and *demanded his business, and how he dared enter his country without permission!*

The Major replied, "I have no design against the *Indians*, but have come to remove the *French, our common enemy, and the occasion of all our troubles ;*" at the same time handing him belts of wampum.

Pontiak replied,—"I stand in your path until to-morrow

morning." As much as to say,—*you must not go further without my leave.*"

It was said of Pontiak,—"He puts on an air of majesty and princely grandeur, and is greatly revered and honored by his subjects." There was more system in his undertakings than has been discovered in any other of his countrymen. At a second meeting he presented Major Rogers with a pipe of peace, which both smoked by turns, and then told him he might pass through the country unmolested, and as a pledge of this, sent one hundred warriors to assist and protect him.

At the beginning of the war of the Revolution, the Americans sent messengers to Pontiak to invite him to meet them in council. He was inclined to do so, but was prevented from time to time by Governor Hamilton of Detroit. His influence, had it been exerted, might have prevented the calamities that fell upon the west and northwest portions of Virginia. These were very severe both before and during the war.

In the early part of 1777 small parties of Indians visited the West Fork of the Monongahela. The family of Charles Grigsby was surprised in the absence of Mr. Grigsby, and his wife and two children were taken captives. Mrs. Grigsby and the younger child, unable to keep up with the rest, were killed, and scalped. Very soon after a daughter of Mr. Coon, engaged in turning flax near Coon's fort, was shot and scalped by Indians that had been lying in ambush near by. About this time mischief of the same kind was done in the neighborhood of Wheeling, by the Indians who were so adroit, as to escape without being observed. Thomas Ryan was killed in the field while at work, and a negro with him was taken captive.

Hitherto the Indians had not come in force, and the country here, as in Pennsylvania was guarded by scouts ranging up and down where the enemy would be likely to come. The inhabitants thus had a sense of security, and did not abandon their homes to seek protection in forts. At this time the only places of refuge for the inhabitants, aside from private forts and block-houses, were at Pittsburg, Redstone, Wheeling, and Point Pleasant. These were garrisoned, but not sufficiently strong to send out detachments to meet an invading foe. Their action was confined to repelling assaults, or the expulsion of small parties of the enemy, committing depredations in their immediate vicinity.

In August '77 the word was brought to Fort Pitt that a large Indian force would soon strike a terrible blow on some of the settlements on the Ohio. The inhabitants along the river after being warned of their danger, very generally retired to the forts, and prepared for the expected assault. The enemy very soon made his appearance at Fort Wheeling, and came quite unexpectedly.

The scouting parties sent out were relied upon to give warning of approaching danger. On the night of September first, Captain Ogal, who with a party of twelve men, had been watching the paths leading to the settlement, and had made no discoveries, came into Wheeling and assured the people that no enemy was near. Yet that very night, three hundred and eighty-nine Indian warriors came near the village, and seeing lights in the Fort, believed the inhabitants were on their guard, and hence thought it better to form an ambuscade, and await the developments of the morning. A cornfield, through which was a road leading to the fort, admirably suited their purpose. Two lines were formed, at some distance from each other, extending from the river across the point to the creek. This cornfield afforded the desired concealment. Six Indians were stationed near the road for a decoy. They could easily be discovered by any one passing by.

Early in the morning two men going to a field for horses having no thought of danger, passed the first line, and came near the six Indians, purposely exposed to view. Beholding these Indians they attempted to escape, when one of the men was shot. The other was allowed to give the alarm at the fort The ruse was successful. No sooner was the report given that the attack was by a party of six Indians, than Captain Mason marched out with fourteen men to the place of action, to punish the audacity of these few Indians. He soon came in sight of them, and marched directly toward where they were. A moment after, they were surrounded by a body of Indians, till then unobserved. To contend against overwhelming numbers was vain. In their endeavor to regain the fort they were almost to a man literlly cut to pieces.

Captain Mason and his sergeant succeeded in passing the front line, but they were discovered and fired upon, as they were ascending a hill. The sergeant was wounded and fell, unable to rise. Seeing his captain pass without a gun, and crippled so that he could move but slowly in advance of his pursuers, he handed him his, and calmly surrendered himself to his fate.

The Captain enfeebled by the loss of blood from two wounds, had little hope of reaching the fort. An Indian with his hatchet raised, was in hot pursuit. He was aware of this, and expected every moment it would descend, and split his skull. He just then bethought himself of his sergeant's gun, and turning instantly, found the Indian so near, he could not bring the gun to bear upon him. Having the advantage of rising ground, he gave the Indian a push with his hand, which thrust him back and the uplifted tomahawk descended with much force to the earth. Before his antagonist could recover himself, and hurl the hatchet at his enfeebled foe, the gun had done its work, and the Indian fell dead at his feet. The Captain could go but a few steps further. He found concealment by the side of a large fallen tree, and was unobserved while the Indians remained about the fort.

The discharge of guns and the shrieks of Captain Mason's men, led Captain Ogal to advance with his twelve scouts to their relief. No sooner did they come near the enemy, than they, too, were surrounded, and cut to pieces in like manner. The Captain being in rear of his men, saw the overwhelming force of the enemy, and fortunately escaped, by throwing himself into a little thicket in the corner of a fence.

While these events were in progress the inhabitants of the village were rushing to the fort, and seeing they were powerless to meet the enemy, prepared to defend themselves as best they could. Scarcely had they come within the walls, and closed its gates, when the enemy with terrific yells came up designing to take the fort by storm. There was a moment's pause,—a voice was heard calling on them to surrender.—It was the voice of the notorious renegade, Simon Girty —He called to them from the end window of a house near the fort, and said, " I have come with a large army to conduct to Detroit such of the inhabitants of the frontier, as are willing to accept of the terms offered by Governor Hamilton. *All who will renounce the cause of the Colonies, and attach themselves to the interests of Great Britain, are assured of protection. Remember the fealty you owe to your Sovereign, and come and join his standard. But if you refuse, or dare to fire a single gun at his men, you will suffer the unrestrained vengeance of the foe I bring against you.*"

Fifteen minutes were allowed for considering this proposition. It was not needed ; they were ready to decide at once.

Colonel Zane who was present, replied as follows : " We have consulted with our wives and children, and we are all resolved to perish, sooner than abandon the cause of liberty and of the Colonies and place ourselves under the protection of a savage army, led by Simon Girty."

"But," said Girty, " what can you do, when there are so many against you ? *It is impossible to withstand the assault, and we will not be able to restrain the Indians, if maddened by your resistance. If you comply with our terms, you will certainly be protected. You had better yield.*"

A shot from the fort just then, caused him to withdraw from the window, and the Indians commenced the assault. Thirty-three men within, were now all that were left to maintain their ground against three hundred and eighty outside the fort. The contest was vigorously maintained for twenty-three hours. The Indians resorted to every device their ingenuity could suggest, while a steady and well directed fire met them from within. The women vied with the men in their activity in repelling the assault. The more resolute assisted in reloading the guns, and in running bullets, while others were busy in supplying the men with water and provisions.

The defence was nobly and successfully maintained. The Indians becoming discouraged, fired the houses outside the fort, killed all the stock they could find, destroyed whatever of value they could not remove, and left at an early hour in the morning. The inhabitants though victorious, found themselves in a very destitute condition. Their houses consumed, furniture, clothing, beds and provisions destroyed or carried away, horses, cattle and hogs killed and lying all about, in fine nothing left but themselves. Saddest of all was the sight of the slain men, who had gone out to fall before the enemy. Three only of those who had left the fort, on that eventful day, returned ; and two of these had been seriously wounded.

CHAPTER VI.

Indian hostilities were general during the year '78 all along the frontier settlements of New York, Pennsylvania and Virginia. The inability of our government to furnish them with the supplies they were accustomed to receive from Europeans, and which from habit they had learned to prize, was clearly the reason of their being retained by the British. The taking of scalps and prisoners had become a lucrative business, and the trade could be carried on with greater impunity among defenceless and scattered homes of our frontier settlements, than in places where a richer booty might have been gained at a greater risk of life.

Had our government been able to supply the Indians with all the blankets, guns, hatchets, powder and lead they wanted they might have been willing to leave these defenceless settlements undisturbed. Or had they been offered fifty shillings for a scalp, and five pounds for a prisoner, they would have shown the same alacrity, had the opportunity been alike favorable, in surprising, killing, scalping, and capturing British subjects, as they did in spreading terror and desolation throughout our American settlements.

By the ease with which Britain could convey from Montreal to the home of the Indian, every article suited to his desire or taste, his favor was gained, and his hostility to the American cause secured.

There were some it is true who maintained their adherence to the American people but most of them took up the hatchet on the other side, and increased greatly the severities through which our fathers passed in their way toward liberty.

Early in 1778 Mr. Van Campen was appointed Lieutenant of a company of six month's men, raised under authority of the State for the protection of the frontier. They were under the superintendence of Colonel Samuel Hunter, then the military head of the County of Norchumberland, a man well fitted for his post, being a true patriot, of sound judgment, thoroughly acquainted with the wants of the country, and prompt in supplying them.

The service of a lieutenant on the frontier was suited to the tastes and habits of young Van Campen, and moreover he was well acquainted with the region where his services would call him, having traversed it many times when in pursuit of game. His command consisted of about twenty young men, alike familiar with the country, expert in the use of the rifle, and acquainted with the Indian mode of warfare.

Early in the month of April he was ordered to go with his men up the North Branch of the Susquehanna river, to the mouth of Fishing Creek, and follow up this three miles, to a compact settlement located in that region, and build a fort for the reception of the inhabitants in case of an attack from the Indians. News had come thus early, of their having visited the outer line of settlements, and of their committing depredations, so that terrified messengers were arriving almost daily, bringing the sad news of houses burned, victims scalped, and of families carried into captivity.

It was no time to be idle; a few days, it might be a few hours, and the savages might be among those whom he was appointed to guard, and repeat these scenes of cruelty and blood.

He and his men without delay entered vigorously upon the work; selecting a site for the fort, on the farm of a Mr. Wheeler; hence when completed it was called Wheeler's Fort. It was built of stockades, and sufficiently large to accommodate all the families of the neighborhood. Anticipating an early approach of the foe they worked with a will, to bring their fort to completion or at least into a condition that would afford some protection in case of an attack.

Mr. C. F. Hill, of Hazleton, Pa., who has interested himself in gathering many historical reminiscences, suggests that Van Campen may have been influenced by the tender passion in selecting a site for this fort. "His intimate friend, Joseph Salmon, was joined with him in this enterprise, and in a short time they completed a stockade fort around the home of Isaiah Wheeler, a settler from New Jersey. Mr. Wheeler had a daughter Ann, for whose hand Major Van Campen and Captain Salmon were rivals; they conducted their rivalry in a spirit of great friendship: there is not a suspicion that it was on her account Major Van Campen selected her home as a very proper site for a fort. Whatever the Major's motive, it is certain the gallant Captain beat him in the race, and won the hand of Miss Wheeler.

But Major Van Campen was not to be out-done, for he built another fort, further down the creek, around the home of the widow of James Mc Clure, who had a daughter Margarette, and who later became Mrs. Van Campen."

The Indians in approaching the border settlements usually came upon the head waters of some of those streams on which settlers were located, and followed them down through valley or mountain defile, until they came near the white man's home, when they would divide, so as to fall in small companies, upon different habitations at the same time.

Their coming now being anticipated, spies were sent out in every direction to look after them, and give warning of their approach, and thus avoid a sudden attack. Before the fort was completed a runner came flying with the speed of the wind, to announce the approach of a large party of savages.

The inhabitants now gathered into the fort with quick and hasty rush, taking with them what valuables they could, and leaving their cheerful homes to the undisputed sway of their foes. Very soon the Indians came prowling around under covert of the woods and all at once with wild yells burst forth upon the peaceful farm houses of the settlement. Fortunately the inmates were not there to become victims of the tomahawk and scalping knife. From the elevated position of the fort, the inhabitants could see their dwellings entered, their feather beds and blankets carried out, and scattered around with frantic cries, and very soon after the flame and smoke leap to the top of their houses, and finally settle down into a quiet heap of embers.

But the loss that thus came to them was more than compensated by the thought, that these sights were not mingled with the dying groans, and death shrieks of their wives and children.

The Indians spent most of the day in pillaging and burning houses; some of them made an attack on the fort but to little purpose. Van Campen and his men were actively engaged in preparing for a vigorous defense, in case of an attempt to storm their unfinished works. They were successful in surrounding the fort at a distance of four rods, with a barricade made with brush and stakes, the ends sharpened and locked into each other, so that it was difficult to remove them, and almost impossible for one to get through.

The Indians seeing this obstruction were disposed to fire at them from a distance, and keep concealed behind the bushes. Their shots were promptly returned, and a brisk firing was kept up all the time till evening.

It was expected that the Indians would renew the attack the next morning, and as the ammunition of the fort was nearly expended, Van Campen sent two of his men to Fort Jenkins about eight miles distant, on the Susquehanna, who returned the next morning before dawn of day, with an ample supply of powder and lead. The remaining hours of darkness were spent in running bullets, and in making needed preparation for the encounter they were looking for on the approaching day. They judged from what they knew of the superior force of the enemy, and from the activity already displayed, that the struggle would be severe.

The day dawned upon them but no enemy appeared.

They might come any moment, and it was no time to relax their vigilance. Yet they needed rest and found opportunity for it by watching in turn, some acting as sentries while others slept, and these in turn serving, after a season of repose. Strict guard was thus kept up during the day, but the enemy did not come, and there was time for rest, especially grateful to the women and children, after the alarms and fatigues of the preceding day and night.

This attack was made in the month of May 1778. Had it been but a few days earlier, it might have proved very disasterous. As it was, not a single life was lost or a single person wounded. The Indians not liking the preparations made to receive them, retired leaving blood on the ground, but nothing else that would indicate their loss. Not suited altogether with this visit they made another attempt to surprise this fort during the month of June. The inhabitants who had taken refuge there in the spring, still made it the home of their wives and children. The men continued to cultivate their farms which were near, and returned to the fort at night. For the pupose of having their cattle more under the protection of the fort, an enclosure was fenced off for them at the head of a small flat near by.

One evening in June, at the time when the women and girls were milking, a sentinel called the attention of Van Campen to a movement in some bushes not far away. On observing them closely it seemed evident that a party of Indians were making their way to the cattle yard. Van Campen immediately selected ten of his sharp shooters, and under cover of a rise of ground crept up between them and the milkers. On ascending the ridge they found themselves within pistol shot of their lurking foe. Van Campen's fire killed the leader. The rest were panic stricken and fled. A volley from his men did no further execution ; it only made the woods roar with the tremendous report of their rifles.

Such an unexpected alarm, however, was sounded in the ears of the dairy women, that they were more frightened than the Indians. They started up on their feet, screamed aloud, and ran with all their might, as though the enemy were after them. The milk pails flew in every direction, the milk was scattered to the winds ;— the best runner got in first. The poor cattle equally frightened, leaped the fence and ran into the woods in every direction, bellowing at a terrific rate. The scene was as wild as can well be imagined, and to those who understood that the danger was all over, laughable in the extreme

To the women and girls it was a serious fright, for when the party, that had occasioned the alarm, returned they found them trembling with anxiety and pale from fear. But they soon regained their composure when assured there was do danger, and were ready now to laugh at the display they had made of their bravery.

As the season advanced Indian hostilities increased, and notwithstanding the vigilance of those on guard, and ranging through the country exposed to the enemy, houses were burned, and families murdered. There were sly and cruel Tories also, as ready to watch their opportunity to plunder and burn, as the savages themselves, and often came with them painted and dressed like Indians, and with difficulty recognized as being other than Indians. Three such men whose families lived on the frontier, and who had been with the British, were accidently discovered by a hunter in one of his excursions after game, as he passed by the place where they lodged. It was in a log shanty that had been deserted by its original proprietor, who had made it his temporary residence and left it in pursuit of some more eligible situation. Surrounded on every side by a wild uncultivated forest, it was well suited to become the retreat of darkly designing men.

Col. Hunter ordered Van Campen to take a few men, as many as he saw fit, and go to their hiding place and overcome them and bring them in as prisoners.

Taking with him five men he started soon after at evening, with the intention of surprising them the next morning before they were up. They traveled nearly all night, and just at the dawn of day drew near the house. Yet before they could enter it, they were unfortunately discovered by one of the party, who happened to be on the outside of the house, near the door and saw them. He immediately stepped back into the dwelling and made it fast without loss of time. Van Campen and his men were equally prompt, pressed up close to the door and called upon them to surrender. This they refused to do, declaring that they would defend themselves to the last moment, and that they would blow out the brains of the first man who attempted to cross the threshold. Van Campen was not the man to be intimidated by threats. He felt that his duty required him to take these men at all hazards. He realized likewise the mischief these men would do if permitted to run at large. He paused not to reflect on the danger, nor did he fear defeat, nor expect to die. No : he expected to force his way in at the head of his men, and with their help take them prisoners, and teach them how to march in good company, toward places whither they had been wont to resort under cover of darkness. A single glance of his eye assured him that there was no alternative but to force a passage. He directed his men, all of them strong, resolute fellows, to take a heavy oak rail lying near by, and drive the end of it against the door until they broke it open ; "Then, my boys," said he, " as soon as there is an opening large enough to admit my body I will enter. *Now my lads, let her drive.*" They did so, and very soon jammed the door to pieces. The next moment Van Campen dashed in among them. They stood with their loaded rifles cocked, prepared to fire and blow out the brains of the first intruder. The first thing that met Van Campen was the muzzle of one of their guns pointing directly in his face. He struck it aside, it went off, the ball passing close to his ear, while the powder exploding in his face, made it black and bloody on one side, burned off the hair about the right ear and temple, and peppered his face to such a degree that many of the grains remained and could be distinctly seen till the last day of his life.

He clinched the fellow that had discharged the gun, and with an energy he could not command at a common time, threw him down. His men followed close upon his heels, and seized the others and wrestled them down after a short but firm resistance. The hands of these men were bound behind them, and they were directed to march before, while the others followed with their loaded rifles, and thus they were taken to the civil authorities of the county for imprisonment.

Thus ended an adventure, in which Van Campen came very near losing his life ; at the time of its occurrence he passed it by with little or no thought, other than self-congratulation for having come out of this skirmish so fortunately ; but in after years he was accustomed to speaking of it as revealing the hand of a kind and over-ruling Providence.

CHAPTER VII.

We come now to contemplate some of the transactions of 1778, made particularly memorable, because of scenes so ill suited to that beautiful land.—

"On Susquehanna's side, fair Wyoming." The valley of Wyoming, widely celebrated in story and in song, was formed by nature for a second paradise. Two parallel mountain ranges mark the course of the Susquehanna, coming down in places so near its waters, as scarcely to leave room for them, and a narrow road upon its bank: in other places receding and leaving an ample space forming the pleasant valley with its broad green fields, or making an opening for the thriving village, or flourishing city.

These ranges here depart from their previous tendency to contract, and by a liberal divergence, with many a pleasing indentation and curve, now forming a bold projection with its steep and rugged ascent, and anon receding, and by gentler slopes and less abrupt elevations reaching upward to their usual height of one thousand feet, they go on extending their line of circumference, in all places picturesque and varied, until they approach each other once more, forming a valley lying north-east and south-west, with an average width of three, and a length of twenty-one miles. Such is the valley of Wyoming a name taken from the Indian,—*Maugh-wau-wa-me,* or extensive plains.

The British officers in command at Niagara, determining to strike a severe blow on the inhabitants of this region, sent forth a detachment of three hundred men under Colonel John Butler, accompanied by five hundred Indians, who marched to the head waters of the Susquehanna, where they halted until they could convert two or three hundred pine trees into as many canoes. In these they sailed down the river until they came to a place called the Three Islands. From this point they marched about twenty miles across the wilderness, passed through a gap in the mountain, and entered the valley near its northern boundary.

They took possession of two forts, surrendered without opposition being occupied by Tories. Colonel John Butler established his headquarters in one of them,—Fort Wintermoot ; the other was burned.

The coming of so large a force though sudden, was not unexpected. The enemy had designedly concealed their purpose, and to allay apprehension had sent forward runners bearing messages of peace, which were deceptive. One of these Indians meeting in the valley an acquaintance, who received him with much cordiality, was presented with the customary social glass of which both partook, and as they talked over old matters the Indian, at the instigation of the other, drank again and again, until he came into a very happy mood, and quite talkative, when his friend by adroit questioning, drew from him the real design of the enemy, which was to allay the fears of the inhabitants while preparations were making for the contemplated invasion.

Suspicions of this had existed before, but now the mask being thrown off, the danger was felt to be real and imminent, and preparations began in earnest for meeting the enemy.

Messengers were sent to General Washington imploring help. Soldiers in the army having families in the valley, were notified of the danger, and requested to hasten home, and the people began to assemble in the forts built for their protection. Colonel Zebulon Butler immediately obtained leave of absence from the army and hastened, as did others, to the relief of the settlement. But though quite a delegation was thus obtained, and through the efforts of Colonel Z. Butler, additions to their number were made from the militia, their force was far inferior to that of the enemy, and had they been fully apprised of his strength, they must have questioned the wisdom of meeting him on ground of his own choosing. As it was they were divided in opinion, some thinking it better to await reinforcements. Others maintaining it as doubtful about the coming of this hoped for aid and that the enemy was increasing daily.

The author has been assured by one conversant with these times, that Colonel Butler was in favor of going forth to meet the enemy, while Colonel Dennison as strenuously maintained the expediency of remaining within the fort, until reinforcements should arrive. Col. Butler seeing it could be decided only by a bold measure, stepped out in front of the fort, and called on all who would go with him to come out on the parade ground. Thereupon a large number went out with him, leaving Col. Dennison and those of his opinion within the fort.

While he, regarding it as a bravado, immediately said,—"*I dare show my head wherever Colonel Butler does;*" and marched out and took his place with him, thus deciding a point intimately connected with the fate of that day. Their bravery outweighed their prudence.

Early in the morning of the third of July, the garrison amounting to nearly four hundred, under the command of Colonel Zebulon Butler, left the fort, and commenced its march against the enemy. Proceeding about two miles they made a halt and sent forward a small detachment of men to ascertain the position of their foes. They were found in a condition of apparent security, seemingly not expecting an engagement. In returning they came across two Indians who fired upon them, and whose fire was returned, but without effect.

The settlers moved rapidly forward, but the Indians had evidently given the alarm, for as they came up they found the emeny drawn out in line, and prepared for battle.

The line was formed a little distance in front of their camp, in a plain thinly covered with pine, shrub-oaks, and undergrowth, and extended from the river about a mile to a marsh at the foot of the mountain.

On coming in view of the enemy, the Americans immediately displayed their ranks in the order of battle, forming a line of equal extent, and attacked from right to left at the same time. Colonel Zebulon Butler commanded the right wing, and was opposed by Colonel John Butler, at the head of the British troops on the enemy's left, while Colonel Dennison commanded the left wing of the Americans, and was opposed by the Indians stationed on the enemy's right.

They were distant from each other about forty rods when the battle commenced, yet from the obstruction of the woods and brush that intervened, little was effected at the first onset. The militia stood the fire well for three or four shots, and some part of the enemy began to give way; but suddenly the wild yell of the savage was heard in the rear of the American left, their leader having conducted a large party of his warriors through the woods, and was successful in turning Dennison's flank without being perceived. The Indians in front, being in the secret of this movement, and who had given way somewhat to render it more effective, now pressed forward, pouring in a heavy and destructive fire before which Dennison's brave men fell very rapidly. To gain time and bring his men into a better position, the order was given,—"*fall back.*" Amid the confusion which prevailed, this command was taken for an order to "*retreat,*" and immediately his line broke, and every effort to restore order proved to be altogether vain.

Very nearly at the same time, Colonel John Butler was enabled to turn the American right wing, and the fire of the British regulars was successful in throwing this part of the line also into confusion.

The irregularity occasioned by mistaking Colonel Dennison's order on the left, was followed by the Indians springing in with the hatchet and striking down the officers, and making fearful havoc among the men. Thus a general rout was given to the American forces, and the Indians pursuing the retreat with wild terrific yells, served to complete the confusion which prevailed. So dreadful was the slaughter, that nearly all who went out in the morning in the full vigor of health, and in hope of victory, were before evening overtaken and killed by the cruel Indian, or the more cruel Tory. Of the four hundred, there were scarcely sixty left to return for the protection of the families that had been bereaved, and were well nigh overwhelmed, as one and another returned, to report the disasters of that terrible day. Among the officers of the militia there fell that day one Lieutenant-Colonel, one Major, ten Captains, six Lieutenants, and two Ensigns. Some of the fugitives escaped by swimming the river, and others by taking refuge in the mountains. As the news of defeat spread through the valley, the women and children sought refuge, some in the woods, and mountains, and different forts, and others still, by passing, in boats down the river. The Indians after satisfying their thirst for blood, turned back to secure the spoils of victory.

In looking over the battle ground, and in wandering through the woods and places adjoining, the Indians not only came across articles left in flight, but also met with stragglers of the defeated army who had not yet found a hiding place, or who were the last to leave the ground where the battle had been fought. These stragglers were taken, a Mr. Lebbens Hammond among the number, to a place where many of the enemy were gathered together, very likely the headquarters of the Indian encampment. Twenty-eight persons had thus been collected, and were made to sit on the ground in a circle, with their feet extended toward its center. Many of the warriors were about them, and some of them appeared to be in consultation about something which from their looks and gestures these prisoners thought must relate to them. They fixed their eyes intently upon them, watching every changing feature of their face, trying to determine by their looks, the tones of their voice, or by their action, something decisive as to their own fate. pending on this consultation.

While thus anxiously awaiting its issue, an old squaw came in bearing a boy, about twelve or thirteen years of age on her back. He was a young fifer, named William Buck, whose father held the office of Captain in one of the regiments, and he had gone out as a musician in the company under his father. He was a beautiful and sprightly lad, and is said to have been one of the most promising boys in the settlement. While the squaw was thus carrying him along in evident delight on her back, intending no doubt to adopt him into her own family, another of her own sex came up behind and planted a hatchet in the boy's head. Young Buck fell off the old squaw's back and sank upon the ground dead. Immediately after there succeeded a contest between these two females. The one fell upon the other with the fury of a maniac, and others came up and joined in the struggle.

This scene occurring at a distance of about four rods from where the warriors were in consultation, drew their attention from the business before them, and led them to interfere in settling the quarrel.

Mr. Hammond watched the progress of this squabble with intense interest, supposing as the event proved, that its issue might have some bearing on his own and his companions' fate. The combatants were soon separated, and the warriors returned to their places, but directly after, she who had been the first aggressor, and called Queen Esther, came to the ring and placing her two hands on the shoulders of two of the prisoners, caused them to lean one side as she stepped between them into the ring, and advanced toward its center, with the deadly weapon in her hand. She came directly toward Mr. Hammond. He supposed she had marked him for her victim. But as she continued to advance, her eye seemed to turn toward the one a little to his left, and coming up planted the hatchet in his head. He sank back upon the ground without a groan. With Hammond, the next moment was one of awful suspense. —On whose head will the next blow fall?—Mine, he thought, may be the one.—The squaw moved on a little further toward his left, and kept on going thus about the ring.—For a few moments his mind was in a state of unutterable anguish and confusion. He thought that death was just before him. But must I sit here and see each one of my brave companions receive the unerring blow, until my turn comes for the awful stroke?—Shall I make no effort to cling to life?—Can there be any hope of escape, though I make an attempt?—But would it not be better to end life in an attempt to escape, than to sit here in silent gloom, and hear the dread sound of that hatchet as it falls upon one and another of my comrades? Such were the thoughts that arose one after another in his mind while this awful wretch continued her murderous course around the ring.

When she had gone about half way round, Mr. Hammond resolved to make an effort for his life. He had little thought of being able to escape, for the warriors were standing in a row about three men deep all around them. Yet he resolved to make the trial, even though he might fail, deeming it better to meet death in a struggle for life, than tamely to submit when a chance was presented for escape. And now that he had formed his resolve, he wondered that the others should sit motionless and quiet;—why do they not start to their feet, and and dashing the old squaw to the ground contend from hand to hand, with their savage foes, until they were stricken down. All sat in mute expectation of the dread moment, the most of them partly bending over with countenances sad and pale.

As the unseemly executioner kept on her way, Mr. Hammond perceived that when raising the hatchet the eyes of all each time were turned toward her;—he thought that would be his best time to make a start. He drew his feet up, little by little, until he had them pretty nearly under him, and when the hatchet was raised over the third one to his right, he started with a bound, and ran with the utmost speed directly toward the ring of savages, pursuing a line straight forward, and to his surprise, the Indians opened to the right and left, and for a moment seemed bewildered by this unexpected movement. He passed through them without being cut down as he expected, and continued to run at his utmost speed. He had not gone over three or four rods from them before they began to send their hatchets after him. For a few moments the hatchets flew about him in every direction. One just grazed his ear,—another passed just before him, and struck quivering in the tree he was passing. The thought flashed upon him to grasp it, but a moment's delay might be fatal, and on he sped. When about ten rods distant, he turned and saw three Indians starting out in pursuit. As he was very fleet on foot, he began to think there was a chance for him to escape. Yet at no great distance before him was a swamp; he might be overtaken there and tomahawked, and he dared not turn to the right or left or they would flank him, he continued to run directly forward. Ten rods further on he looked around and saw he was gaining on them. He endeavored to increase his speed somewhat. In a few moments he descended into a little hollow. This took him out of thier sight. He saw before him a large pine tree partly surrounded by bushes. He sprang in behind it, and stood with his back close against it, hoping to elude observation.

The next moment the Indians came bounding by him, one on his left, and two on his right; they went on without stopping, and were presently out of sight. But they would soon reach the swamp, and would there be led to think they had left him behind, and would no doubt return in a short time, and might discover his place of concealment. He had no weapon for defense, and after all might become their victim. He was not satisfied to remain where he was, but looked about for a better place, more especially to find something on which he could lay his hand to offer some resistance to a second capture. He found at a little distance from him the remains of an old pine tree, that had laid on the ground until it was perfectly decayed and from which the knots had fallen out. He found one with quite a lengthy arm, and with the knot at the end, and placing his knee across it, found it capable of sustaining a heavy blow without breaking.

Thus equipped he returned to his secret covert for he saw no better, and felt happy in the consciousness of not being entirely unarmed in case of an attack. He now awaited with some anxiety the return of those in pursuit, intending to keep a good outlook, and in case he was discovered, to rush out and if possible, administer the first blow. It was not long before he saw one of the Indians coming toward him, and examining carefully the thickets in his way. Now, thought he, I shall be discovered, and must be prepared to give him battle. But when within a few rods of his place of concealment, the Indian caught sight of the head of some one raised up from behind a log that lay a few rods to Hammond's right, and he immediately turned in that direction. He did not go far before the settler, as it proved to be, arose and shot him through, and dropped back again behind the log. How fortunate this!—thought Mr. Hammond. He was evidently spared from a contest that might have been doubtful, yet it was not certain whether it would turn to his advantage or not, for the firing might bring other Indians to the place. But there were guns discharging constantly in every part of the forest, so that this particular spot would not be likely to attract attention more than any other, and it gave him more assurance when he found a friend near by, in case of the return of the other two Indians who had started out in pursuit. They did not come; and if they had, it might not have been well for them, for the friend near by could be distinctly heard reloading his rifle.

It was now a little after sunset and twilight began to throw her mellow shades around him. Soon it would be dark, when he would try and make his way back to the fort. He kept his place until the darkness assured him of comparative safety, and then ventured to address, in a low voice the companion he had found near. He gave him to understand that he was a friend, and that they must come near each other for mutual protection and aid.

They came together and began to direct their way toward the fort. They proceeded cautiously, every now and then coming upon a dead or wounded soldier. Mr. Hammond searched for a time among the slain for a gun, but the Indians had been over the ground and taken them away. He kept on his way with his war-club, trusting to this in case of danger. Passing off the battle-ground, they soon came to the fort. They did not know but that in the meantime it had come into the hands of the enemy, and they approached it with caution. They crept up silently to the gate, and soon were able to discern voices with which they were familiar.

On making themselves known they were admitted into the fort, and rejoiced in being able to meet with friends, though in circumstances of deep sorrow and affliction.

Mr. Hammond, as far as he was able, related to them the scenes that transpired after the battle, and of his marvelous escape, and as there were not men enough to defend the fort, and as it would no doubt have to be surrendered to the enemy the next day, he was advised to continue on down the river until he was beyond the reach of the Indians. In accordance with this advice, he and his companion continued to move further on, and thus made good their escape.*

Mr. Hammond's case presents a very remarkable instance of daring. It is certainly wonderful that he should have effected his escape, when surrounded by a dense crowd of dusky warriors, and it is not less surprising that he should have eluded the three who started out in pursuit, when there were so many chances against him.

The deliberate murder of so many prisoners of war, and the other cruelties that have been recorded as having transpired there at this time, go very far toward justifying the impression, that there were enacted some of the bloodiest and most revolting scenes on record. No wonder there has been an effort to deny them, for they naturally tax our credulity, and lead us to suppose they must have been committed by beings outside of the range of our common humanity.

We turn with pleasure to an act relieving somewhat the darkness of the picture we have been contemplating. It is of a young man named Samuel Carey, about nineteen years of age, who was among the few prisoners taken. He had been captured by Roland Montour, an Indian Captain, and was taken by him to a young warrior who had been wounded and was dying. Montour asked the young warrior if Carey should be slain, or if he should be taken to his father and mother to be adopted into their family in his stead. The young warrior with his expiring breath desired that he should be re-

---

*Statements given to the author by the late Amariah Hammond, Esq., of Dansville, Livingston Co., N. Y.

ceived into his father's family in his place. Carey was then painted, and received the dying Indian's name, and when he reached the Indian country, was taken and adopted as had been arranged.*

*Annals of Luzerne County by Stewart Pierce.

CHAPTER VIII.

It has been said of the battle of Wyoming that " the sun never shed its rays on a bloodier field. From Wintermoot's to Fort Forty, the broad plain was strewn with the dead and mangled bodies of one hundred and sixty-one brave men who perished in a conflict which no resource of art, and courage of soul on their part, could render equal."*

In view of the superior force of the enemy and their own depleted numbers there was no thought of holding the fort against them. To avoid being made prisoner Colonel Zubulon Butler left the valley and retired to Guadenhutten. Fifteen regulars belonging to Captain Hewitt's company retired to Fort Augusta for the same reason. The women and children of the Lackawanna valley fled toward the upper settlements on the Delaware; those of Pittston and Wilksbarre toiled over the mountains, and through the great swamp to the lower settlement; while those of Hanover, Plymouth and Newport escaped to Fort Augusta.†

On the morning of the Fourth of July, Colonel John Butler, with his British and Indian forces appeared before Fort Forty and demanded its surrender.

Colonel Dennison being in command, gave answer to this summons, and entered into articles of capitulation.

---
*Annals of Luzerne Co.   †Ib.

It was stipulated that the settlers should be disarmed and their garrison demolished ; that all the prisoners and public stores should be given up ; that the property of the people called Tories should be made good, and they be permitted to remain peaceably upon their farms. In behalf of the settlers it was stipulated that their lives and property should be preserved, and that they should be left in the unmolested occupancy of their farms.

The British officer advised that in case there were any spirituous liquors in store, to destroy them, for if the Indians were to get hold of them, he would be unable to restrain them from whatever acts of violence they might choose to commit.

When the time came, as agreed upon for the surrender of the fort, both British and Indians were in attendance, and the gates being opened, they were allowed to enter and take possession of whatever articles had been given up in the terms of capitulation. The Indians as soon as they came in began to look about with a sort of idle curiosity in every part of the fort. This they continued to do for some time and seemed as much gratified as little children with anything they saw that was new. Yet having become satisfied with this, they began to lay their hands on whatever they could find, and appropriated to themselves whatever they chose. They wandered about in a most reckless manner, siezed on everything within their reach and wantonly secured it.

Large and nice feather beds had been brought into the fort for safe keeping. The feathers, to them seemed of no account, but the ticking they thought had some value, hence the beds were ripped open and the feathers emptied out on the ground. Occasionally gusts of wind would take them up, and whirl them in clouds in the air. This gave them infinite amusement, and each time they were lifted up and whirled around above their heads was hailed with yells of delight and peal after peal of laughter.

Colonel Butler then said to Col. Dennison that he would not be able to restrain the Indians from pilfering and that if the women had articles of clothing they wished to preserve they had better put them on, for if they were left in sight they would certainly be taken. The women therefore selected whatever they considered of most value and dressed without special regard to the number of garments they had on. But after the savages had plundered everything they could find, they began to examine closely the dress of the inhabitants, and finding they had more on than seemed essential for a warm day in July, went to work and stripped off this fine clothing leaving on the women nothing but a couple of under garments, while they tore from the men everything but their shirts and pantaloons. They may have thought they did well to escape with their lives.

For a time they regarded their fate as quite uncertain, since their treatment had been so different from what had been expected in view of the articles of capitulation. Colonel Butler himself seemed to be at a loss what to do with so many women and children; he could not expect to carry them back to Niagara as prisoners without subjecting them to unheard of sufferings, and they could not remain where they were without the means of subsistence, he determined therefore to let them remove to the settlements east of them on the Delaware.

In accordance therefore with this decision the men in the fort with their families, together with those bereaved of husband and father, amounting to about sixty removed from Fort Forty, and taking a path across the mountains after a journey attended by many hardships, came to the valley of the Delaware where were settlers who met them with kindness and hospitality.

Such as had taken refuge in Fort Wyoming made a surrender to the enemy on similar terms and shared alike with them in a violation of the articles of capitulation.*

Van Campen having been sent in another direction, was away when the sad events just related were transpiring, and on his return was advancing toward the place when he met an express on Shawnee Flatts who said "*All was lost, that all the men had been cut off by the*

---

*In closing his account of the battle of Wyoming, Colonel Stone remarks,—"It does not appear that anything like a massacre followed the capitulation. Nor in the events of the preceding day is there good evidence of the perpetration of any specific acts of cruelty, other than such as are usual in the general rout of a battle-field—save only the unexampled atrocities of the Tories, thirsting probably for revenge in regard to other questions than that of allegience to the King. In a subsequent work by the same author he says,—"During the flight to Fort Forty the scene was that of horrible slaughter. Nor did the darkness put an end to the work of death. No assault was made upon the fort that night; but many of the prisoners taken were put to death by torture. The place of these murders was about two miles north of Fort Forty, upon a rock around which the Indians formed themselves in a circle. Sixteen of the prisoners placed in a ring around the rock, near the river, were held by stout Indians, while the squaws struck their heads open with a tomahawk. Only one individual, a powerful man named Hammond, by a desperate effort. escaped." My informant whose account is given in the text, thinks there must be a mistake about these men being held by stout Indians. The evidence subsequently given to Col. Stone, must have led him to make this admission. With some little variation it is essentially the same thing we have given, only not quite so circumstantial as that given by the man who was the principal actor in the scence. J. N. H.

British and Indians and that the fort was about to be surrendered to the invading party."

Finding he could be of no assistance and that if he advanced he and his party would in all probability fall into the hands of the enemy, he turned about and went back to Northumberland.

Soon after his return, he was sent to take charge of the garrison at Fort Wheeler ; and directly after an order came from Colonel Hunter, to take charge of a company of militia-men from Lancaster County, and circuit about the settlements and see if any strolling parties of Indians could be discovered in the region.

These men had come as volunteers from the southern part of Pennsylvania, and as at present there was no special call for their service elsewhere, it was thought their time would be well employed in guarding the settlements from sudden inroad and surprise. They had brought their officers with them and were prepared for any duty, but as they were unacquainted with the woods, the command was given to Lieut. Van Campen.

Entering cheerfully on a duty that led him once more to visit his old haunts, he prepared at once to march through the woods with the men of Lancaster They accordingly set out in fine spirits, and many protestations of their desire to meet and punish the enemy, that had wrought such disaster among the settlements.

Captain Salmon a particular friend of Van Campen's joined the expedition. He was something of a *limb*, and he and Van Campen were rarely out together without finding some occasion for amusement.

At the close of their first day's march they came to a

house in an open clearing deserted by its proprietors, where they proposed to encamp for the night. As the nights were now becoming cold a large fire was made in the house, and when the time came for taking rest the militia men took their places very near the fire. Capt. Salmon and Van Campen finding the room taken up so that little warmth could be had from the fire, had a place near the door. A large black dog had followed the Lancaster men, and as the room was full without him, he had been left outside to shirk for himself. Very soon after, as all had taken their places on the floor, everything became quiet and still. The militia-men soon fell into a profound sleep, as their snoring seemed to indicate, and as during the day they had been on the outlook for Indian warriors, it is not improbable they may have had some thoughts of them in their dreams. They may have thought of them as very near and watching their opportunity to spring from their covert and deliver the death-dealing blow. All seemed to be enjoying the rest of night, with the exception of the poor black dog, who was uneasy, and evidently dissatisfied with his single quarters in the open air. He came to the door and tried to get in. The door was hung on wooden hinges, and when it was opened or shut made a creaking noise that seemed alarmingly loud in a still night. It did not shut very close, but being warped a little, left an opening near the bottom an inch or more in width. The dog in trying to get in thrust his nose into this crack and forced the door a little further open. This movement made such a creaking it aroused the militia-men from their slumbers. One raised up and said,—" What's that,—

what's that?"—Another said,—"I heard a noise." A third affirmed,—"So did I." Another still,—"I believe it's the Indians."

For a few moments they were very uneasy, listening anxiously with the expectation of hearing something more. They were told by Salmon and Van Campen that it probably was nothing very serious and that they had better lie down again. They very soon settled down once more into a quiet sleep, when Salmon whispered in Van Campen's ear, "The next time the dog attempts to come in, we'll play them a little trick."

With this in view he watched his opportunity when the dark knight of the chase should put in a second appearance. He soon came and forced his whole head through the opening made. Just at this moment Salmon pushed against the door with his foot, and caught the dog by the neck. Old growler finding himself in this plight gave a terrific yell. In an instant the men started to their feet, some of them crying out, "*The war-whoop,—The war-whoop—The Indians are upon us,—The Indians are upon us.*" By this time the dog had been relieved, and an Irishman who was in the company sprang to the door, and placing his back against it, called for help. "*Och,*" said he, "*they'll burst the doo-er open, —they'll burst the doo-er open;—give us some help, men, —give us some help,—the Engens 'll be arter a comin in.*"

To Salmon and Van Campen the scene was comical in the extreme, but they started up as though something must be done, and in a few moments all were under arms and ready for action. The stalwart Irishman was ordered to leave the door. He jumped as though expecting to be made the first victim. He darted forward with such haste, he stumbled and fell his whole length on the floor. The men were so intent on watching the door, that this mishap occasioned little merriment to any but Salmon and Van Campen. They could not help enjoying it, and with an amused feeling watched the earnest expectation of the men, who looked as though they were expecting the sudden entrance of a party of Indians. But no one came in, they could hear no noise without, not even the tread of a single warrior.

Van Campen ordered the door to be opened, and to their surprise only one dark visage made its appearance, and this was the face of the old black dog, that came quietly walking in when there was no impediment in the way. Captain Salmon could contain himself no longer; but laughed outright, telling the men it was their dog that had raised *the Indian war-whoop.* They seemed a little chagrined at this, but presently as they saw there was no danger, they joined in the laugh, and it passed off as a good joke.

Starting out again the next morning they proceeded on their way through the woods, and keeping up their march most of the time during the day, penetrated the wilderness to a considerable distance without meeting the enemy. Yet they advanced with the same care and circumspection as they would have done had they known their foes were in that region and prepared to meet them.

When night was coming on they made choice of a low piece of ground, called Eve's swamp, as their encampment. It was too cold to do without a fire and as the ground was low and surrounded by a thick growth of young trees, the light from their fire would not be seen at a distance and hence would not be likely to attract the enemy They built but one fire, partly from necessity in providing for their evening meal, after which Van Campen and Salmon took a stroll around, partly to see if any lurking foe might be near, and partly to ascertain the safety of their position, and whether the light of their fire could be seen at any considerable distance.

Becoming satisfied as to this, they found on their return that the soldiers had disposed themselves quite advantageously about the fire, each one seeking for himself a position of comfort and leaving their officers to do the same. The most comfortable situations the camp afforded were now occupied, and Van Campen and Salmon settled themselves upon the best ground they could find and composed their minds for sleep. They were comfortable for a time, but soon began to be so cold it was impossible to sleep.

The militia men had recovered from the disturbance of the previous night, and were having a very comfortable time. Van Campen thought there might be a chance if they were startled a little, to gain a more comfortable position. So taking up his hatchet he struck the handle against a small staddle that was near, and the stroke resounded with a loud cracking noise. It had the desired effect, for the men instantly took the alarm and the inquiry passed from one to another,—"*Didn't you hear a stick crack just now,—there must be some one around.*" One said *he heard it plainly*, another, *he could hear them walk*,—meaning the Indians.

After hearing them talk for a few minutes, Van Campen said to them,—" *You had better lie down ; I think no enemy is near, very likely it was something else that made the noise,—you need rest, and may as well try and get what you can*" They dropped down again and were soon fast asleep. After waiting awhile to let them all forget their troubles, Van Campen took his tomahawk and gave the tree another stroke. This startled them more than it had done before. Now they felt confident the enemy was lurking about them in the woods. All were wide awake and ready to move. One swore he would not stay where he was ; another said he would not lie near the fire to be shot at, and the agitation seemed to be very general.

Van Campen and Salmon let them talk until they had fully opened their minds, and then Van Campen said it might be advisable for them to take a station a little distance from the fire, and keep a good look out, *while he and Capt Salmon would camp down near it*, and if anything stirred, or showed signs of the approach of the enemy they were to give him notice.

They kept up a watch, coming occasionally to the fire to warm, while Van Campen and Capt. Salmon remained in their places and were quite comfortable until daylight. Nothing, however, was said about the tomahawk handle, but the soldiers were commended for their good conduct and watchful care during the night.

The **route** pursued by our party after this was the one usually taken by scouts in this section of country. They proceeded first to the head waters of Green Creek, crossed over through Eve's swamp to little Fishing Creek, thence to Chilisquaka, and from this directed their march to the Muncey Mountains and over these to Muncey Creek, up which they followed for nearly a day's travel.

On their route they discovered no traces which led them to infer the presence of Indians. It was now becoming late in the season, and the probabilities were becoming greater that they would not visit this region again before the opening of another season. From this point they commenced their return homeward, taking very nearly the same direction pursued in going out. They returned therefore to their stations, Lieut. Van Campen to Fort Wheeler, and the militia-men to a Mr. McClure's farm where they had their quarters.

Not long after this Van Campen projected another expedition somewhat different from the one just described. It was not unusual for parties to disguise themselves as Indians and go out into parts of the country frequented by them, that in this way they might better ascertain their position and numbers. Fearful that there might yet be some few, still lurking around and ready to commit some depredation. Lieut. Van Campen and his friend Capt. Salmon went out in disguise to see if they could make any discoveries. They were gone longer than had been expected and their friends began to be anxious concerning them, and were fearing they might have been killed or taken prisoners.

The reason of their long absence was because of their delay with the hope of making some discoveries at a notch in Nob Mountain, through which the Indians were accustomed to pass on their way to attack the settlements, or waylay and shoot people on or near the river.

They lingered around this point until they were satisfied there would be no Indians to make their appearance before another year, and then set out on their return homeward.

On their way they ascended the summit of a hill covered by oak trees. They came to an opening whence they had a view of the valley below, through which they were to pass. On observing it carefully they saw a party of men led by some one, and from the course they were taking they concluded this company would ascend the hill and pass right by them. Who they were they did not know; were they Lancaster men, or were they not?—was the question that arose in their minds. From certain things they observed, they concluded it must be a company of soldiers without much experience, and the thought occurred to them that they would give them a little start.

Fixing their eye on a large oak tree that appeared to be in the direct line of their march they concluded to await the coming of the company to this tree and then plant a couple of balls two or three feet above their heads in the tree. As soon as the officer at the head of this company came up to this tree, Van Campen and Salmon fired from different stations, then raised the war-whoop and began to jump from tree to tree, so as to make it appear as though a number of Indians were on the ground.

These soldiers did not wait for another discharge of guns, but turned and ran with all possible speed back to the fort. It was about five miles distant, and when they arrived there they created a great alarm; said they had been fired at by a large party of Indians;—they heard their war-whoop, and saw them jump. "Yes," said the officer,—"some of their balls struck the tree over my head, and only just missed me."

Van Campen and Salmon came in the same day, and great joy was expressed at seeing them alive and safe. There was a hearty shaking of hands and many congratulations in view of their escape, and inquiries it they did not see Indians? They answered No; but said they had seen moccasin tracks, meaning their own, and that on the route they were going they heard firing, and supposed it must have been from the same party that attacked the scout. The real facts in the case they thought it prudent not to divulge.

It may be thought that the statements here made are not very creditable for the Lancaster men. They conducted no differently from multitudes of others under like circumstances. The truth is they were unaccustomed to the field; they had not been hardened by exposure to danger. Reports were rife of the terrible and cruel nature of Indian warfare, there was a general and constant recital of their bloody deeds and it is not in the least surprising that in coming suddenly upon what they supposed a large party, the most of whom were in ambush, and the demonstration made simply a feint to lure them into a fight with overwhelming numbers, it is not strange they thought it prudent to retire from what may have been considered a very unequal contest.

Their flight from what they supposed to be a large party of Indians was not a circumstance without a parallel in the history of the war. Our brave Washington had frequently to complain of the instability of the militia-men, so much so, he was led to believe they did more injury to the service than good. The want of firmness in the hour of danger did not belong to the militia of Lancaster any more than to those of any other section of the country.

Near the close of the season an expedition of about two hundred men under the command of Col. Hartley, set out for the enemy's country. "In our route," says the Colonel, "we met with great rains, prodigious swamps, mountains, defiles, and rocks impeded our march. We waded and swam the river Lycoming upward of twenty times." They marched into the very heart of the enemy's country, destroyed Queen Esther's town, and put the savages to flight in several engagements. On his return march, Col. Hartley was attacked below Wyalusing by two hundred Indians, whom he routed, their loss being fifteen killed and thirty wounded. His own loss was four killed and ten wounded.*

From the events recorded of this year it will be seen that the sufferings of the people on the frontiers of Pennsylvania were such as to cast a gloom over the entire region, yet it naturally resulted in stimulating them to greater exertion in providing for their defence in the future.

This same year also, was fruitful in disaster among the frontier settlements of New York.

---

*Annals of Luzerne County.

CHAPTER IX.

The unexampled barbarities committed by the Indians and British, led General Washington to turn his thought to this part of the great American conflict. With little outlay of means themselves, an immense destruction of life and property resulted from their murderous inroads; leading him to believe that the most effective remedy would be to strike a blow at their homes, and break up if possible, those hives that sent forth these swarms to prey upon the defenceless.

To effect this one thousand men were ordered to be placed under the command of Gen. McIntosh who was to proceed directly against the Sandusky towns. Between two and three hundred soldiers were to be under the command of Col. Clark to go against the Indians of Illinois. The success of these two expeditions, it was thought, would tend greatly to diminish the inroads made by the savages coming from these famous recruiting grounds for Indian invasions, and contribute much to the safety of the frontier settlements.

Col. Clark, with the men that were to go on his expedition, immediately left Fort Pitt and went down the Ohio river as far as the falls where he landed his men, concealed his boats, and marched directly toward Kaskaskia. The provisions they carried were soon exhausted, obliging them to subsist on roots for two days.

Their bravery and patriotism equaled the occasion, and they passed on with unabated vigor. Fortunately they met with no opposition, not even a straggling Indian appeared in sight. These indications they regarded as omens of success, and elated with the prospect, hastened forward, reaching Kaskaskia in the night. They entered it unseen and without being heard, and took possession of the town and fort without opposition. The inhabitants were unconscious of danger until it was upon them. Separated as they were from the American settlements by immense forests, whose stillness seemed to inspire in them a sense of security and peace, they were surprised and taken without dreaming of the impending danger; and not one was allowed to escape to give the alarm to adjacent towns.

Col. Clark's sudden and bloodless victory put him in possession of a band of horses, and mounting on them a detachment of men, he sent them against other towns higher up the Mississippi, three of which were in like manner surprised and taken. The governor of Kaskaskia had in his possession papers from Quebec, Detroit and Mackinaw, directing him to incite the Indians to war, and promising remuneration for the blood they might shed. These papers were sent with the governor to Virginia; for though regarded within the limits of that State, yet it was so distant and so occupied by hostile savages, that no attempt had hitherto been made to extend her jurisdiction over it, yet as it now became hers by conquest as well as charter, the General Assembly erected it into a county to be called Illinois; appointed for it a temporary government, a regiment of infantry and a troop of cavalry, and placed it under the command of its intrepid and enterprising conqueror.

When the news of Col. Clark's achievments reached Detroit, Governor Hamilton resolved to expel him from Kaskaskia, and capture him and his soldiers. Raising an army of six hundred men, principally Indians, he left Detroit, determined to take from Col. Clark his well-earned laurels. Advancing toward Fort Vincent on the Wabash, he arrived there about the middle of December. The fort was considerably out of repair and he immediately set about improving its condition, designing it for a repository of warlike implements such as he might need, in carrying out the ambitious projects he had in view.

Meanwhile to give employment to his men, he sent most of them abroad to harass the settlements bordering on the Ohio, retaining only a single company for the defense of the fort.

Col. Clark busied himself in trying to bring the surrounding Indian tribes into correspondence with the United States, working on the fears of some, persuading others that their best interest would thus be secured.

The aid promised him fell far short of what had been contemplated, yet his enterprise and activity seemed in a measure to compensate for his deficiency in numbers. He was in the heart of the Indian country, surrounded by powerful and hostile tribes, yet he not only maintained his conquest, but by his adroit management, his undaunted courage, and his genius tor exploits of a daring character, he anticipated combinations formed against him, and acted in a way that struck terror to the heart of his foes, and caused even the strongest to stand in awe of him.

Some time passed before the news of Governor Hamilton's purpose to take him and his little army reached him. It failed to occasion him any alarm. Its influence might be seen in the preparations he began to make for the coming of the foe. His force was small;—winter was coming on;—he was so far away, and the difficulties so great, he could not expect reinforcements;—what could he do? He did not despair;—nor had he any thought of abandoning his post. He and his men talked the matter over, and resolved to maintain their ground or die in the attempt.

The Indians had no doubt received the intelligence, for they began to lurk around and *put on airs.* But the Colonel gave no sign of uneasiness, and commenced quietly to concentrate his men and prepare for action.

It so happened that while these preparations were going on, a Spanish merchant called one day at Kaskaskia, and during his conversation with the Colonel, incidentally remarked that he had recently been at St. Vincent.

The Colonel then remarked,—"I suppose Governor Hamilton has quite a large force there."—"No," said the Spaniard,—"his force is not large."—"What has become of his men?—I understood he had a large force and was coming to pay us a visit." "The most of his men have been sent away to different points along the Ohio River. He has not a very large number of men in the fort." "Ah,"—said the Colonel,—"I supposed he had."—The Colonel was not long in deciding what to do. He saw before him a grand opportunity, and embraced it. He made no further preparations to resist an attack, but resolved to become the assailant, and began at once to prepare for the expedition. A galley mounting two four pounders, and four swivels, was furnished with a company of men, and its commander was ordered to ascend the Wabash and station himself a few miles below St. Vincent's, and to allow no one to pass until the arrival of the main army. Then garrisoning Kaskaskia with militia, and arranging the inhabitants for the protection of the other towns, Col. Clark set out on his march across the country, on the 7th of February 1779, at the head of one hundred and thirty intrepid and brave men.

Such were the difficulties to be encountered that less resolute spirits would have quailed before them. The weather was cold, and in crossing the overflowed lands of the Wabash they were obliged to wade through water and ice, in places up to their breasts, making their advance toilsome and slow. Yet strange to say these heroic men toiled on, overcoming every obstacle, and arrived at St. Vincent's on the evening of the twenty-third of February, and almost at the same time with the galley sent on before them. The army had not been discovered on the way ; the enemy had not been informed of their coming, but here they were with the trial of their powers and strength to be put to the test.

At seven o'clock the next morning they marched up to commence the assault. The inhabitants instead of interposing any obstacle received the troops with gladness, and joined in the attack on the fort. For eighteen hours the garrison resisted the continued efforts of the assailants. But when night came on, Colonel Clark had an entrenchment thrown up, within rifle shot of the enemy's strongest battery, and in the morning such a well directed fire was poured in upon it from this point, that in fifteen minutes two pieces of cannon were silenced without any loss to themselves. The advantages thus gained induced Hamilton to demand a parley, when he intimated his design to surrender. The terms by which the governor and garrison became prisoners of war, were soon arranged, and a considerable quantity of military stores came into the hands of the conquerors.

The capture of Governor Hamilton was justly regarded as a matter of no small importance. He was a man at once bold and active, and believed to be the chief instigator of the Indians in their work of devastation and death. His design in sending out the larger portion of his men to harass the frontier settlements on the Ohio, was but a part of his plan to involve the entire region west of the Alleghany mountains in a bloody and destructive war. He who had planned all this, and was determined to sweep away all the American settlements in Western Virginia, was now a prisoner in the hands of the enemy. It is not surprising the event created much rejoicing, nor that a man who had rendered himself so obnoxious to the people, should have been treated with more than ordinary rigor. By order of the Governor of Virginia, the Governor of Detroit was manacled with irons and confined in jail.

While the siege was in progress Col. Clark was informed that a party of Indians sent out by Hamilton to harass the frontiers, was returning, and were near St. Vincent's with two prisoners. He at once sent a detachment of men to give them battle, which resulted in taking nine Indians and liberating the two prisoners.

The prompt, energetic, and self-sacrificing action of Colonel Clark excited universal admiration, and it certainly merits the highest praise, evincing a rare genius as a commander, and presenting qualities found only in men of the very first order in generalship.

The expedition under General McIntosh was not alike successful, and having been projected at the same time, seems to have been somewhat eclipsed by the brilliant success that attended the other. His command was to consist of a thousand men, not already in the field and prepared to march toward the point designated, but men that were to be enlisted for the service. At a distance from the thickly settled part of the country, to enlist, equip, and organize so large a force was no small undertaking. The time consumed in this wearisome labor, occupied the season best suited to a successful military movement.

Hence it being late and anxious to achieve what he could for the security of the frontier, he penetrated the enemy's country as far as Tuscarawa where it was resolved to build and garrison a fort, and wait for further operations until the opening of spring. A fort named Laurens was erected on the banks of the Tuscarawa, a garrison of one hundred and fifty men, under the command of Col. John Gibson was left for its protection, while the main army returned to Fort Pitt.

It was some little time before the Indians became

aware of the erection of Fort Laurens, and they were not a little disturbed in view of this trespass on their territory, and began immediately to devise schemes to annoy their enemy. Early in January a body of Indians approached Fort Laurens without being perceived, and during the night succeeded in catching the horses outside the fort, and taking off their bells carried them into the woods some distance away. Concealing themselves in the prairie grass, along the path leading from the fort, they commenced rattling the bells in the morning, at the farther end of their line of ambush. Sixteen men were sent out to bring in the horses. Allured by the sound of bells, they followed the path along which the Indians lay concealed. All at once they arose and opened upon them a destructive fire from front and rear. Fourteen were killed and two were taken prisoners. Toward the close of the same day, an army of eight hundred and eighty-seven warriors, painted and equipped for war, marched in single file in full view of the garrison, and encamped on elevated ground on the opposite side of the river. The Indians thus invested the fort, making little or no demonstrations against it, and remained here for six weeks, when they were led to withdraw. Such was the overwhelming force of the enemy that the garrison could do nothing more than maintain their position, and the service they rendered was simply to hold the fort. These two expeditions were directed against the western Indians; another expedition was now in contemplation to march into the Seneca country, or Western New York.

General Sullivan was appointed its leader, and Fort

Laurens was ordered to be evacuated that its garrison might be added to the force that was being gathered for that expedition.*

*Archives of Pennsylvania.

CHAPTER X.

In accordance with a determination to punish the Indians, as intimated in the preceding chapter, and as ordered by Congress in the instructions given to the Commander in chief, "To take the most effectual means for protecting the inhabitants, and chastising the Indians for their continued depredations," an expedition was planned for carrying the war into the very heart of the country occupied by the Six Nations.—They were regarded as very warlike tribes and having been for a long time in alliance with, and under the care of Great Britain, they rendered her very important service, and served greatly to increase the severities endured by the people while engaged in the Revolutionary struggle.

By their enterprise and prowess, they had gained ascendency over many other tribes, and they laid claim to a very extensive region of country. They were considerably removed from barbarism, cultivated the soil to some extent, and in their social regulations, partook of the order which characterizes more civilized communities. The expedition was designed to invade the region occupied by this confederation, lay waste their villages, destroy their crops and whatever else might be found, by which the Indian interests might be afflicted.

General Sullivan having been appointed to the principal charge of the campaign, entered on the work of preparation and selected Wyoming as the gathering place of a part of his force, and the supplies needed for the enterprise. Here were gathered the troops to march from Pennsylvania, up the Susquehanna Valley to Tioga Point, where they were to meet another portion of the army from the North under the command of General Clinton, and having formed a junction, they were to proceed up the valley of the Chemung to the rich and beautiful country of the Seneca and Cayuga tribes.

The history of Van Campen during the summer of 1779, connects him with this campaign, and we shall be led to speak of it somewhat in detail. For two or three months previous to the time of starting, he was occupied in collecting military stores. In the capacity of Quartermaster, he attended to the purchase of provisions, obtaining them of the settlers up and down the river by means of boats, and having to oversee the shipping and unshipping of these, was engaged for the most part, with the details of this business.

On one of his trips with these boats he fell in with a young man whose appearance betrayed a more than ordinary supply of self-conceit. He was not far from twenty years of age, well proportioned, and somewhat above the ordinary stature. He may have heard or known something of Van Campen's engagement with the Indian-land-man; at all events he seemed to be "spoiling" for some trial of his strength, so, as he was walking on the bank of the river, he came up to Van Campen, who was coming toward his boats, moored near by, and politely inquired,—" *Would you like to be laid on your back, sir?*"

Perceiving that the young man had a somewhat exalted idea of his bodily powers, and hoping, though he had been for sometime out of practice, to give him a lesson he would be likely to remember, and would be of some advantage to him in the future, he replied,—"*I have no objection, sir, if it can be done fairly.*"

They accordingly prepared to wrestle, and came up and took their hold. It was on a little grass plat near the river, where the bank was considerably high and steep. Van Campen before taking hold, determined what disposition he would make of the fellow and worked, in their maneuvers for this purpose. He managed to get him near the edge of the bank, and when he had him in the right position, fell back, raised him with his hands and knees and threw him over his head down the bank, landing him head foremost in the sand and water, and partly under one end of a boat. The unfortunate youth gathered in his mouth a goodly supply of sand and water, and might perhaps have been in some danger of being drowned, but there were men by, who helped him out, and though well pleased with the way in which he was served, were disposed to render him what assistance he needed.

After clearing his mouth so as to be able to speak, he said to his antagonist,—"*I will remember you for this, sir.*"

To which was replied,—"*You are welcome to think of me as long as you live.*"

The young man had no doubt reason to complain of the treatment he had received as being too harsh, but as he was the aggressor, and as his mishap was occasioned by his unwonted vanity, he is perhaps not entitled to the sympathy he might otherwise have received.

On the 31st of July, Gen. Sullivan having completed his arrangements, began to ascend the river from Wyoming toward Tioga Point. At the same time a fleet of boats under the command of Commodore John Morrison, sailed up the Susquehanna bearing in them the stores for the army. "His baggage occupied one hundred and twenty boats and two thousand horses, the former of which were arranged in regular order on the river and were propelled against the stream with setting poles, by soldiers, having a sufficient guard of troops to accompany them. The horses which carried the provisions for the daily subsistence of the troops, passed along the narrow path in single file, and formed a line extending about six miles.

The boats presented a beautiful appearance as they moved in order from their moorings, and as they passed the fort received a grand salute. which was returned by the loud cheers of the boatmen. The whole scene offered a military display surpassing any which had ever been exhibited at Wyoming, and was well calculated to make a powerful impression upon the minds of those lurking parties of savages which still continued to range upon the mountains from which all these movements were visible for many miles."*

Van Campen, being obliged as Quartermaster, to have the care of all the stores, ascended the river in one of the boats. He attended to the distribution of the pro-

---

*Chapman's History of Wyoming.

visions among the several captains and companies of boatmen, and gave an account of the same to the Commissary General of the Army.

They reached Tioga on the 11th of August, and there halted until General Clinton should join them with the forces under his command. In the meantime the Indians had been concentrating at Chemung, a large village about eleven miles above, on a branch bearing the same name.

While remaining here they proved very troublesome neighbors. They waylaid every path to watch and cut off any small party that might be sent out, or any individual so unfortunate as to stray too far from the army. They inflicted several injuries of this kind, in cutting off small companies sent out to look after the pack horses belonging to the army, that had been suffered to run loose in the woods.

They were wont to wander off to what were called Queen Esther's Flatts, and to a plain about six miles distant, covered with underbrush, and a few large oak trees.

General Sullivan thought that by sending a small party who should advance with caution to some place in the vicinity of the plain and there form an ambush, the movements of these savages might be discovered, and they would be able to play them the same game in return. Having formed his plan he called on Van Campen, and desired him to head the party and try and carry his design into execution. The plain six miles above was fixed upon as the place of trial. It was proposed to go to this place or near it, station a sentinel in the bushy top of some oak tree, who would indicate by some signal the presence of Indians if seen crossing the plain, to the party in ambush, who would be prepared to give them battle.

Major Adam Hoops, one of Sullivan's aids brought Van Campen his instructions, directing him to go as near the enemy as he judged prudent, and there make his arrangements for carrying out the plan,—which was to let the sentinel in the tree top watch for the Indians, and on discovering any, he was to let down a cord loaded with lead, to which was attached a piece of white paper; this he was to let down a given number of feet for a given number of the enemy, and if passing to the right or left, this was to be indicated by a corresponding movement of the paper.

Having received his instructions Van Campen took with him a small company of men, and proceeding to the appointed place, selected the tree and the ground for his ambnsh. His sentry with the cord prepared for giving the signal, ascended to the point of observation, where seating himself on a limb, and leaning against the the body of the tree, he could overlook the plain, and easily distinguish any movement upon its borders. From their ambush they had a fair view of the sentinel, and they all kept an eye upon him to obtain the first intimation of an approaching enemy.

After watching for about an hour, they saw the paper begin slowly to descend until it fell about five feet and stopped. Van Campen said to his men,—"My good fellows, we'll soon have sport,—there are but five of them." Presently the paper lowered about five feet more. He then observed, "We'll have something more to do,—there are ten of them." The paper continued gradually to descend until it reached a distance of about fifteen feet. He then added,—"We shall now, my brave fellows, have enough of it, for we are about equally manned."

Before the words were fairly out of his mouth, the sentry came tumbling down through the limbs to the ground, and fell near the body of the tree. The cause of the descent of the paper then flashed upon their minds, and they began to laugh at their mistake.

It was quite apparent the sentry had fallen asleep, and had unconsciously let the paper fall, and he himself, losing his balance, had come down headlong with it. The soldiers were disposed to be somewhat mirthful over the event, but to the sentry it was quite a serious disaster. One of his shoulders was put out of joint, and in other respects he found himself bruised and injured. Yet when casualties involving so much more, were things of daily occurrence, this was little thought of.

After remaining some time without making any discoveries, Van Campen returned and reported his proceedings to General Sullivan; the General inquired, "How do you like the plan?"

To which he replied,—"The plan I think is a good one, but I came very near losing a man by it."

"How so, sir?"

"Why, my sentry fell asleep and came down the tree in a hurry, head foremost, and unjointed a shoulder."

"Why didn't you dispatch the rascal?"

"I had no orders, sir, to kill my own men."

The General and his officers laughed.

Having performed this service much to the satisfaction of the commanding officer, Van Campen was entrusted with another, more hazardous than the one just related, yet well suited to his adventurous spirit. General Sullivan contemplated an attack on the Indians, gathered in force some little distance above, and wishing to know their numbers and situation, he desired some one to inspect the enemy while they were encamped for sleep, and ascertain as to these points.

Van Campen was selected for this dangerous enterprise. Having no dread about visiting the resting-place of the savage in the still hour of night, and fond of the excitement of adventure, though attended with danger, he cheerfully entered upon the undertaking. He did not anticipate trouble, a buoyant spirit raised him above fear; and though confident of being able to perform this service, and return in safety, he omitted no care that prudence might suggest as a protection against harm. He obtained an Indian dress, consisting of breech-cloth, leggins, moccasins, and a cap ornamented with feathers, and painting himself a tawny color he donned the savage costume, and with a companion habited in the same way, left the camp after dark and proceeded to execute his commission.

The two advanced cautiously to a fording place in the Chemung. It might be guarded, but finding no impediment in the way they crossed over, and ascended a mountain which brought them in sight of the enemy's fires. For a few moments they stood here, casting their eyes over the plain below, and beholding the lights that here and there gleamed through the surrounding darkness. After talking over the hazardous work before them, they began slowly to advance, keeping a good lookout for the foe, knowing full well that if discovered, their lives would pay the penalty of their temerity. Were there sentinels on the watch to discover them, or wakeful Indians to discern their strange appearance and give the alarm? Fortunately their approach was not discovered, and they waited until all were down and as they believed, asleep, and then drew near the camp.

Here Van Campen left his companion, directing him to remain until his return, but adding that in case he should hear the report of guns, he might know there was trouble, and he should try and get back to the army the best way he could.

With slow and weary tread Van Campen came within the enemy's encampment. He found there were several fires, and the Indians were lying about them apparently in profound sleep. He saw the dusky forms of warriors all around him. He heard the low hum that attended the breathing of sleeping men. Every now and then he could see one of them turn over, or move in some way to better his position. It was a dangerous place to be in and prudence suggested that he had better not stay here very long. He remained here long enough, however to count the number of men in that encampment, and the counting the number of fires that indicated the number of encampments he estimated their force at about seven hundred. Having made these observations he silently worked his way back to his companion, and both of them returned to their own camp in safety. It was now about the dawn of day, and their coming was welcomed with joy, and after giving his report to the General, who was gratified with his success, Van Campen sought rest after the watchings and fatigues of the night.

On the afternoon of the day of his return, Mr. Adam Hoops, one of General Sullivan's aids, came to Van Campen's tent, and requested him to wait upon the General. He went, and as he came into the General's presence, saw that he appeared in a very pleasant mood, when he said,—" Well sir, you have learned the way to Chemung,—what say you about leading the advance guard against the Indians?" At the same time adding, —" It's a post of honor and of danger too."—"That will suit me,"—replied Van Campen, "I am ready to meet danger."

"Go, then," said he, "select your men, and be ready." In obedience to this order he prepared for the expedition, made choice of his men, and was ready to start at a moment's warning. The order soon came and they took up their line of march a little after sunset.

General Samuel Hand of the Pennsylvania line, had been appointed to command the detachment, consisting of eleven hundred men. Van Campen marched on before the main body, at the head of twenty-six men, with orders to advance as far as the Narrows, and halt until the main body came up.

On coming to this place they waited until the others came up, when they all received the order from General Hand, in a low but emphatic voice,—" Soldiers cut your way through,—cut your way through."

They did so, and entered the Indian camp and village at the break of day. The Indians had left, evidently in great haste, from the indications betokening their flight. Their trail seemed to lead up the river, and pausing a few minutes for rest they pushed on after them.

They set fire to the village and followed up the river about two miles where they came to a ridge, called from its shape, Hog Back Hill.

As they came near this place Van Campen remarked to his men,—" Here we must look out for an Indian ambuscade, it seems so well suited for one."

" Be on your guard, my brave fellows, we shall be likely to have it as hot as we can sup it."—Every eye now turned to the hill, and as they began to ascend, they saw a stir in the bushes at the top, and presently the muzzles of rifles darted out toward them like hatchel teeth. A deadly fire followed a moment after, *and sixteen of Van Campen's men, fell at his side, some wounded, the most of them killed.* There was not a moment for reflection. Another fire would sweep away the remaining part of the advance guard. They were near the river bank. As quick as thought Van Campen ordered his men to reserve their fire and fall behind the bank of the river. " Quick," said he "*they will be out in a moment to scalp,—then will be our turn, let every shot tell.*" No sooner had their position been taken, than six or seven stout fellows rushed out, with knife and tomahawk in hand, to kill the wounded and take the scalps. " Now is our chance, boys." Van Campen took the leader, and his men took care of the others.

General Hand now came up at quick step, advanced within a few rods of the enemy, and ordered his men to fire and charge with the bayonet.

This movement routed the enemy and put him to flight. After this engagement they took up their dead and wounded and came back the next night, to their former camp.

On examining his clothes after the battle Van Campen found that there had been some sharp shooting; two or three bullet holes had been made through them, and a ball had just grazed his side. They had no further encounter with the enemy until after the arrival of General Clinton, with the other part of the army.

General Clinton as we have seen was to descend the Susquehanna and meet General Sullivan at Tioga Point. His preparations were made in view of this and depended on receiving a notice of Sullivan's advance, and on receiving this he set out for the place of meeting.

General Clinton conceived the idea of conveying his troops in boats down the Susquehanna to Tioga Point. One of its principal branches takes its rise from the waters of Otsego Lake. The General kept back the water by throwing a dam across its outlet, thus accumulating a large volume of water and was ready on receiving the order to open his reservoir, and be wafted by its swollen tide into the vicinity of the other army. The order came and he opened his flood-gates, embarked with his troops upon the stream, and was wafted by its proud wave bearing its burden in triumph to its point of destination. The sudden and unexpected rise of water without any visible cause to produce it occasioned great alarm among the Indians who ascribed the cause of this unusual inundation to the Great Spirit, who thus manifested his displeasure with them and had sent this flood to inundate their fields of corn, and destroy their crop for the year.

The sudden bursting forth of such a flood, in a dry time, when the river was low and with no heavy rains to precede it, might well occasion surprise and alarm. By means of the flood, this expedition, served by a flotilla of more than two hundred boats, descended the river, through a wild and for the most part uncultivated region, on a stream which heretofore had only been navigated by a little bark canoe.

To the other division of the army, that had already reached Tioga Point, this sudden rise of the water was alike surprising and unaccountable. They viewed the flood as it came with a rush that filled the channel and swept over the banks that could not hold it, and wondered what should have occasioned so singular a phenomenon. While yet held in astonishment and admiration of the sudden grandeur and majesty of the stream' their eyes were greeted by the appearance of Clinton and his host, as they came quietly floating down on the bosom of the mighty current.

By the junction of the force under Clinton, with the troops under Sullivan, the whole army that was to march into the Indian country amounted to five thousand.

This campaign had been in contemplation for so long a time and its object was so generally understood, that the Indians had become advised of its design, and kept themselves informed of its movements. They had collected a considerable force, and had made preparations to oppose its progress at a point, selected with much judgment above the Narrows. They were differently estimated at from eight to fifteen hundred, including Indians, British troops, and rangers. Their own authority gives the number of five hundred and fifty Indians, led by their famous warrior Brant, and two hundred and fifty whites, commanded by Colonels John Butler, Sir John and Guy Jackson, Major Walter N. Butler, and Captain McDonald.

As Sullivan's army advanced they determined to risk a general engagement at the point where they had taken their position. This they had fortified by a breast-work of logs and trees, formed on a rising ground, and extending nearly a mile in length. The river wound about their rear, and protected their right wing, their front and left were only exposed to attack. A little stream now called Baldwin's Creek, ran in front, and on the left was a high ridge nearly parallel with the general course of the river, which terminated a little below the breast-work; and further on to the left was still another ridge, running in the same direction and leading to the rear of the Americans.

The ground was covered with pine interspersed with low shrub oaks, many of which to conceal their works, had been cut and stuck in front of them, and had the appearance of trees that had grown there. The road, after crossing a deep brook at the foot of the hill, turned to the right, and ran nearly parallel with the breast-work, so as to expose the entire flank of the army to their fire, if it advanced without discovering their position. Parties communicating with each other, were stationed on both hills, so as to fall on the flank and rear of Sullivan as soon as the action should commence.

The position of the enemy was discovered at about eleven o'clock in the morning of the 29th of August, by Major Parr who commanded the advance guard. General Hand immediately formed the light infantry in a wood about four hundred yards from the enemy, and waited for the main body of the army. During this time a continual skirmish was kept up between the rifle corps of Parr and the Indians, who sallied forth from their works in small parties, fired and then retreated as though they wished to be incautiously pursued by the enemy. The woods were made alive by the wild yell of the savage which resounded from every point, filling the mind with enlarged ideas of the number of their warriors.

General Sullivan formed his line on ground rising directly opposite the works of the enemy, where he had a full view of the preparations made to receive him. Supposing the hills on his right were occupied by the enemy, he ordered Gen. Poor to take possession of them, and by coming in behind to cut off his retreat.

While Gen. Poor was marching to execute his command, and to give him time to fall in behind the enemy, General Sullivan ordered the riflemen under Major Parr, to move toward their line and keep up a running fire, adopting the cautious mode of warfare peculiar to their foes, of fighting from behind trees, stumps or logs, each one taking care to expose himself as little as possible, and all watching and shooting, whenever they could catch a glimpse of the enemy.

Van Campen took a station with the rest, as had been directed, and seeing a stump near, threw himself down behind it. He had not more than fairly taken his place before he heard the report of a gun, from which a ball came whizzing toward him, and entered the stump where he had sought protection. He saw that it came from a large tree directly opposite.

A few minutes after his antagonist planted another bullet in the stump. Perceiving immediately after this fire that a few hazel bushes obstructed his view, in case he should return the shot, Van Campen sprang out, and with his knife lopped them down, and instantly returned to his position. Directly after another ball struck the stump, and putting his eye out a little behind it he caught a glimpse of the Indian, as he was reloading his rifle. In ramming down the charge he threw out his hips from the tree so far, that Van Campen thought a well directed shot might hit him. Then watching his opportunity, with his finger on the trigger of his gun, and aiming close to the bark of the tree, the hips of the Indian again coming in sight, he touched off his rifle, and the ball speeding its unerring course hit the mark.

The Indian bounded into the air with a yell, halloed "*ca-hoo*," and sank upon the ground. "No more shots came from that tree," says Van Campen, "and I concluded I had silenced that battery."

At this time the musketry who had been listening to the brisk firing of the rifle, mingled with the loud shouts and fierce yells of the Indian, became impatient to be led into action. They feared the riflemen would defeat the enemy, and carry off all the honor.

Sullivan learning this from his aids, and that the men could be held back no longer, gave the order for them to advance The main body then moved toward the enemy's line, the artillery at the same time opening a fire upon them, so that their works were stormed and carried in a few minutes at the point of the bayonet.

Meanwhile, Gen Poor pushed up the mountain, which had indeed been possessed by the enemy, and in his course met with much opposition. Yet he continued to advance pressing the Indians back at the point of the bayonet, and occasionally opening upon them a brisk fire, but they retreated from one point to another, delaying his progress by an irregular fire, until he gained the summit of the hill. Perceiving that by this movement, their flank was left uncovered, and that they were in danger of being surrounded, the savages fled with the utmost percipitation, thus leaving the Americans masters of the field.

The battle had been contested manfully on the part of the Indians and their allies. No effort had been spared adapted to give them success, or inspire the hope of victory, but their adversaries were equally active, and by their superiority of force, soon gained the ascendency. In vain did the Indian chief fly from place to place to encourage his trusty braves to resist to the last extremity, the progress of an enemy sent to destroy their corn and lay waste their villages. In vain does he call upon them to nerve their arms to ward off the blow aimed at their homes, and drive away the gaunt and haggard visage of famine. Their well devised plans did not succeed, their utmost endeavor failed. They were driven from their works, they had been met at every point, they were threatened with having the enemy gain their rear and shut off their escape, when they raised the retreat-halloo, precipitately abandoned their works, and fled across the river, leaving many of their packs, tomahawks and scalping knives behind them. The contest had been severe, and their flight was so hurried that they left eleven of their dead on the field, a thing very unusual with the Indians, who use every precaution to hide their loss from their foes. They were pursued in their flight about two miles, yet it was so rapid they suffered but little; only eight scalps were taken from them. The loss of the Americans has been differently reported.

Mr. Van Campen says the popular estimation at the time was about seventy. The houses of the village near by were burned and the corn fields destroyed. The Americans held their encampment the night after the battle on the field where their victory had been won.

The reader will no doubt be interested with a circumstance in connection with this battle, which came to light several years after the restoration of peace between the parties engaged in this conflict.

Mr. Van Campen was often visited at his residence in Angelica, Allegany Co., N. Y., by the Indians who lived in Caneadea, a town of theirs a few miles below on the Genesee River. He was known by them as having been engaged in the Revolutionary war, and as having had something to do with the Indians and they may have had some curiosity to see him. They were kindly received and well treated and very frequently paid him a visit. The author remembers seeing them there often, when he was but a lad from five to eight years old.

Among those that used to come and see him was an Indian named Shongo, a war chief, a tall finely built fellow, who called one day on Mr. Van Campen on some business and when this was over, they fell into conversation among other things, about the campaign of Sullivan, and the battle below Newtown.* Van Campen told him he was there, and with Major Parr's company of riflemen when they fought behind trees and bushes. That he was behind a stump that was fired into by a large Indian who stood behind a large oak tree directly opposite, that he shot at him when he was loading his gun, and from the way he jumped he supposed he must have hit him.

Shongo here interrupted him by exclaiming,—*Cowaugh,—I same Indian.*

He then turned up his breech cloth, and showed the scar. He said he fell to the ground and had to be carried off, being unable to do anything more during the remaining part of the action.

Mr. Van Campen speaks of him as possessing an uncommonly stout, military figure, about six feet high, fine head, roman nose, full chest, well proportioned limbs, a dignified and quite pleasant countenance. He says of him,—"*I have seldom if ever seen a more noble looking fellow of any nation or tribe of men.* During the war of 1813, he visited my house more than once to consult with me about the course it would be best for the Indians to pursue. He lived to an advanced age and has been dead several years." He must still be remembered by the early settlers of Angelica, and those living below in the neighborhood of Caneadea, on the Genesee river.

But the brave fellow is now no more and the race of which he was a noble representative, has melted away before the sweeping tide of white immigration until now scarcely a vestige remains behind.

---

*Present site of Elmira, N. Y.

CHAPTER XI.

By the battle of Newtown an important point had been gained. The Indians had here brought together their principal force. Their position had been chosen with judgment, their preparations skillfully made, and they were situated so as to meet the enemy advantageously. They no doubt hoped to strike a heavy blow on this campaign, and possibly arrest its progress. Their failure would discourage them from making an effectual resistance at other places. Such indeed was the result of this battle. They were thoroughly routed, and continued their flight until they arrived early the next day at their village, Catherine's Town, at the head of Seneca Lake; where the warriors said to the women,—" *We are conquered and must fly;—we have had many killed, and vast numbers wounded.*"*

From their encampment at Newtown, the Americans sent back to Tioga, whatever of their baggage, artillery and wagons, were not needed in advancing farther. While remaining here Van Campen was sent with a detachment to destroy an Indian village at the head of Baldwin's Creek.

He found it deserted, and having burned the houses, about twenty, returned to the army. On the 31st of

---

*Sullivan's official report, as quoted by Col. Stone. The statement is perhaps somewhat exaggerated.

August they marched in the direction of Catherine's Town, destroying cornfields, and whatever other Indian possession they found on the way.

The route pursued led them through a wild uncultivated region, over places hitherto traveled only by the wandering savage, making their advance very fatiguing and difficult. Had the Indians been less precipitate in their retreat, they might have greatly annoyed our army, as in its course it passed through narrows, and dangerous defiles, and over streams they were obliged to wade; at any, or all of these places they might have been severely harassed, had the opportunities presented been diligently and persistently improved. But they were thoroughly demoralized, and hastened to remove their families beyond the reach of the invading army.

The route pursued by Gen. Sullivan led him across the high land that formed the dividing line of waters flowing eastward into the Chemung, and those flowing westward and emptying into the Seneca Lake. On this high ground was a widely extended hemlock swamp, through which their course lay, very difficult to pass, from the nature of the ground, and because of the fallen trees, tangled vines, and brush-wood in the way. The frequent miring of their pack-horses, and the uncertain foot-hold for the men, together with the impediments they were obliged to overcome, rendered their progress a constant scene of anxiety and trouble, and had a wily enemy been present still further to annoy, the climax of their difficulties would have been reached.

It was late in the afternoon when the army came to this swamp, and the General was advised not to enter it until the next day, but he rejected the counsel, and pressed on, without reaching the other side, a large part of the army being obliged to pass the night amid the discomforts and gloom of that dismal place. Two streams of water find their way out of this swamp in opposite directions as just intimated. The army after having passed the swamp, followed the course of the stream emptying into the head of Seneca Lake,

On elevated ground affording a beautiful prospect of woodland and lake, was the Indian village of *Catherine's Town*, the residence of the notorious Catharine Montour. It was pleasantly situated, surrounded by corn-fields, and orchards, and numbered about thirty houses. Coming to this they found no one to dispute their possession, the Indians, panic-stricken had fled, leaving their homes to be at the disposal of the enemy. It seemed a very stern order that required the destruction of the homes and property of the Indians, but this was required by the Commander-in-chief, and so their houses, cornfields, and orchards were destroyed, and not a vestige left in the track of the army on which the Indian warrior could find subsistence. Every settlement in the region was burned, every cornfield leveled with the ground, and the stately fruit trees cut down.

From Catherine's Town the army continued its march down along the eastern border of the Seneca Lake, burning Kendaia, a town of about twenty-houses on the way, crossing the outlet on the 7th of September, and advancing to Kanadaseaga, the capital of the Seneca nation. Here General Sullivan expected to find the enemy fortified, and prepared for another engagement, and in approaching the town, separated his army into three divisions, designing to come upon it suddenly from three points, and take it by surprise. But though the war chiefs endeavored to bring their men to make another stand, they could not be persuaded; declaring it to be utterly useless to contend with such a powerful army. Their capital, therefore, popularly known as the Seneca Castle, and later as the Indian Castle, was found deserted, not a man appearing to offer any resistance to the invading force.

This was one of the largest towns the General found in his march through the Indian country. Being the seat of government, the chief men of the nation had their residence here. Their dwellings though rudely constructed, were quite comfortable, and their grounds were laid out in gardens, or planted with corn. In several of their edifices they aspired to something more than rude log cabins, they were of hewn logs, and were by no means unsightly. The abundance of their fruit trees, and the luxurious growth, and variety of their vegetables were evidences of a people considerably advanced toward civilization. But here, alas! as well as elsewhere, a ruthless hand was laid on everything belonging to the Indian, whatever may have been its value as representing his character or culture; all that could mark the ancient glory of their nation was reduced to ashes, or laid in ruins.

Tradition still hallows the place where the ancient council fire burned, and where the distinguished men of a noble race met to discuss matters of polity, questions relating to the interests of their nation, receive embassadors, an occasion ever attended with much ceremony, and dignified speech, weigh carefully the subject matter of their mission, resulting often in lengthy debate, marked by passages of superior eloquence, these things presenting still further evidences of their intelligence and culture, have attracted the attention and curiosity of the civilized world, and have led to deep and earnest inquiries after their history. Relics of them have been gathered and preserved, and whatever has tended to throw light upon their origin and history has been treasured as a thing of value.

Often has the regret arisen that these noble trees were cut down, yet some of them had a vitality that made them unwilling to die, and they sprouted again and became trees ; long may they live.

The army having accomplished the destruction of Kanadeseaga, and one or two other towns and settlements near, moved forward upon Kanandaigua, and arrived there in two days. This was likewise considered a place of considerable importance, and the houses, twenty-three in number, which some who saw them at this time, regarded as quite elegant, but sad, to say, they were all destroyed. There were large fields of corn destroyed here also, and it was regarded then, as it ever has been since, a very beautiful country.

From this they proceeded to Honeoye, a town about half the size of Kanandaigua, destroying its houses, and cornfields. A strong garrison was left here in charge of the heavy stores of the army, while it advanced upon the still larger town of Genesee. This was a very important town, the frequent gathering place of large assemblies, and numbering one hundred and twenty-eight houses, many of them large and well built, and being situated in a very fertile region, and one widely cultivated, their possessions here were highly appreciated and perhaps valued more than any which had hitherto fallen into the hands of the army.

The Indians being apprised of Sullivan's design to come here also, began to meditate resistance. They felt assurred of the destruction of all their towns, if the enemy should advance farther without being molested; and concluding that defeat would add but little to the extremity of their case, they determined to way-lay the path of the invading army, and strike one more blow in defense of their homes. Sullivan's advance therefore from Honeoye, was very carefully watched. The riflemen who marched in front and on the flank, when coming to high ground, where the Indian had an opportunity to observe their movements, very often caught glimpses of him fleeing, like a deer started up in the track of the hunter, from the place where he had been viewing the progress of the army. These indications led to the suspicion of some design on the part of the Indians, to make an attack, and led them to advance with caution.

The army kept on its march, however, without being molested, and soon arrived at the head of Connissius Lake, where it was obliged to halt and devise means to cross its inlet. An extensive and marshy ground and water of considerable depth, obstrncted their farther progress, until a rude bridge should be constructed to enable the army to cross with safety. This place presented an opportunity favorable, and they expected here a severe encounter with the enemy.

A detachment of the army under Gen. Hand gained the opposite side to protect their work, while a small party under Lieut. Boyd was sent to watch the movements of the Indians, and reconnoiter the next town. Genesee being a town of much importance, and their last stronghold, it was supposed they would resolutely resist its being taken. Boyd with twenty-six men, and two faithful Oneida Indians as guides, started out on this undertaking late in the afternoon, and having discharged his duty with all secrecy and dispatch, during the hours of night, was on his return to the main detachment, when he discovered two Indians running at a distance before him. He was disposed to pursue them, but was advised by his trusty guides not to follow them, "Since," said they, "it is *only an artifice by which they intend to draw us into an ambush, where we shall suddenly be surrounded by a large force and shall be cut off.*"

These Oneidas well understood the design of the enemy, they had been trained in Indian strategy, and the apparent timidity of the two that started up and fled before them, aroused their suspicions, and they were not mistaken. The Indians by some means had learned of this detachment that had gone out under Boyd and they resolved to prevent its retnrn. Hence they formed an ambuscade on the course they thought would be pursued, and were eagerly watching its approach.

Boyd notwithstanding the advice that had been given, and anxious to come up with the fugitives, and thinking he might with safety follow a short distance farther after them, kept on, until one of them was killed, and his scalp taken. He was shot by the famous Murphy, one of the party, who ran on ahead of the others and by his fleetness came so near his victim, there was no chance for his escape.

Timothy Murphy was a native of Pennsylvania, of dark complexion, having a keen black eye, and features though well formed, marked by hardihood from much exposure in camp. He was about five feet nine inches high, and his limbs finely turned, gave indications of great muscular activity and strength. He was not a Virginian, as some have represented, was well known to Van Campen, having lived on the farm of Van Campen's father, and was more or less intimate with the family, until his father moved into the vicinity of Northumberland. Murphy was one of the brave spirits of the revolution, and his name is extensively known from his having taken an active part in border warfare. His adventurous spirit led him into deeds of daring that were lagely tinctured with the marvellous, and stories of remarkable daring that should properly have been ascribed to other men, have interested and delighted many a barroom audience, with Murphy as the grand hero of the occasion. The author was once told by Harvey Watson Esq. of Schoharie, N. Y., that in stopping over night at a hotel on one occasion, he heard related among many other very remarkable things performed by Murphy, the story of *Putnam and the wolf*, representing Murphy as the brave actor in the scene. Telling also of the way he captured some Indians, one time. He was in the woods splitting a log to make rails, and had the log partly opened when the Indians came upon him, and claimed him as their prisoner. He promised to go with them shortly, he wanted to split the log open first, and wished they would help him, some to stand on one side and some on the other and pull while he was to drive the wedge home, and finish opening it. While driving the wedge further in, either by accident or design, the wedge flew out and the gap closing up again, fastened their hands firmly in the log, so they could not remove them, and were effectually caught and became his prisoners, instead of he theirs.

But there was no need of manufacturing incidents; enough of well authenticated facts can be presented to establish for him the character of almost reckless daring. Having always had the good fortune to escape whenever pursued by the enemy, he never had any fear of falling into his hands. He was so fleet of foot, he could out run the swiftest Indian, and having a double-barrelled rifle, so as to be able to shoot twice without reloading, the dusky warriors regarded him with almost superstitious veneration. He never missed his aim, and the fact of his shooting twice in succession was well understood. Frequently making war on his own account, he was often in danger, yet he relied on his trusty rifle, and a nimble foot to bring him off in safety. If Indians started after him and followed in hot pursuit, he would turn upon the foremost and with one shot bring him to the ground, if still further pressed, he would wheel and bring down another.

The second fire would generally put an end to all further pursuit. The savages became alarmed, and thought he must possess some wizard power by which he was enabled to shoot as long as he pleased without having any trouble to reload.

Learning finally that he could only shoot twice without reloading they were sure to wait until they heard the second report before venturing near. On one occasion when hotly pursued by several Indians, he ran until he had distanced all but two,—and as these followed hard on, he turned and shot down the leading one, and, catching up the rifle of the expiring warrior, shot down the other. Hearing two reports others came rushing on, and Murphy, with his remaining charge shot down one of his pursuers, when the others turned about, saying, "*It is no use to follow a man who can keep on firing all day.*"

On the occasion we are now considering, Murphy, as was his custom, scalped the Indian he had killed, and with his usual coolness, took from him the leggins he had on, which were of good cloth, and of bright scarlet color, and appropriated them to his own use.

Lieutenant Boyd, as his Oneida guides had feared, advanced too far. He had no thought of the enemy until he was in their midst, and saw them rising every where around him. It was a trying moment. No less than five hundred warriors now stood up to prevent his return to the army!—What could he do but surrender to the enemy?—What hope could he have of escape?—There was none:—Yet he resolved to make a trial. Perceiving it as his only alternative, he selected a point in the enemy's line that he thought weaker than at other places, and determined upon forcing a passage. It was a bold measure; but he thought he might accomplish it. Directing the fire of his company upon the line of Indian warriors, he saw them fall before the deadly aim of his men, and then they rushed into the breach, but were repulsed, yet what was very singular, without the loss of a single man. They made another attempt and were defeated with loss. But not discouraged, he and his brave comrades made one more trial, and in the desperate struggle most of the party fell; yet three of them made their escape, among them was the ever fortunate Murphy. He was pursued and finding his leggins so small as to impede his flight he paused a moment to cut them open; this done he continued his race and made good his escape. Boyd and one of his soldiers named Parker, together with the two Oneidas, were taken prisoners. Boyd finding himself in the hands of the enemy, solicited an interview with their leader Brant, determining as a last resort to try the honor and fidelity of the Indian chief. This distinguished warrior, Thayendanegea, being near by, immediately presented himself, when Lieutenant Boyd by a signal understood only by the initiated, made himself known as a free mason, thus claiming the sympathy and protection of a distressed brother. The appeal was recognized by Brant, from whom he received the strongest assurances of the protection of his life. But the fate of one of the Oneidas was very different. His story is one of deep interest.

He had early enlisted in the American cause, and had already been of great service to the army. He was active bold and persevering, and was much beloved by the officers under whom he served. In this expedition he had acted as General Sullivan's guide. He had been faithful to his trust, leading the troops with the utmost fidelity, through the country inhabited by his red brethren. But now he was a prisoner in the hands of the enemy.

It appears from the circumstances following his capture that when he entered the American service, he had an elder brother who was about to join himself to the fortunes of the British, and who besought him, with all the earnestness of a brother's love, to go with him and with his people into the service of the crown.—His entreaties were unavailing, the younger brother clave to his choice; and they parted, each to pursue his own course in the uncertain paths of war.

They had not met since the time when by mutual consent they had left each other; but now the young Oneida is brought, a captive, into the presence of his brother from whom he had been long separated. They mutually recognized each other, and as the eyes of the elder were rivited in earnest gaze upon the mild features of the younger, they suddenly glowed with unwonted fire, and it was clearly perceived from his changed manner that his soul was kindled with revenge.—He approached him haughtily, and with a proud and dignified air, and addressed him as follows :—

"Brother! you have merited death! The hatchet or the war-club shall finish your career!—When I begged you to follow me in the fortunes of war, you were deaf to my cries; you spurned my entreaties!

"Brother! you have merited death and shall have your deserts!—When the rebels raised their hatchets to fight their good master, you sharpened your knife, you brightened your rifle, and led on our foes to the fields of our fathers!

"Brother! you have merited death and shall die by our hands!—When those rebels had driven us from the fields of our fathers to seek out new homes, it was you who could dare to step forth as their pilot, and conduct them to the doors of our wigwams, to butcher our children, and put us to death!—But though you have merited death, and shall die on this spot, my hands shall not be stained with the blood of a brother!—Who will strike?"

There was a moment's pause, and then the bright hatchet of Little Beard, an Indian Sachem, gleamed like a flash of lightning through the air, and the young Oneida chief lay dead at his feet. The other Indian captive who was also an Oneida chief, was then assured by Little Beard, that he need apprehend no fears for his life, that they were fighting against the whites, and that in due time he would be restored to his liberty. Yet through want of confidence in the good faith of the chief, or from some other cause, he watched his opportunity and effected his escape.

The instance just related presenting to view the high sense of honor existing among some, at least of the red men of the forest has been contrasted with one related by Chapman of the pale faced man, that occurred at the close of the battle of Wyoming in '78. At a short distance below the battle ground, is a large island called Monockonoc, where some fugitives found concealment among the logs and brushwood upon it. They had thrown their arms away in their flight and were without the means of defense. One or more of the enemy in pursuit saw them swimming across to the island and fired at them, but without effect, while swimming. Coming still nearer they crossed over bringing their guns. Wiping them and reloading they began to look about and discover the hiding place of the fugitives. Passing slowly about and examining every covert one of them discovered his own brother in concealment. They represented different sides of the struggle, the concealed one looking upon his Tory brother and understanding the deep seated hatred borne toward those called rebels, realized his peril when discovered and accosted, in sarcastic tone, with chilling words, "*So, it is you, is it?*" Leaving his place of concealment and coming forward a few steps he dropped on his knees and begged of his brother to spare his life, declaring his willingness to live with, and serve him, and even to become his slave during all his remaining days, if *he would only spare his life.* "*All this is mighty fine,*"—replied the cruel-hearted brother,—"*but you are a d—d rebel,*" and deliberately levelled his rifle and shot him.

Let us now return from this digression. From the field of battle Lieutenant Boyd and his fellow captive, Parker, were conducted to Little Beard's town where they came in company with Colonel Butler and a detachment of his rangers. The honor of Brant had been pledged for his safety, and while under his supervision there can be no doubt he would have religiously observed his promise; but the active habit of this warrior, and the special care devolving on him at this crisis, keeping him constantly in motion he left the camp on duty and placed Boyd under the care of Butler. No sooner had Brant left than Butler began to question the prisoner about the situation, numbers, and intentions of General Sullivan and his troops.

Boyd unwilling to betray the cause of his country even by a single word, declined giving any answer that would implicate his friends. Butler provoked by the steady and unswerving reticence of his prisoner, threatened to deliver him over to the tender mercies of the Indians, and Boyd still relying on the kind assurances of the Mohawk chief persisted in refusing; when his cruel inquisitor, true to his bloody threat delivered him up to Little Beard and his clan, the most ferocious of the Seneca tribe.

The noble fellow met his fate with a truly manly and independent spirit, facing his tormentors with a look proudly indignant, while they proceed to execute their horrid designs with a refinement of cruelty unparalleled in any of the accounts given of this war.

They first stripped him of his clothing, then tied him to a sapling, where the Indians gratified their fiendish tastes by throwing the tomahawk at him so near as to strike a little above his head, and by brandishing their scalping knives around him in a most frightful manner, accompanying their motions with terrific yells and dancing about him with frantic demonstrations of joy.

They next proceeded to pull out his nails; this done they cut off his nose and plucked out one of his eyes. In addition to these enormities they cut out his tongue and stabbed him in several places. Their more than savage cruelty did not end here. As if to tear him from life by the most excruciating pains they made a small incision in his abdomen, took out one of his intestines, and fastened it to the tree. The suffering man was then unbound, and with brute force was compelled to move around the tree, until his entrails were literally drawn from his body and wound about its trunk. They ended his torments by severing his head from his body. A tale like this is too agonizing to be read, to horrible to be written down, and become one of the sober realities of history.

CHAPTER XII.

Northumberland is pleasantly located on the level and fertile bottom lands of the Susquehanna, on a point between its north and west branches, formed by a gentle bend in the river, where these branches unite their waters, and flow on to their final destination. Its position is commanding and beautiful, combining the attractions of mountain and river scenery, pleasing in the variety and grandeur of the prospect afforded. On the opposite side of the river was the village of Sunbury, and Fort Augusta, and on the south side of West Branch, was Blue Hill some three hundred feet high, surmounted by John Mason's leaning Tower, built for an observatory, and so placed as to overlook a fearful precipice. The view afforded from this tower, in its day, was surpassingly magnificent. The location of this town at the junction of these noble streams, which drained an immense region of rich and valuable land, was regarded at an early day, as affording important facilities for commerce. Immense quantities of lumber passed down these streams. Southern Pennsylvania and Maryland were not well supplied with trees, the most desirable for building, while above on these streams and their tributaries, the country was covered with immense forests of white pine, whose stately forms were crowded into every valley and covered every hill. Finer timber for building purposes never grew, and when the war was over and the title to the land settled, men flocked hither in swarms, and sounds of the woodman's axe began to reverberate through the valleys, and along the hills, and the cracking, and loud sweep, and heavy resounding fall of these lords of the forest, were sounds most familiar to the ear. These trees were cut into logs, and the logs were soon converted into lumber, and then followed the busy scene of making rafts, and releasing them at high water, from their moorings; away they glided, passing with the current down the river, under the guidance of a skillful pilot and his helpers, until they reached tide-water, where the lumber was sold, and the avails used by the early settler to pay for his land, and provide for his home Northumberland was a pleasant and convenient place to stop on the way, and many an incident of historic value, if it could be gathered, would be found connected with this grand old town.

Several, whose names adorn our history, had their homes here. Jonathan Walker, father of Robert J., Secretary of the United States Treasury; Robert C. Grier, the well-known Jurist; Thomas Cooper, the lawyer and philosopher, who in 1820 became president of Columbia College, South Carolina, and Joseph Priestly, the famous chemist and scientist;—all had their homes here. Colonel Williamson, who was connected with large land-holdings, and agent of the Pulteny land-purchase, established his headquarters here, while opening up the extensive region he had in charge for settlement.*

---

*A. J. McCall's Early Hist. of Bath.

But among those whose names will be remembered as residents of Northumberland, none are more entitled to grateful remembrance than that of a woman,—Mrs. John Boyd. At the time of the breaking out of the war of the revolution, this widowed mother was living in Northumberland. Her family consisted of herself and three sons, John, Thomas and William. It was when the spirit of the revolution began to animate the bosoms of the Americans, and when they perceived that everything must be laid on the altar of liberty. The frontier settlements were writhing under the blows inflicted by the cruel Indian, and Mrs. Boyd like a truly Spartan mother, devoted her boys to the cause of her country. It was a solemn and noble resolve, and marked by the deep piety of her heart. Calling them before her she expressed the deep interest she felt in the success of those engaged in the struggle for liberty, and with what pleasure she had beheld the sacrifices which others were willing to make in its behalf; at the same time stating that she was willing to pledge *her* all, in the sacred cause of freedom. Her sons were dearer to her than any thing of earth, and these she was ready to lay upon the altar of her country's rights. She did so with this solemn injunction, "That they should never disgrace their swords, *with the least spot or stain of cowardice.*"

They all with an eager spirit, entered the army. William fell in the battle of Brandywine, John was a prisoner to the Indians, at one time, with Mr. Van Campen, and the sad fate of Thomas the younger, which was brought upon him by refusing to dishonor the cause in which he had enlisted, even by a single word, shows but too well how he regarded the solemn charge of his noble-hearted mother. How afflicting to her must have been the melancholy intelligence, that was brought back concerning her darling boy! He was a youth of promise; intelligent, sprightly and brave, the path of honor was before him, and he bid fair to press his way forward, until he should be permitted to bask in the clear light of a well-earned fame.

He was about six feet high, finely proportioned, rather light of complexion, and possessed an active, vigorous frame. The severity with which he was made to part with life, has enlisted for him an universal sympathy, and his name will ever be remembered as one of the gallant heroes of the revolution.

As soon as the detachment under Gen. Hand, heard the news of the skirmishing of Boyd's party, it moved rapidly forward, ascended the hill which arose at no great distance from the head of the lake, and in their route fell in with the packs and baggage of the Indians. They concluded from the situation of the place, that the enemy had selected this point, with the design of making an attack, since it afforded them a sort of central position, whence they could send their parties to harass their foes, and to which they might retreat whenever they were driven back. Not stopping here Gen. Hand pressed on to the scene of action, and soon came to where the enemy had been busy in removing their dead; but the Indians not awaiting his approach precipitately fled, leaving one of their number with the dead riflemen.

They then attended to the burial of those who had fallen in the engagement, and waited until they were joined the next day by the main army, when they marched together as far as Fall Brook, where they camped for the night. Gen. Sullivan learning here that the enemy had fled from all their towns, made a disposition of his army for the destruction of their villages and plantations. Generals Poor and Maxwell were sent to destroy those below, while Generals Hand and Clinton were sent to destroy those that were above the place of their encampment.

On the next day the work of destruction commenced, each division of the army advancing to its appointed field of operation. Maj. Parr of Gen. Clinton's brigade crossed the Genesee river to burn Little Beardstown, and here found the lifeless bodies of Boyd and Parker. He immediately proceeded to give them the honor of a decent burial, selecting a spot which, from its situation might be easily remembered by those who were their companions in arms. It was on the bank of Little Beard's Creek where a little stream forms a junction with it, in a break of the bank under a clump of wild plum trees.

This spot has been kept in mind by tradition and there is now an appropriate mound which marks the place,* that may be seen by every traveler through the region visited by this campaign, on the road leading between Geneseo and Moscow.

---

*This mound has of late been encroached upon by the waters of the creek, and a small part taken away. The town of Leicester has lately fortified the bank, in such a manner, it is hoped, as will prevent any farther encroachment.
A large oak tree standing only a few rods distant from the mound, is claimed by some of the old citizens of the neighborhood, to have been at the time (1779) the "sapling" to which Lieut. Boyd was tied, and the owner of the ground on which it stands, guards it with jealous care. ED.

From the sad offices of the grave, the troops turned again to the work of destruction, and in a few days the beautiful country of the Genesee, was one wide scene of desolation. The territory which had been thus laid waste, was the finest that had been visited by the army. Upon first casting their eyes over it, the soldiers beheld it with astonishment and joy. It presented, then, the same delightful and open view, which it spreads out to the beholder, now. The mind and the heart were feasted, as they ran out in vision over a plain which stretched far into the distance, meeting here and there a beautiful grove, on every side corn-fields, that were bowing to the breeze, and whose broad and ample bosom gave the most enlarged ideas of plenty.

The Indians had here come together in great numbers, and here they had the largest village which Sullivan had met with on his route, and in speaking of it, he uses the same exaggerated style he employs in describing the other villages he passed through. "The town of Genesee contained one hundred and twenty-eight houses, mostly large and *very elegant*. It was beautifully situated, almost encircled with a clear flat, extending a number of miles; over which extensive fields of corn were waving, together with every kind of vegetable that could be conceived of.*

From the glowing colors in which General Sullivan describes the country he passed through, Col. Stone has doubtless been led into an error in speaking of the high state of civilization to which the Senecas and Cayugas had arrived. He says, "It is apprehended that but few

---

*Sullivan's Report, as quoted by Stone.

of the present generation are aware of the advances which the Indians in the wide and beautiful country of the Cayugas and Senecas, had made in the march of civilization. They had several towns, and many large villages, laid out with a considerable degree of regularity. They had *framed houses*, some of them well finished, having chimneys, and painted." Mr. Van Campen says that the story of their framed houses is all a *fudge:* at least in that part of their country passed through by the army of Sullivan. His own memory may be trusted, upon this point, for, if the houses had been upon the magnificent scale represented, the fact could not not have altogether escaped his recollection. And the reasons which he gives in support of his position tend very much to confirm his opinion.

He says that "In a country where there are framed houses, there is generally found such a thing as a saw-mill. But there were no saw-mills on our route. Yet framed houses are sometimes found in a country where there are no saw-mills. Yes; but it is in a region to which lumber can easily be transported, and in one where the inhabitants have advanced considerably in the arts of commerce. At the time of the war there were very few saw-mills in the whole country; there was but one to my knowledge above Wilksbarre, in the whole region watered by the Susquehanna; and as for the houses being painted, it couldn't have been with anything but *mud:* many of them we found daubed over with this." Indeed, it would be contrary to the native indolence and slovenly habits of the Indian, to suppose that he would go to any great labor, or pains in rearing for himself a dwelling, other than that which could be formed of materials near at hand, and then too, without any surprising exercise of skill. He delighted more, in his hunting grounds and the chase, than in any great display about his place of living. Mr. Van Campen says that their houses were generally built by fixing large posts in the ground, at a convenient distance from each other, between which poles were woven. This formed the covering of the sides; the roof was made by laying bark upon poles, which were properly placed as a support. To afford greater warmth, the sides were plastered with mud. The houses that were found on the route were all of this description, and if they were framed, this is the manner in which it was done, and the painting was doubtless such as has been described.

It cannot be denied, however, that the Indians had advanced far, in the arts of peace. Their wide and flourishing corn-fields, and their fine orchards of the apple and peach tree, were no fiction; they presented evidences of a cultivation, which was extraordinary, when we consider how naturally averse the American Indians were, to any thing like patient industry. Yet the labor which was bestowed upon these, was, doubtless, performed by the faithful squaw, since she was doomed by her lord to bear the principal drudgeries of life.

After laying waste the beautiful country of the Genesee, Sullivan pursued the Indians no further. It doubtless belonged to the original design of this campaign, that the army should proceed as far as Niagara and there strike a decisive blow upon the Indians and British.

But from some cause, which has been left unexplained, the expedition was stopped here, and the Indians were allowed to seek their last resort of strength, without being molested in the least. Niagara remained the head quarters of the British rangers, blood-thirsty Tories, and cruel Indians, whence parties could be still sent out on the work of devastation and death, among the uncertain homes of the frontier settlers. But Sullivan, as though he had accomplished the end of his campaign, relinquished all further enterprise and started home, marching with his army in very much the same route they had come.

Still, if the destruction of property was the only end of this undertaking, it must be confessed that the work of desolation was well completed. The country which a month previous, appeared like a beautiful and flourshing garden, now presented little less than a dreary waste, or a smoking heap of ruins. A better description of the scene cannot perhaps be given than that from the pen of Stone. "The axe and the torch soon transformed the whole of that beautiful region from the character of a garden to a scene of drear and sickening desolation. Forty Indian towns the largest containing one hundred and twenty-eight houses, were destroyed, corn, gathered and ungathered to the amount of one hundred and sixty thousand bushels, shared the same fate; their fruit trees were cut down; and the Indians were hunted like wild beasts, till neither house, nor fruit tree, nor field of corn, nor inhabitant remained in the whole country. The gardens were enriched with great quantities of useful vegetables of different kinds. The size of the corn-fields, as well as the high degree of cultivation in which they were kept, excited wonder ; and the ears of corn were so remarkably large, that many of them measured twenty-two inches in length."

" So numerous were the fruit trees, that in one orchard they cut down fifteen hundred of them."

Several towns were destroyed on their way back, by detachments sent into the region of Cayuga Lake, the main body of the army pursuing the most direct route to Tioga, at which place it arrived on the 30th of September. In a few days it resumed its return march, down the Susquehanna, and passing through Wyoming, arrived at Easton, on the 15th of October. It had traversed a large extent of territory, the distance thence to the Genesee Castle being not less than two hundred and eighty miles. Besides the victory at Newtown the army achieved but little, yet it had marched over a broad extent of country, and sorely afflicted the Indian in the destruction of his towns, and in the desolation of his favorite retreats ; but as for himself, he had not been crippled, nor his ferocious spirit subdued. If any thing his spirit was more restless ; like a galled tiger, he had gone back to his lair, and was only waiting for an opportunity to burst from his retreat, and seize upon his foe with a more deadly grasp.

The part performed by Mr. Van Campen in the expedition above Tioga, was only that of a volunteer. Belonging to the boat department, having to superintend, as we have seen, the military stores, his services ended when he reached that place ; yet he could not bear the inactivity of awaiting the return of the army, he chose rather to throw himself in with the fortunes of the campaign, and endure its fatigues and dangers, than remain at a distance from the field of strife.

Upon his return he was taken sick with a fever, and was removed to the fort, which he had built early in the preceding year upon the waters of Fishing Creek. Here his father resided, his house having been burned by the Indians at the time of making their attack upon the settlement, as has already been described, in the spring of '78. Van Campen recovered his health during the winter and was prepared for entering upon the duties of the coming year.

CHAPTER XIII.

Much reliance had been placed on the campaign of Sullivan, by the inhabitants of the frontier settlements, to afford them protection against further molestation from the Indians. These had been driven back so far from their homes, and had suffered such a complete overthrow it was fondly hoped they would not very soon visit the frontier. It was supposed by some that they had been completely vanquished, and that now it was perfectly safe for the farmer to return to his employments and, as soon as the spring should open, commence the labor of cultivating his soil.

But the Indian though he had been driven back had not been conquered. On the contrary, he had been wrought up to a spirit of desperation, by the ravages made upon his territory in the destruction of his home, and of the altars of his fathers.

Many of the settlers, especially those in the vicinity of Wyoming, had been so much interrupted during the preceding years, in their labors on the farm, and the products of many had been so completely destroyed by the Indians and British rangers, that it was deemed necessary for the husbandman to engage in an early cultivation of the soil.

While the inhabitants, therefore, were preparing to enter upon the peaceful occupation of their farms, their unsubdued foes were meditating designs of mischief, and ere long were prepared to plant themselves, like so many sentinels, along the outskirts of the settlements, and watch for the favorable opportunity to spring from their hiding places, upon the unarmed laborer, and make him the victim of the tomahawk, or hurry him away as a captive, whose fate was to be entirely at the beck of savage caprice. Instances of plunder, burning, murder and capture began early to circulate along the frontier, so that it was soon apparent, that the enemy was abroad and intent upon doing all the mischief within his power. But in every instance the Indian did not escape unpunished for his deeds of cruelty.

Among the inhabitants of the territory open to his incursions, there were those who possessed a most resolute, daring spirit, who were not to be intimidated by the enemy, and who were not slow to extricate themselves from danger. One of these, as we have had occasion already to mention, was Lebbeus Hammond; and another almost equally fearless, named Bennett, was a brave companion with him, and both of them inhabitants of the beautiful valley of Wyoming.

This place had been protected after the massacre in '78 by troops of the regular army stationed at Wilksbarre Fort. Some of the inhabitants that remained, removed from this fort early in the succeeding year to the upper part of the valley, and fortified themselves by building a garrison of twenty-eight houses standing in a semi-circle, the base of which was formed by the river, each one being placed three feet within the other, so that the rear of every successive house could be defended, from the preceding one. In the center of the semi-circle a large gate led into the open space enclosed by the buildings. The two that were next the river were constructed so as to guard against an attack from Indians, creeping along the bank, all had a communication from one to the other in the upper story, and along on the top was a promenade for sentries.

Here Bennett and Hammond, with nearly thirty of the settlers, lived during the summer of '79, and cultivated about one hundred acres of corn, which gave an amply supply of food for the winter. Their fortification appeared quite formidable at a distance, so much so that a large party of Indians, which lay upon the opposite mountain previous to the campaign of Sullivan, did not venture to make an attack upon it as they had designed. It was guarded by three sentinels, two of which promenaded the tops of the houses, and one the bank of the river. Having spent the summer and winter here without an attack, Bennett resolved in the spring, to go and cultivate his own farm which lay a few miles above. His friends remonstrated with him upon the danger of going off alone, so far from the garrison, saying that "He would certainly be killed or taken prisoner by the Indians." Yet he persisted in his determination, affirming that there was no danger,—that the Indians would not certainly venture this year to attack the settlements, and if they did, he relied much upon a famous hunting dog of his, to warn him of the approach of the enemy. This dog, he said, could smell an Indian before he was within rifle shot, and would give the alarm. Trusting, therefore, to the faithfulness of his sagacious old pet, he took with him his son, who was quite a boy, and went up to his farm and commenced ploughing. He placed two rifles at each side of the field where his furrows ended, believing that in case of an attack, his son and himself could reach one of the two rifles.

Thus they worked for the space of two days without any interruption, returning at night to the garrison. They had been watched, however, by a company of savages, numbering seven, who had inspected their every movement. On the third day they were accompanied on their way back to their work, by Mr. Lebbeus Hammond, who went in pursuit of a pair of horses, which had strayed from their enclosure. He was also warned of the danger of going out alone in the woods, yet he apprehended nothing of the kind, and would allow no company to go with him as a guard. He expected to find his horses in the direction of Bennett's farm and they proceeded on together, each shouldering his rifle. Not meeting with the animals of which he was in pursuit, before reaching the farm, Bennett volunteered, with his boy and dog, to go with him further; but he refused, saying that there was no danger, and that he would soon return. He then proceeded up the river alone, until he found his horses, and having caught them, mounted one and was returning, leading the other. As he came in sight of Bennett's farm, his eyes were fixed in that direction, earnestly watching him and his boy as they were at work in the field. He had no thought of the savage, nor the most distant idea that he was in the vicinity of danger. Yet while he was looking towards his friends, and eagerly expecting another sight, when they should pass the point, which at that moment obscured the view, his path was immediately beset with Indians, who siezed his horses before he was aware, and afforded him no opportunity for escape. Seeing himself so completely in their power he thought it best to offer no resistance, but to make the best of the circumstances into which he was thrown. They made him dismount, then bonnd him and laid him on the ground. While he was lying here he could see some of them creep along behind the fence, which obscured them from Bennett, and there could see the latter pass and re-pass, where the view was open, while the Indians were watching for the most favorable moment to take him. He wondered where Bennett's dog could be, all this while, and was expecting every moment that he would sound the alarm. But the dog, which had been doted upon so much, proved himself a coward; Hammond caught a glimpse of him running away, with his tail down, and at full speed. The Indians watched Bennett and his boy, as they ploughed round after round, unconscious that the keen eyes of their foes were upon them. But finally, as they were just beginning to cross the field with another furrow, these slipped over the fence, and came behind them with noiseless tread, and placed a hand upon the shoulder of himself and boy. Seeing that there was no opportunity for escape, he also gave up without making any resistance, and they were about to take him away, leaving his team standing in the harness. Bennett, with characteristic bravery, swore he would not go with them, until they would allow him to unhitch his horses, so that they might be able to get their living while he was gone.

The Indians generously performed this service with their knives, and then led him on till they came to where they had left Hammond. The two recognized each other with a smile, and were not a little gratified that their fortunes were thus thrown together. Unloosing Hammond, they began to march with their prisoners, up the river, leading his horses only a short distance with them, for they appeared to be concerned lest their trail would lead to detection. They therefore slipped off the halters and let them go.

We have seen that Hammond possessed a bold and courageous spirit; he was gifted with another trait of character, which is not unfrequently found to be the handmaid of bravery. As he walked along by his Indian guard, he soon forgot his troubles and broke forth into an airy whistle, or made the woods echo to the notes of some playful song. He threw off his cares with as much ease as though they had been no burden, and tripped along with so light and merry a heart, as to impart to the savages themselves, a high gratification, and make them more at ease concerning their prisoner.

Bennett, either from the circumstance of his having a family or from some other cause, could not be so light of heart. His boy was with him, and the sympathies of a father were doubtless laden with a deep anxiety for the welfare of his child, and the savages regarded him with a more cautious eye. Yet as they advanced the prisoners had an opportunity to pass a word or two, sufficient to become acquainted with each other's designs. Hammond informed Bennett that he did not intend to stay long with his company, and when they came to a place which favored his design, he spoke and said, "Now, here Bennett, is a spot where I can get away from the Indians as easy as to turn my hand over. I can start and run and the best of them can't catch me. There are trees in the way and I will risk their bringing me down with a rifle. I can run like a bird."—Bennett plead with him not to go—that he should have some sympathy with him and his boy—that, should he leave them, they would certainly be tomahawked. He begged of him for the sake of his boy, to remain. He said that if they went along peaceably, their lives would in all probability be spared, and that a journey through to Niagara, would not be a very great undertaking, and that they would be likely to get back by winter. Hammond told him that he would not go through with them to Niagara, but that, if they would help him kill the party which had taken them, he would go further. To this they assented and determined to embrace the first opportunity to execute their designs; if possible, during the coming night. They traveled on until darkness overtook them, Hammond cheering their way with a merry whistle or with a song. At night they encamped near a running brook, and after having brought together a sufficient supply of wood and taken supper, they made preparations for the night. The prisoners were tied and made to lie down, each one between two Indians. Thus situated they were presented with little hope of making their escape, yet they had a full opportunity of reflecting upon the curious fortunes of the day, and of imagining the depth of anxiety which must be felt by those whom they had left at home. We leave this party here to describe the progress of another, of the same character, and of similar history.

There was little apprehension, as we have stated in the commencement of the present chapter, among the settlers of the frontier, concerning an attack from the Indians in the spring of 1780. They had been so completely routed the year before, that it was supposed they would not venture again upon their missions of plunder and death. The inhabitants of Fort Wheeler, among others, entertained the same opinion and Mr. Van Campen having recovered from his sickness, was called upon by his father to go and assist in re-building his house, which had been burned by the Indians, and make preparation for raising grain. He therefore left the fort, late in the month of March, in company with his father, a younger brother, an uncle and cousin, and one Peter Pence, who proceeded to take possession of their farms, his uncle of one, and his father of another. They were about half a mile apart and four miles distant from the fort. Here, each party fixing an encampment, commenced its preparations for making sugar and for rearing their dwellings. Not anticipating danger, they had only two rifles, one with each company, and in other respects, were wholly unprepared for an attack from their foes.

The Indians in making their descent upon the frontier settlements, usually proceeded in a body until they came into the vicinity of these, where they would separate into small parties, and for the purpose of striking greater terror upon the inhabitants, attack them at different points along the line open to their incursions They usually came as far as the Wyalusing Flats and from that point, a part would go to the settlements on the Delaware, some descend the east branch of the Susquehanna, and others the west branch of the same river. In the present instance, the party of seven which had made prisoners of Bennett and Hammond, was accompanied by ten others, who, as soon as they came into the neighborhood of Wyoming, struck off, that they might fall upon the inhabitants below. The latter party descended the river and in the vicinity of Shawnee Flats, came upon one named Asa Upson, whom they killed, and a boy called Rogers who was taken prisoner. They next advanced to the waters of Fishing Creek, where they discovered Van Campen's uncle who with his son and Peter Pence, was at work. His uncle they killed, and took the boy and Peter along with them as prisoners. Taking possession of the rifle, they marched on with their prisoners up the creek, and soon saw before them the appearance of other settlers. It was Van Campen with his father and brother. Securing their prisoners, they crept cautiously up, and suddenly burst upon this unsuspecting company. The father was thrust through with a spear, and as he fell, the Indian released his hold and it stood upright, from his transfixed breast. The warrior, taking his knife from his girdle, scalped his victim, who was lying in the agonies of death, and then cut the throat of the dying man, from ear to ear. The little brother, who stood by Van Campen's side, as he saw this last act, raised his eyes, and with an agonizing look, said, "*Father is killed.*" In an instant the hatchet was gleaming over *his* head, and the next moment, the little boy, too, was struggling with his dying pangs. Van Campen was seized by two warriors, who each laid hold of one of his arms, and another coming up, took the scalp from his expiring brother and threw him across the fire. Then the warrior who had killed and had been scalping his father, placed one foot on the body, and drew out his spear. But his thirst for blood was still unquenched; with the reeking blade he came towards Van Campen, and aiming at his body made a violent thrust. But the latter perceiving the movement, quickly shrank to one side, and the spear passed through his vest and shirt, and made a slight wound in his flesh. The Indians, who had hold of him, then seized the weapon and secured his arms behind him, appearing to be satisfied with the number slain.

This was a trying scene for Van Campen. His honored father lay before him, a slaughtered victim. The dark smoke which went curling up towards heaven, from the fire near, bore in its deep folds, the incense of a brother's blood,—too darling a sacrifice to be met with an unblanched cheek. Yet what could he say—or, what do? His little brother had no doubt fallen, because of the agony he had expressed for his dying father;—should he, too, allow the deep current of his emotions, to break away from their pent up channel, and overwhelm him with a flood of grief? This would be to expose himself to certain death. Yet he would as soon die, almost, as live, with the deep sorrow that was pressing him down to the earth. But amid the whole, he preserved his countenance erect—not a single muscle of his face betrayed the agitation within—and there was no sign which gave the least indication of fear. The savages, beholding his apparent indifference, ceased from the fury of their rage and the tumultuous wave passed over, leaving him the lone survivor of the wrecks around. They took him prisoner and pursued their march up Fishing Creek, leading along two of his father's horses, upon which they had mounted their baggage.

Upon coming to the vicinity of a place called Huntington, they again discovered inhabitants, and dispatched four of their number to go and take a survey of the scene before them, and then come back and report. They were fortunately discovered by the settlers, who immediately fled, but the Indians shot at them and wounded a Captain Ransom in the shoulder. Proceeding on their way they came, the next morning, to the head of what was called Hunlock's Creek, and the Indians again perceived that they were in the vicinity of inhabitants. It was the place of one Pike, who was with his wife and child at a camp, engaged in making sugar. Here one of the Indians, who could speak a little English, told Van Campen that he must stand out in an open place, and call to those that were near, and have them come towards him, threatening to put him to death if he did not do as he was ordered. All the others concealed themselves and Van Campen, thinking it best to obey them, rather than lose his life, called aloud as though he desired some assistance. He was answered—"What do you want?"—"Come here," was the reply. In a moment Pike came running up, and when he was just at hand, the savages rushed out upon him, with their tomahawks, and brandished one over his head. The poor fellow immediately dropped on his knees and begged for quarters. They appeared to be pleased with the success of their little stratagem, and with the manner in which they had frightened him, and were willing to spare his life.

Pike then led them to his camp where they found his wife and child; these they stripped of all their clothing, except a thin, light garment and one of the savages, more blood-thirsty than the others, took the little child by the heels and swung it around, with the intention of dashing out its brains against a tree. The infant screamed, and the poor mother, with a frantic shriek, flew to its relief, catching hold of the warrior's arm. The Indian chief, Mohawk, who was one of this party, beholding the situation of the woman came up and took away the child from this cruel wretch, and gave it to the agonized mother. He then gave her the clothing which had been torn from her, and taking out his paint box, painted her, and pointing in the direction he wished her to go, said, "*Joggo*, squaw." She departed and traveling on foot arrived safely at Wyoming, where she gave a report of what had transpired.

A few extracts from a diary, which was kept by Lieutenant Jenkins, of the valley of Wyoming, and which belongs to the time of which we have been speaking may not be uninteresting to the reader.*

"March 27th.—Bennett and son, and Hammond taken and carried off, supposed by the Indians. The same day Upson scalped near William Stewart's house, and young Rogers taken.

"March 28th.—Several scouting parties sent out, but make no discoveries of the enemy.

---

*As quoted by Stone in his History of Wyoming.

"March 29th.—Esquire Franklin went to Huntington, on a scout, and was attacked by the Indians, at or near his own house, and two of his party murdered—Ransom and Parker.*

"March 30th.—Mrs. Pike came in this day, and informed that she and her husband were in the woods making sugar, and were surrounded by a party of about thirty Indians, (there were only ten,) who had several prisoners with them, and two horses. They took her husband and carried him off with them, and painted her and sent her in. They killed the horses before they left the cabin where she was. One of the prisoners told her that the Indians had killed three or four men at Fishing Creek."

Taking Pike with them the Indians, after having killed the two horses, as just mentioned, proceeded on their way, crossing the mountain and coming to what was called Little Tunkhannock Creek, in the mouth of which stream, they had concealed their canoes. They embarked in these, crossed over the Susquehanna, and paddled along the edge of the stream until they came to the mouth of Big Tunkhannock Creek; after passing by which, they went on shore, cutting holes in the bottoms of their little barks and sent them floating down the river. They passed along up through the valley of the Susquehanna, without meeting with any thing worthy

---

*Mr. Van Campen says that Ransom was only wounded in the shoulder, and that he recovered his health, and was well afterwards. He does not know that any one was killed at that time, and supposes there was not from the fact that no scalp was taken. They might have killed Parker, however, without taking his scalp.

of note, till they came to Meshoppen Creek, where the prisoners discovered something very strange in the appearance of their captors. Their countenances suddenly were lighted up with revenge; their eyes darted fire, and their every look was kindled with the strong expressions of rage. The prisoners saw around them no cause for this unexpected change in their actions, and wondered what could be the matter. They were led to entertain the most fearful apprehensions, concerning their fate, beginning to anticipate a sudden and terrible death. Another glance at the party, which we have left, is here necessary to explain the reason of these movements.

Hammond and Bennett were lying between their captors; it was the first night after they were taken, and they were in hopes that some opportunity would present itself, for rising upon the party by which they were detained. Bennett, who was really a brave man, had some hesitation about acting, for fear that a failure might decide the fate of his boy. He did not wish to engage without a strong probability of success. The thoughts of each one was occupied, while the warriors were held in profound sleep; Bennett, for the reasons given, viewing their proposed enterprise somewhat reluctantly, and Hammond, watching for the favorable moment to arrive, when they could perform the work of death and escape.

They continued thus until nearly the break of day, when the Indians arose, and unbinding their prisoners, took them down to a little creek, near which they had encamped, that they might perform their accustomed morning ablution. Upon returning, Hammond whispered to Bennett, that now would be their time to watch their opportunity for making an attack.—Bennett answered that they had better not. There was no chance for the other to urge his purpose, and they went back to their places, without saying anything more. The Indians then laid down, and their prisoners with them, to take another nap, but the latter were left unbound. As soon as the savages were again in the soft embraces of sleep, Hammond passed the signal over to Bennett, and the latter shook his head. The other could not remonstrate, for their communications must be made in silence, he therefore remained in the greatest anxiety, until the time for action had passed, and the broad light of day soon chased away the dreams which hung around the slumbering warrior. Hammond then gave Bennett to understand, that he would not go one step farther with him, that they had enjoyed as fair an opportunity as they could have desired, for making an escape, and he had not been willing to embrace it, and that now he should be left to make his way along as best he could, for he, Hammond, was determined to take his first chance for flight. Bennett well understood the fleetness, as well as the decision of the other, and was perfectly assured that he would make his escape, if he once resolved to do so. He therefore besought his companion, that he would go with him one day longer, stating the embarrassment he felt, on account of his boy, and that the circumstances with which they had been favored, were such as they had not anticipated, and that he was in a measure unprepared to act; but he might rely upon it, that he would not fail to co-operate with him, in anything he should propose during the coming night. Hammond was persuaded to continue with them another day; and during their progress, the two prisoners managed to be together as much as possible without incurring suspicion, so that their plans for the proposed attack, were well matured before it came night. But though they had used great caution in conversing with each other, the savages had observed that they were more than usually intimate, and began to watch them with a more careful eye, every now and then bringing upon them a dark and significant frown. Hammond resorted again to his music, but it failed of producing its wonted effect. The melody of his voice passed over them, as though it had been unheard, and the clear and lively notes of his whistle, fell upon their ears without starting any thing, which even bordered upon a smile. They all looked gruffly and sullen, not excepting the one with whom Hammond had become quite a favorite, on account of his pleasing songs and insinuating manners. The latter finding that his efforts to please were in vain, relaxed into his accustomed careless manner, and stepped along as though he was beyond the reach of trouble.

Bennett, on the contrary, bore upon him the marks of anxiety. It was but too apparent from his looks, that he apprehended another failure, and the Indians conceiving, perhaps, some dislike, treated him rather roughly, placing upon him, in addition to his own, the pack which had before been carried by Hammond.

When it came night they were pinioned more closely than than they had been before, and the hope of destroying these savages, began to desert them. Yet they looked forward to the morning, when they expected to be unloosed, as they were on the one previous. Their encampment was near Meshoppen Creek, and they anxiously awaited the time when the savages would go down to the creek to wash, trusting that they would be left unbound, when they returned.

Soon the first light of morning began to send up a few timorous rays in the east, and the Indians, true to their habit, arose, unloosed their prisoners, and went down to the creek, as had been anticipated. But when they came back they were careful to make fast their captives between two warriors, leaving the boy only, unbound. They were thus disappointed, and began to give up all ideas of making an escape. Hammond, especially, was impatient, and was tossed about with restless anxiety. He was lying near the Indian who had been rather prepossessed in his favor, and this fellow, who was called English, spoke to him and said, "Lie still, Yankee;—Yankee—sleep." Hammond answered that he couldn't sleep the cord hurt him so. With this the Indian slipped out his knife to him, that he might loosen his fetters a little, and be able to obtain more rest. Hammond was very careful to use the knife in relieving himself from bondage, and having silently cut himself loose, handed the instrument over to Bennett, who used it with equal success.

It had been previously agreed upon, in case of their being free to make an attack, that Hammond should take a war-spear, Bennett the wood-hatchet, having been careful to observe where it was placed, and the little boy was to stand by the guns, that had been stacked against a tree. He was not to fire unless a warrior should attempt to take possession of them.—One of the Indians, upon returning from the creek, had not laid down with the others, but sat by the fire with his blanket partly over his head, and was engaged in picking and eating the roasted head of a deer. He sat with his face turned partly from them, and they were in hopes of creeping out from their places without being discovered. When all the rest were asleep, they began slowly to draw themselves out from between the warriors, and were so happy as to remove, without causing them to awake. Hammond then took one of the spears that were sticking in the ground at the head of where each one lay, and motioning to Bennett to be ready, came up behind the Indian that was taking his repast, and aiming for his heart, plunged the spear through his body. He sprang forward with a yell, upon the fire immediately before him. This started the other warriors, and as they arose up, Bennett sank his hatchet into the heads of four. Hammond had been detained in endeavoring to extricate his spear. He had made such a violent thrust, that this passed through the Indian's breast bone, which closed in upon, and fastened it so that he could not draw it out.

Two of the party made their escape. The boy standing by the guns attempted to fire at them. but finding the first, second, and third rifles he took up unloaded, they were so far away when the fourth, containing a charge was taken, it was in vain to fire. It was supposed, however, that one of them had been wounded by Bennett, who caught up a spear and hurled at him, striking him in the back.

They were thus left masters of the field, five of their enemies lying dead on the ground. Yet it was dangerous to remain long where they were, and selecting from their booty what they chose, they threw the remainder on the burning logs, as also the bodies of the Indians slain, and directed their course toward Wyoming and reached their homes in safety.

It was at this place that the Indians, who were leading along the company of prisoners, of which Mr. Van Campen was one, became so much altered in their manners and aspect. They were expecting to meet the warriors from whom they had parted, as soon as they should reach the Wyalusing Flats, which were a few miles above. But here they undoubtedly saw the marks of death, and were led to entertain fears concerning the fate of their companions. How much they saw, we cannot tell, yet they must have seen enough to have revealed a part, if not the whole of the secret of the sad disaster which was brought upon their friends; for Mr. Van Campen says that, "When they came to this place, they showed signs of great anger, and their eyes darted fire, as they looked at one another, and at the prisoners."

But Van Campen like Hammond, did not fancy the idea, even if his life should be spared, of a journey through to Niagara, the head-quarters of the Indians. The night after Pike was taken, he began to meditate an attack upon his captors. Himself, with other prisoners they pinioned, and while they were thus lying around their night-fire, he began to reflect upon the scenes through which they had been hurried. These arose one after another to his mind, and prevented him from obtaining sleep, which seemed to settle on all but him. The scene of a murdered father, and of a tomahawked brother, was presented to his view, and he was now lying with the perpetrators of these horrid acts. The prospect before him was uncertain ; he might die by a lingering and cruel death after he reached the end of their journey, or he might fall under the hatchet by the way. In either event, it would be far better for him to make some effort to escape, even though that effort should cost him his life. The only probable way of escape, that presented itself to his mind, was to consult with his fellow prisoners, and resolve upon the destruction of the whole party.

He had an opportunity of communicating his designs to them during the next day. They regarded it, however, as a scheme entirely visionary, for three men to think of dispatching ten Indians. Yet he spread before them the advantages which three men, awake, and active, would have over ten that were asleep—stated to them further, that as they were the first prisoners which would be taken in, after the destruction of the Indian villages and corn by Sullivan, the summer before, they would in all probability be tied to the stake, and subjected to a cruel and lingering death. He told them that now they had an inch of ground upon which to fight, and they might perhaps gain their point; but if they failed, it would only be death, and they might as well die one way as another.

That day passed and at night, the Indians encamped and secured their prisoners as before. The morning came, and as they proceeded on their way, Van Campen renewed his suggestions to dispatch them on the coming night, and urged them to decide the question without any further delay. They were removing continually from their home, into the heart of the enemy's country, and if they should advance too far, they might not be able to return again, even if they should effect their escape. The prisoners agreed to make a trial, but they were at a loss to know how it should be done. Van Campen said, "Disarm them, and take each a tomahawk, and come to close work at once. There are three of us, and if we plant our blows with judgment, three times three will make nine. The tenth we can kill at our leisure." They were suited with this proposal in part; but were not decided about using the tomahawk altogether. One of them proposed to fire at those on one side, with a gun, while two of the three were using the hatchet. Van Campen urged in opposition to this, that it would be a very uncertain way of making an attack; the first shot fired might give the alarm, and their enemies might rise, and see that it was only the prisoners, and defeat them before they carried their project into execution.

He was obliged, however, to yield to tneir plan.—Peter Pence was to take charge of the guns, Pike and Van Campen were to wield the tomahawk. When it came night the prisoners cut and carried a goodly supply of wood so that the Indians might have a large fire, and then they were tied as usual, and laid in their places. While they were lying here one of the savages had occasion to use his knife and dropped it at Van Campen's feet, and he immediately turned one foot over it, thus hiding it from view. Presently they all laid down, and were soon in the soft embraces of sleep. About mid-

[Illustrated by Dennis D. McKibben]

VAN CAMPEN'S ENCOUNTER WITH MOHAWK.

night, Van Campen arose and looked around. Every thing appeared favorable, and he began to think of entering upon the work of death. He had few misgivings of heart; a father's and a brother's blood was calling for vengeance, and this steeled his mind to sympathy and nerved his arm for action. He immediately went with the knife to Pence—whom he cut loose, and he in turn performed the same office for him He then cut Pike loose, and they all forthwith began silently to disarm the Indians. The guns were stationed against a tree near the encampment. Pence then prepared himself to shoot, Pike and Van Campen took their places with the tomahawk. The latter was to kill three on the right wing, the former two on the left.—That moment Pike's two awoke, and were getting up; Pike proved a coward, and laid down. It was a critical moment. Van Campen saw that there was no time to be lost; their heads were turned up fair, and he planted the hatchet deep into them and then turned to the destruction of his own three men. As he was striking his tomahawk in the head of the last, Pence fired and did good execution, killing four. The only one left, started with a bound away from the fire, but perceiving that the attack was from the prisoners, he gave the war-whoop, and darted for the guns.— Van Campen was quick to intercept him, and the contest then turned between the two. As the latter raised the hatchet, the other quickly turned to run from him, yet he followed and struck at his head, but missed his aim, the tomahawk entering the back of the Indian's neck, who immediately fell; and Van Campen's foot slipping, he, too, came down by his side, and they both clinched, each as they were, on the ground. The warrior with his naked arm, caught Van Campen around the neck, and hugged him so close that he could hardly breathe. They had a most violent and doubtful struggle, Van Campen at one moment being uppermost, and then the Indian, from whose wound the blood ran freely into the face of the other, getting into his eyes, and almost obscuring his sight. During the whole scuffle, the warrior kept feeling around behind him for his scalping knife, which, if he had obtained, would have shortly ended the strife. Van Campen perceiving this, and being almost suffocated with blood, was wrought up to an agony of feeling, and bringing one of his feet up, caught his toes in the warriors belt, and gave a violent spring, which threw them several feet apart. They both rose at the same time and the savage took to his heels and ran. It was a minute or more before Van Campen cleared his eyes so that he could see; he was a little time in hunting the tomahawk, which had fallen from the wound, and had been partly covered up during the scuffle, so that when he was prepared for pursuit, the other had gone too far to be overtaken. He was the only one who escaped, and made out to return to his own people. This fact Mr. Van Campen learned from the Indian's own mouth, several years after the war. The warrior's name was Mohawk. He was a stout, active, and daring fellow, and and held the office of Chief in one of his tribes.*

As soon as Van Campen ended his struggle with Mohawk, he returned to his fellow prisoners. Pike, however, was powerless. He was found on his knees endeavoring to pray, while Pence was cursing and swearing at

---

*See Appendix, Note "A."

him most furiously, charging him with being a rascally coward, and telling him that it was no time to pray, when he ought to be fighting. Nine Indians were lying dead upon the ground, and the season of strife had ended, leaving the prisoners masters of the field. They took possession of all the guns, blankets and match-coats. There were twelve guns, ten owned by the party, and two that had been taken from Van Campen and his uncle. They then scalped the warriors they had killed, and recovered those that had been taken from their friends, Van Campen stringing them all on his belt for safe keeping.

This scene was performed in less time, perhaps, than has been occupied in describing it, and as there were several hours of the night yet remaining, Van Campen thought best to remove from the fire, and be on their guard lest the Indian who had escaped might fall in with another parrty of warriors, and lead them back to recover what had been lost.

The two little boys, who were also prisoners, had taken the alarm and fled from the scene of action. While Van Campen was at his station, eagerly watching for the appearance of day, his attention was arrested by hearing the tread of some one, not far distant, and turning his eye in the direction whence the sound proceeded, he could just distinguish the outlines of some one who was coming towards him. He immediately cocked his rifle, and held it to the tree, behind which he was standing, with his eye upon the object, which he supposed to be an Indian, and waited for its appearance, with his finger on the trigger of his gun. It came nearer and nearer, and just as he was on the point of firing, the thought struck him that he might be aiming at one of the little boys. He immediately called out—" Who's there?" Young Rogers answered—" It's me." The answer, in a voice that was known, came upon him like an electric shock. His arms dropped powerless by his side, and if, but a few moments before, he had shown himself equal to the most daring act of bravery, he now seemed to manifest the trepidation of fear. The thought that he was just upon the point of firing at the young innocent by his side, almost unmanned him;—the effect, which the slaughter he had just made, produced on his mind, was nothing in comparison. But fortunately the boy was unharmed, and Van Campen was spared the painful thoughts which he must have endured, had he taken the life of the lad at whom he was aiming.

The prisoners kept possession of the battle-ground until morning, and then gathering whatever of the Indian baggage they could carry, began to thread their way towards home.

There is another scene of interest, growing out of the one which we have been describing, which gives us some further insight to the history of the Indian Chief, Mohawk, and which will serve to impress the reader with a just idea of the number of depredations that occurred at that period. While the two parties of Indian warriors, whose progress we have been describing, were executing the purpose of their mission, the celebrated war-chief, Brant, was decending with a company of Tories and Indians, into the region of Schoharie. On his way he came across a company of fourteen men, who had been sent out under the command of Captain Alexander Harper, to inspect the movements of the suspicious Tory, who, it was susposed, was about commencing the labor of making maple sugar, and to engage himself in the manufacture of the same article. While in the execution of the command, and without a thought of the presence of the lurking savage, he was approached by the party under Brant, the first monition of whose coming, he had in the loss of three of his men who were engaged at work. Next appeared the Mohawk chief, who immediately rushed in with the uplifted tomahawk, and advancing to Capt. Harper, observed,—" Harper I am sorry to find you here !" " Why are you sorry Captain Brant ?" was the reply. " Because," replied the chief, " I *must* kill you, although we were school-mates in our youth "—at the same time raising the hatchet, as though about to strike. But his arm suddenly dropped, and fixing his keen eye upon Harper he inquired,—" Are there any regular troops at the fort in Schoharie ?" Harper, as quick as thought, determining in his answer, to startle the Indian chief, and prevent, if possible, his descent upon the settlements, told him, though contrary to the truth, that the forts had been strengthened a few days before, by the arrival of three hundred Continental troops. This information, given with a look of the utmost assurance, served to disconcert, for a moment, the noble warrior, and, preventing the further shedding of blood, he called a council of his subordinate chiefs. The fate of the prisoners was made the subject of debate. Long and earnestly did the Indians contend that they should be put to death, yet Brant, whose word was regarded as law, decided in their favor, and they were permitted to live.

The conviction produced on the mind of this warrior, of the presence of so large a force, determined him to retrace his steps to Niagara, and taking his prisoners he commenced his return march. It was not, however, without again questioning Harper, giving him to understand that he strongly suspected the truth of his statement, yet the prisoner bore so well, the severe scrutiny of the Indian's eye, that the warrior was once more misled by the sincerity which was apparent in every look of his informant, and abandoned the idea of striking his intended blow upon the settlements of Schoharie. The warriors, disappointed in their expectation of plunder, demanded the lives of the little band they had taken, yet the Mohawk chief promised them safety, if they would be conducted by him to Niagara as prisoners of war.

Their march was commenced, attended with pain, difficulty and adventure. Having to carry along the spoils, which the Indian had taken on his route, the prisoners found themselves subjected to the most oppressive burdens, and were ready at times, to sink under the fatigues of the way. But a resolute mind sustained their drooping spirits, and enabled them to keep pace, though with much effort, with the progress of their foes. As they proceeded on their course, Brant fell in with a Tory, who was well acquainted with the party he had taken, and who urged him to give them all to the tomahawk and the scalping knife, stating that their news respecting the arrival of troops was nothing but a fabrication. Harper was then made to pass through the trying ordeal of another examination, yet so well did he counterfeit the signs of sincerity and truth that the glittering tomahawk was again withdrawn from over his head.

The party of warriors continued their march, descending the Delaware a sufficient distance, then crossing over to Oghkwaga, where they constructed floats, with which they sailed down the Susquehanna as far as Tioga Point. Here the prisoners were visited with a new and unexpected trial. *"During his march from Niagara on this expedition, Brant had detached eleven of his warriors to fall upon the Minisink settlements for prisoners.† This detachment, as it subsequently appeared, had succeeded in taking captive five athletic men, whom they secured and brought with them as far as Tioga Point.‡ The Indians sleep very soundly, and the five prisoners had resolved at the first opportunity to make their escape. While encamped at this place during the night, one of the men succeeded in extricating his hands from the binding cords, and with the utmost caution unloosed his four companions. The Indians were locked in the arms of deep sleep around them. Silently, without causing a leaf to rustle, they each snatched a tomahawk from the girdles of their unconscious enemies, and in a moment nine of them were quivering in the agonies of

---

*See Stone's Life of Brant, Vol. 2, page 59.

†His warriors did not, as we have seen, descend the Delaware for prisoners, but fell upon the settlements bordering upon the Susquehanna, and the original party consisted of seventeen instead of eleven. Whenever the Indians invaded the settlements on the Delaware, it was usually with a larger company than eleven, since the inhabitants living along this river were quite numerous, and an incursion among them was attended with considerable danger, while on the contrary, the scouts dispatched into the valley of the Susquehanna, a more thinly settled region, did not often exceed the number mentioned.

‡The number taken agrees exactly with that of the captives, among whom was Mr, Van Campen, three of them men, and two boys. The party advanced till within about fifteen miles of Tioga Point,

death. The two others were awakened, and springing upon their feet attempted to escape.—One of them was struck with a hatchet between the shoulders, but the other fled."* The narrative continues—"As Brant and his warriors approached this point of their journey, some of his Indians having raised a whoop, it was instantly returned by a single voice with the *death yell!* Startled at this unexpected signal, Brant's warriors rushed forward to ascertain the cause. But they were not long in doubt, the lone warrior met them, and soon related to his brethren the melancholy fate of his companions. The effect upon the warriors who gathered in a group to hear the recital, was inexpressibly fearful. Rage, and a desire for revenge seemed to kindle every bosom, and light every eye, as with burning coals.—They gathered round the prisoners in a circle, and began to make unequivocal preparations for hacking them to pieces. Harper and his men of course gave up for lost not doubting that their doom was fixed and irreversible. But at this moment deliverance came from an unexpected quarter. While their knives were unsheathing, and their hatchets glittering as they were flourished in the sunbeams, the only survivor of the murdered party rushed into the circle." Himself a chief, he waved his hand as a signal by which to command attention and notify them of his desire to

---

*This story agrees, in time, place, and circumstance, as perfectly with the one which has been related of Mr. Van Campen, as is possible for stories to agree which come from different authorities. The number of prisoners is the same, and the manner in which the escaping warrior was wounded is also the same; but as the number of the party was stated as being eleven, it was necessary to account for the good fortune of one who was not there.

speak. The warriors immediately turned their eyes upon their unfortunate comrade, and were anxiously awaiting the first words that should break from his lips. He commenced his speech with all the authority and dignity of an Indian sachem; but what was their surprise to find, that as he advanced, his plea was in favor of the unfortunate victims upon whom they were about to let loose the fury of their rage. The prisoners, too, could understand from the changed looks of those around them, that the noble chief was making his address in their behalf, and Harper, who was somewhat acquainted with the Indian tongue, understood its import as follows: "Warriors, your looks are changed! The tale of our butchered brothers, has fired you to take revenge. But where—the hands that are stained with blood? Are these men guilty of the slain warriors? Take no blood from the innocent! The Great Spirit will be angry!" His appeal produced the desired effect. The burning eye of the warrior ceased to shoot forth the deep fire of revenge, and the savage looks, that had encompassed the prisoners with the terrific forms of vengeance, suddenly died away, and gave to their agonized spirits the feeble wings of hope.

It so happened, that this chief, who must have been Mohawk, had years before been acquainted with the prisoners, whom he saw when he was brought to the main body of Indians, and beholding their situation, he generously interposed in their favor.

The biographer of Brant justly says of this deed,--"It was a noble action, worthy of the proudest era of chivalry, and, in the palmy days of Greece and Rome, would have insured him almost 'an apotheosis and rites divine.' The interposition of Pocahontas, in favor of Captain Smith, before the rude court of Powhattan, was perhaps more romantic; but when the motive which prompted the generous action of the princess is considered, the transaction now under review, exhibits the most genuine benevolence. Pocahontas was moved by the tender passion—the Mohawk sachem by the feelings of magnanimity, and the eternal principles of justice. It is a matter of regret that the name of this high-souled warrior is lost, as, alas! have been too many that might have served to relieve the dark and vengeful portraitures of Indian character, which it has so well pleased the white man to draw! The prisoners themselves, were so impressed with the manner of their signal deliverance, that they justly attributed it to a direct interposition of the providence of God."

Harper and his men, were taken to Niagara, and after an imprisonment of three years, by an exchange of prisoners were permitted to return to their own country and homes.

That the noble actor in this scene, was the warrior who escaped from the hatchet of Van Campen, there can be but little doubt, for the story of each is the same in every particular, excepting the number of Indians in the party, one account given it as ten, the other, as eleven. The deed seems, too, to be characteristic of the chief, Mohawk, for we have seen him before, generously interposing in behalf of Mrs. Pike's child, whose brains one of his men was about to dash out against a tree; at the same time, freely surrendering her clothing, and sending her in the direction of safety, with this mark upon her, to shield her from the violence of any savages whom she might meet.

We will return again to the party of Mr. Van Campen, which had rendered itself free by the slaughter of its captors. They remained in safety, each one at his station until the approach of morning light, when they constrcted a raft, and having placed upon it, the Indian baggage which fell into their hands, set sail for Wyoming the nearest settlement on the river. They had not gone far, however, before their raft began to give way, and after using their utmort endeavors to keep it together, they were obliged to run the crazy thing ashore and betake themselves to the more laborious journey by land. They left behind, a great portion of their baggage, but took with them, the guns and ammunition. Late in the afternoon they arrived at Wyalusing, and marching thence, came to the Narrows at evening.

Near this place, they discovered a smoke before them, rising from the low ground bordering on the river, and saw also a raft lying at the shore, by which appearances, they were led to conclude, that a party of Indians had passed them during the course of the day, and had halted for the night. They had no other alternative than to rout them, or go over a mountain, which lay before them, and in crossing which they would be obliged to encounter the deep snow that was still lying upon the north side. Yet they might incur some danger in making an attack upon the enemy, but they concluded, from the size of the raft that the party must be small, and as they had made the first discovery, they supposed that the advantage would be on their side. They were well armed, each being supplied with two rifles, and the only fear that entered Van Campen's mind, was, that Pike would prove a coward as he had done before. Yet he thought it best to ascertain the numbers and situation of the enemy, and if every thing was favorable, he was to give the signal for attack. He crept down the hill silently, and came so near as to behold the fire and packs, but saw no Indians. Concluding that they had gone out to hunt for meat, he motioned his men to come on. They came, and taking the packs from the deserted camp, threw them on the raft, that was near by, and with paddles and setting poles drove her briskly for the opposite side of the river. When they had passed nearly out of the reach of gun-shot, two Indians came up to the bank, whence the raft had been taken, and beholding it merrily conveying off another party, drew up their rifles and fired, but without doing any injury. They soon passed under cover of an island, and coasted along its border, leaving the Indians out of sight. They descended the river several miles, until they supposed themselves out of the reach of the enemy, and drew up to the shore. They landed on an island, and being damp and cold, began to look about for some means of making a fire. Having collected the materials they kindled one in a deep hole, where they were out of sight and could imagine themselves perfectly shielded from being discovered by the enemy.

They had not been long at their encampment before their attention was arrested by the breaking of snow crust near by, which sounded like the noise of some one stepping. Pike was the first to take the alarm.—He said that the Indians had followed them, and they would certainly be shot down where they were. He became quite annoying, with his anxiety and his fears, so much so that Van Campen, with a view to make him quiet, threatened to shoot him if he did not keep still. He was silent for a moment, and the stepping began to be heard more distinctly, and seemed to be approaching nearer and nearer the fire. Van Campen took his position and stood with his rifle cocked, and prepared to put a ball through the unknown assailant as soon as he should come in sight. At length the enemy, which had been the occasion of so much alarm, presented itself in the form of a noble raccoon, and, as it came within the gleaming of the firelight, was a fair object for the rifle. Van Campen shot, and hit him.—The animal gave a squeal, and Pike, mistaking it, perhaps, for the yell of an Indian, was frightened out of his wits, jumped up, and halloed at the utmost stretch of his voice, "Quarters! quarters! gentlemen; for heaven's sake, quarters!" Van Campen, taking up the raccoon by one of its legs, threw it down near the fire and said, "Here, you cowardly rascal! skin that, and let's have the *quarters* for supper." Pike was better at cooking than he was at fighting, and soon had the animal ready for the coals upon which it was laid to broil. It was a fine treat for them, and they ate it with many a hearty laugh, and a good joke at Pike, for his excellent "*quarters.*" They rested during the night without any further alarm, aud in the morning, embarked upon their float, and began to sail down the river. They pursued their course along the silent stream, without interruption, and reached Wyoming at evening. They were received with many demonstrations of joy, their coming being as little anticipated, as life from the dead.

CHAPTER XIV.

After resting at Wyoming a day, Van Campen procured a canoe, and with Pence and his little cousin began to go down the river toward Northumberland, going by night, it being more safe than journeying by day He arrived before dawn at Fort Jenkins.

"Fort Jenkins was situated on the north bank, of the north branch of the Susquehanna, five miles below the town of Berwick, on the public road leading to Bloomsburg, in Columbia county, Pa.—at that time in Wyoming township, Northumberland county. It was situated on a high plateau of ground overlooking the river, and from the southern bank must have formed a prominent, and imposing sight.

The tract of land on which it stood was surveyed by Charles Stewart, Depty Surveyor in Oct. 1774, for Daniel Reese, who afterward lived and died at or near the town of Lewisburg, on the west branch. He conveyed the tract of land about four hundred acres, Feb. 25th, 1775, to James Jenkins a merchant of Philadelphia, who built a house upon it and made substantial improvements. After the war broke out the Indian depredations which followed, made it necessary in the spring of 1778, to surround this block-house with palisades of hewn logs, set upright in the earth, twelve feet in height, forming a structure which was called Fort Jenkins. It was sixty feet in width and eighty feet in length, and enclosed a substantial block-house, supplied with a hearth of brick brought up the river in boats for that purpose. The well inside the fort was a very substantial one seventy-five feet in depth and walled up. It still remains and does duty as a farm house well."*

Near this point Van Campen found Col. Kelly encamped with about one hundred men. In view of the late Indian depredations he had raised this company and gone out in pursuit of the enemy. He had been up the west branch of the Susquehanna, and had thence crossed over to the north branch, and the head of the Chilisquaka, to Fishing Creek. Passing through the gap at the end of Nob Mountain, he came to where Van Campen's father and uncle had been killed. He found their bodies as the savages had left them. That of his brother had nearly been consumed by the fire, yet the parts left were committed to the earth with the remains of the other two.

From Col. Kelley, Van Campen learned that his mother and her surviving family, were safely lodged in the fort. To him the anticipated meeting with his dearest earthly friend, was a subject of joy; how much more to her, who, with the deep love of a mother's heart, was to clasp in her arms the form of her first born child; a son whom she had wept over as dead, and whom she expected never more to behold. But though an ardent desire impelled him to seek an immediate entrance into the fort, prudence would not allow him to rush directly into the

---

*C. F. Hill Esq. from the Wilksbarre Record

presence of his mother. Her grief at the loss of a husband who had been so inhumanly slain, of a son that had fallen under the Indian's tomahawk, and of another carried away captive, to be the subject, perhaps, of more excruciating pain, was too overwhelming for her feelings, and she well nigh sank under the weight of her sorrow.

Supposing that the interview would be overpowering to her, the Colonel was sent in to prepare the way for his coming, and laying aside his belt of scalps, he soon after went in himself. The meeting, though introduced with the utmost caution, produced almost the anticipated effect. It was one of mingled joy and woe, in which every feeling of delight at seeing her returning son, was immediately met and driven back, by an opposing current of sorrow, at the thoughts of those, whose remembrance still drew forth the tears of grief.

As soon as these emotions subsided sufficiently to allow of the inquiries, she questioned him concerning his capture, and the way in which he had escaped. These he related to her in the manner in which the several events took place, and as the reader has already been acquainted with the facts, they need not be repeated.

Before Mr. Van Campen's return, the commission of ensign, in the continental service, had been sent him of a company to be commanded by Capt. Thomas Robison. He had no knowledge of this, before it came, yet as he was led by his disposition to follow the life of a soldier, he accepted of the office, and spent most of the ensuing summer in obtaining recruits, to fill out the company to which he belonged, and formed a part of the quota that Pennsylvania was to raise for the army. Leaving Fort

Jenkins he proceeded to Northumberland where he received his papers and prepared to enter upon the duties of his office.

We have had occasion to speak of Col. Kelly more than once. and as he was very prominent in the region where the scenes we have been contemplating transpired, some further account of him will no doubt be very acceptable to the reader.

John Kelly was a native of Lancaster Co., Pa., and was born in February, 1744. He was a noble stalwart man, resolute and fearless, six feet two inches in height, strong, active and insensible to fatigue. After the purchase from the Indians by the Proprietaries of Pennsylvania, in 1768 he left his native county and settled in Buffalo Valley, and endured the hardships common to settlers in a new country.

He served in the Revolutionary war and distinguished himself in the battles of Trenton and Princeton. While on one of their retreats Colonel Potter sent an order to Major Kelly to have a certain bridge cut down to prevent the advance of the British, who were then in sight. Kelly sent for an axe, but represented that the enterprise would be hazardous. Still the British advance must be stopped, and the order was not withdrawn.

He said he would cut down the bridge, for he would not order another to do what some would say he was afraid to do himself. Before all the logs on which the bridge rested were cut off, he was within the range of British fire, and several balls struck the log on which he was standing. The last log broke down sooner than he expected, and he fell with it into the swollen stream.

The American soldiers moved on, not believing it possible for him to make his escape. But by great exertions he reached the shore through high water and floating timber and followed the troops. The fact is noted in history that our retreating army was saved by the destruction of that bridge but the way it was done and the man who did it are not mentioned.

After his discharge Major Kelly returned to his farm and family, and during the three succeeding years Indians were very troublesome to the settlements on the west branch. He became Colonel of a regiment and his duty required him to guard the valley against the incursions of the savages. When the "Big Runaway" occurred he was one of the first to return. For at least two harvests, reapers took their rifles to the field and some watched while others wrought.

At one time Col. Kelly had command of scouting parties in the valley, and very often was out in person. Many nights he has laid on the branches of trees to keep out of the mud, without a fire, because it would indicate his position to the enemy. He became well skilled in Indian warfare and was a terror to their marauding bands.

So greatly was he feared by the savages that they resolved on his destruction, but being too cowardly to attack him openly, sought his life by stealth. He had reason to believe they were prowling around one night, and rising early and looking through the crevices of his log house he saw two lying with their arms in a position to shoot him when he opened the door. Being of a quick turn of mind, he determined to thwart their design, fixed his own rifle and arranged to open the door with a string and watch them at the same time. The moment he pulled the door open two balls came into the house and the Indians arose to advance. He immediately fired and wounded one, when they both retreated. After waiting to see if there were others, he followed them by the blood, but they escaped.

For many years Col. Kelly held the office of Justice of the Peace, and in the administration of justice, exhibited the same anxiety to do right, that had characterized him in his military service. At any time he would forego his own fees, and if the parties were poor, pay the constable's cost to bring about a compromise.

He was a Presbyterian and a devout Christian, but entertained much hatred toward the Indians. At one time a movement was set on foot by the Presbytery of Northumberland to evangelize the savages. When Col. Kelly was called on for a contribution he said he would not give one cent to send preachers among them, but he would give any sum required to buy ropes to hang them.

He died February 18, 1832, at the age of eighty-eight, greatly respected by his neighbors and friends, and was laid to rest in the Presbyterian burying ground in Lewisburg. On the 8th of April, 1835, amid great military display, a plain monument to his memory was unveiled, and an appropriate oration delivered by James Merrill, Esq. Early in the spring of 1856 the monument, together with his remains, were removed to the new cemetery on the western borders of the borough.

Sarah Kelly, his wife, died suddenly Jan. 2d, 1831.*

---

*Taken from the Biographical Annals of the West Branch. J. F. Meginnis, Williamsport, Pa.

We will present also what few items we have of the history of Capt. Joseph Salmon. Van Campen and he had been companions from childhood. When the war of the Revolution was about to be declared, they engaged with one heart in practicing with the rifle for the British they expected to meet on the sea-board, and with the tomahawk to be prepared to meet the Indian on the frontier. They seemed to be so well suited to each other that their companionship was ever a source of pleasure, and they were never more happy, than when as soldiers they were out on duty together. The reader has already become acquainted with some of their exploits as they were called to lead scouting parties through the woods in guarding the frontier settlements.

It will be remembered that he accompanied those sent to capture the inhabitants af Catawissa, suspected of betraying the cause of the Colonies, and how adroitly he and Van Campen effected their capture.

Capt. Salmon was living at this time on the north branch below Danville on the main road, where he was taken prisoner by a party of Indians, on a Sabbath day, March 8, 1781. After traveling four days, his captors turned him over to another party, among whom was an acquaintance of Salmon's called Shenap, who said to the Captain, "Solly, you shan't be hurt." They soon fell in with a large body of savages, who had another prisoner named Williamson.

On coming to where they were to run the gauntlet, Williamson refused and was beaten to death. The captain understanding the thing better started rapidly and plunged through fearlessly, receiving but a few trifling bruises. After the race Shenap came up, and shaking him by the hand laughingly said,—"*Solly you run like debill,—you run like hoss.*" He was exchanged in a short time and returned to his home in safety.

After the war and upon the first organization of the militia which was directly after the termination of hostilities, Mr. Salmon was chosen to fill the office of Colonel. Mr. Van Campen's name was mentioned as an opposing candidate, but he declined to enter the lists against his old friend, and accepted the nomination as first major, and was elected almost unanimously, three votes only out of about five hundred being cast against him. This was the title by which afterwards he was universally recognized.

Colonel Salmon continued to reside for a long time in the neighborhood of his early conflicts, and married, as is supposed, Miss Anna Wheeler, the girl of his choice, and left a very respectable family. He died universally respected and beloved.

CAAPTER XV.

On the left bank of the Susquehanna, at the mouth of Catawissa Creek, is the large and flourishing village of Catawissa, containing a population of more than two thousand. Some four miles above, on Fishing Creek, which forms its northern and western boundary, is the town of Bloomsburg. These towns are pleasantly and beautifully located, and from elevations near present scenery, so varied by mountain, valley, and river, as to hold the attention of the beholder in long and rapt admiration. For many a mile upward he will behold the winding and silvery line of the wide and beautiful Susquehanna, gleaming in the sunlight, and forming an ever radiant border, of wide, green, and fertile fields; beyond them on the south, rising up in its grandeur, the Catawissa Mountain, to the north the conspicuous form of Nob Mountain, and the valley of Fishing Creek, loosing itself as it becomes enveloped in forest and mountain scenery, while about him on every side will bespeak evidences of thrift, and bustle of a large and growing town.

Strange that amid scenes where nature has been so lavish in her gifts, there should have lurked darkly designing men, intent on fighting against freedom and the right. Yet here at an early day were settlers, belonging to the Society of Friends, and others called Tories, the two supposed to be more or less affiliated in their views, and conduct, who were strongly suspected of favoring the cause of the British, and of holding treasonable correspondence with them.

In a region where unparalled suffering had been endured from British and Indian invasions, the aid and comfort afforded by these people to the enemy, would naturally arouse attention, and compel observation. The different condition of things in this neighborhood when contrasted with those of adjoining neighborhoods, could hardly fail of attracting attention While others had to leave their homes, and seek protection within the sheltering walls of neighboring forts ; these would remain unmolested, and enjoy quiet and peace. While other neighborhoods were severely harassed, the people killed, if found outside of their forts, their property destroyed, and themselves subject to captivity and death ;—these would suffer no loss, and carry on the labor of their farms without being annoyed, or distressed by the disasters that universally prevailed elsewhere. The most casual observer would not fail to note this difference.

It was likewise very apparent that their situation was quite favorable for carrying on a treasonable correspondence with the enemy without being discovered, They were surrounded by mountains on one side, and by the Susquehanna River on the other, so that the enemy could reach them, and they the enemy, without being abserved. "*But murder will out*," and a chain of circumstances began at length to be formed, so linked together, that the minds of patriotic men were well convinced of the presence of an enemy among them. In addition to the circumstances already mentioned we may note one or two others, proper to be added as links, to the chain above referred to.

Justice Hewitt, in a letter to the president of the Council of Safety for Columbia County, (Aug. 20, 1780.) says that the "disaffected families" in every incursion of the enemy into this county, fly to them, (viz. inhabitants of Catawissa and Fishing Creeek,) for protection, whilst the *well affected are obliged to vacate the county, or shut themselves up in garrison.*" He also states, by the confession of Casper Reaney, Duncan Beeth, and others, that they were sent to Niagara by David Fowler and others, and that the Indians came to that place in a peaceable manner last spring :—" *Together with many more circumstances which might be produced.*" "*He therefore prays the Honorable Council to grant such relief as in their wisdom they may think proper.*"

From a deposition by Henry O'Neill before this same justice, (Thomas Hewitt), evidence is given of the correspondence and familiarity of the Indians with the people of Catawissa.

Thus ample testimony is afforded that the settlements named were more or less implicated in the disasters and sufferings endured by the others, and that the safety of the country demanded their removal.

The Hon. Wm. McClay, addressing President Reed, from Sunbury, April 2nd, 1780, writes, "I will not trouble you with the distresses of this county. They will no doubt be painted to the Council in lively colors, and indeed the picture cannot be overcharged, nor should I at this time write to you, but for a strong belief and persuasion that a body of Indians are lodged about the head of Fishing and Muncy creeks. They were with us to the very beginning of the deep snow last year, they are with us now before the snow is quite gone. This country might be examined. This is what we wish. Many of our hunters who went late last fall into that country (which is a fine one for hunting) were so alarmed with constant reports of guns, which they could not believe were white men's, that they returned suddenly back. We are not strong enough to spare men to examine this country and dislodge them."*

Col. Hunter had decided on making a demonstration on this Tory Settlement, and had arranged with Captain Klader of Northampton county to join him in the enterprise. The Tories learning of this design, had no doubt sent word to their British and Indian friends to aid them at this juncture. And they had come on the ground in large force, before the arrival of Captain Klader and his men. On the 6th of Sept. 1780, the British and Indians to the number of two hundred and fifty or three hundred men appeared before Fort Rice, and made a vigorous attack, which was kept up until after night, when they set fire to the buildings and haystacks in the neighborhood. The garrison at Fort Jenkins was sent to the relief of Fort Rice. Col. Kelly with one hundred men and Col. Purdy from the Juniata with one hundred and ten men arrived upon the scene. The enemy having destroyed Bosley's mills near Fort Rice, now broke up into smaller bodies, and retreated in different directions. One body of not less than forty British and Indians, left Fort

---

*Col. Freeze's Hist. of Columbia County.

Rice, went by the way of Knob mountain, passing near where Van Campen's father, uncle, and brother had been killed the previous spring, thence by way of Cabin Run to Fort Jenkins, which had been evacuated and destroyed the fort and all the buildings in the vicinity. The well inside the fort was filled with the chared remains of the logs and buildings. All at Fort Jenkins was utterly destroyed except the young orchard, planted by James Jenkins, and just beginning to bear.

This party evidently understood that Captain Klader would soon be expected to meet Col. Hunter, and proceeded up the river to, what is now the town of Berwick, where they crossed over, and followed the path leading from the Susquehanna to Northampton, a distance of about seven miles from Nescopeck, here they lay in ambush, awaiting the arrival of Capt. Klader and his company. At high noon on the 10th of Sept. 1780, four days after the attack on Fort Rice, these unfortunate patriots, while taking their noonday repast were surrounded by this murderous band and were nearly all either killed, or taken prisoners.

Their concealed and terrible enemies had hovered about their track, ready to take advantage of the first unguarded moment. As the soldiers drew near the end of their journey they supposed themselves safe, and were elated with the hope of soon joining with their brethren in arms, to assist in defending the invaded, and distressed frontier to the north and west. They had come to what had been a Scotch settlement, but now, because of the border troubles, wholly deserted. Here were open and cleared fields, covered with a luxuriant growth of grass, and beautiful with wild and fragrant flowers. Before them were pastures rich with the green coloring of early summer, sprinkled here and there with the snowy heads of the modest white clover.

Here was a place too inviting to be passed by without pausing to enjoy the luxury of the scene. It was especially tempting to men weary from the fatigues and hardships of the long march. They needed relaxation and refreshment, since they had been for days before tearing their way through thickets of brush and briers, clambering over rocks, and logs, and opening as they did on what appeared an earthly paradise, they would naturally cast aside every thought of danger, and give themselves up to the luxury of needed repose.

What enemy could invade so delightful a place? Its very appearance one would think sufficient to lull to peace the rough elements of war. They surrendered themselves to the enjoyment of the hour in a very thoughtless unguarded manner. One went one way, another went another, as suited him, each following his own fancy, without order, without placing a sentinel. Their guns scattered here and there, some leaning against stumps, or logs, some perhaps stacked, others lying flat on the ground. The position of the men resembled much that of their fire-arms. Some were lying on the ground indulging in a smoke, one man was leaning against a tree with his shoes off and cleaning them out, others had gone off for grapes, which were there in abundance, and one had climbed a tree and was picking and eating grapes.

Such was the condition these men were in, when the enemy came suddenly upon them, and with hatchet and gun, hewed and shot them down. Some escaped and one or two were taken prisoners, but most of them were killed. A great uncle of the Engle brothers now living in Hazleton and vicinity, escaped over Nescopec mountain. Abraham Klader, brother of the officer in command, concealed himself in little Nescopec Creek, by clinging to a tree, that had fallen across the stream, and keeping his face only above the water until the enemy disappeared, when he emerged from his concealment, and succeeded in reaching his home. Frederick Shickler also escaped on Buck mountain by avoiding the Indian trail, leaving it to his right and by keeping out of sight of the Indians, whose yells he could hear as they followed on in pursuit.

Lieut. Moyer, Ensign Scoby, and a private soldier were taken prisoners; the Lieutenant escaped, the other two were taken through to Niagara.

As soon as the result of this action became known, at the instance of Col. Balliet a large company of men was raised who went to this place and burned ten of the bodies of those that had fallen. At a later period Col. Hunter directed Van Campen to take a company of men, and go and see what discoveries he could make, and bury what dead he could find.

He was not aware of the service already performed, and reported to his superior officer, that he had buried their dead. Some have detected a discrepancy in the two statements referring to the same transaction. The author conceives them both to be true. It will be remembered that Catain Klader's men were widely scattered; they were doubtless left where they had fallen. The man in the tree after grapes, was shot and fell heavily on the ground beneath. Others were shot or killed one in one place, and another in another, while a number may have been killed and their bodies disfigured as represented in the account of Col. Balliet, and their bodies lying near each other. It is said of Capt. Klader that he performed prodigies of valor, killing of the enemy four, and according to others seven, before yielding to the superior force of the enemy. They in turn inflicting upon him, and his companions perhaps, every indignity possible, these forming the ten bodies no doubt buried by Col. Balliet's company.

The author supposes the coming of Van Campen to have been later than that of the other party. He remembers distinctly that in giving his account, Van Campen said the only way they could bury the men found there, was by taking a blanket and fastening the sides securely to two poles ; that without handling them the bodies were rolled on to this blanket, and emptied into the grave prepared to receive them ; two men acting as bearers, and holding in their hands the ends of these poles.

They were evidently in a state of decomposition, quite in advance of those bodies found and cared for by the other party.

C. F. Hill, Esq., of Hazleton, Pa., to whom the author is indebted for the facts contained in this chapter, in speaking of Capt. Klader, says,—"That after performing deeds of valor that caused his name to be viewed with feelings akin to veneration, he was finally killed and scalped, and subsequently buried, as were others also of the party, on what is now the farm of Samuel Wagner, about half a mile from Conyngham. We visited Wagner's farm a few days since, in the company of S. D. Engle, of this borough, and were conducted by Anthony Fisher, a man whose locks are whitened by the frosts of ninety winters, to the spot where the brave Klader rests, but no traces of the grave can now be seen. The oak tree under whose branches he lay, and upon which were the initials of his name, D. K., was sacriligiously cut down fifteen years ago, and even the stump is decayed and gone. Mr. Fisher many years ago was intimately acquainted with with John Wertz, who had belonged to the party that buried the slain, and marked their leader's grave by cutting the initials spoken of above. As the old man leaned on his staff and surveyed the spot, he gave expression to feelings of deep regret, that the tree was not permitted to stand as a memorial of the heroic deeds of those by-gone days. Well might they have exclaimed, who revered the memory of the hero of Sugarloaf Valley,—

"Woodman spare that tree !
Touch not a single bough !"

Colonel Hunter, the commanding officer of the county of Northumberland, intent on putting an end to the sufferings endured by the people, and originating in this neighborhood, directed Capt. Robison to go with his company and bring in its inhabitants, saying, "If they were not friendly to the British cause, it would be better for them to be removed, and if they were, it was vastly important they should be taken from a point where they had the opportunity of causing so much mischief to the country."

Captain Robison therefore made his preparations and

started with his men to execute this commission. Van Campen, as he belonged to the company, was one of the number and his friend Salmon, went as volunteer, though not having any command. A Lieutenant Hays, also a volunteer, went with them and on their setting out, was very profuse in his professions of bravery, and engaged the attention of the men in telling them what he would do, if he had the command;—how he would hunt the enemy in every hiding place, and drive them from every refuge, until they were exterminated;—in short he would accomplish wonders.

Salmon and Van Campen were considerably amused with his bravado style, declaring even in the hearing of his superior officers what he would achieve, if he only were in command, and they thought it would not be amiss to apply some test to his professed bravery.

Having formed their plan, they communicated the same to Capt. Robison. They told him they had brought with them their Indian dress, and proposed that as soon as they should arrive at the house of a Mr. Gaskin, which was nine miles above Northumberland, he should halt and allow them sufficient time to change their dress, and paint, and requested him after this to send Hays to the river, to examine and see if he could see any moccasin tracks. Their plan was approved, and as soon as they came to the place appointed, Capt. Robison ordered his men to halt, when Van Campen and Salmon slipped away from the company unobserved, and under cover of the river bank, arrayed themselves in the Indian costume, and having taken upon each other the tawny color, they awaited the coming of the boasting Lieutenant, each selecting a tree behind which they stood until he came in sight.

Captain Robison after waiting a sufficient time, allowing his men to rest and slake their thirst, requested Lieutenant Hays to go to the river, and see if he could discover any moccasin tracks in the sand. In a moment he was on his way, and the Captain whispered to his men that they might look for a little sport, as Van Campen and Salmon in their Indian dress, were going to try the Lieutenant's courage.

Hays was a tall, red-headed man, and as he came up and began to bend his lank form over the bank, with a rather suspicious look, Van Campen and Salmon thrust their tawny faces from behind the trees, gave the Indian war-whoop, and fired their rifles over his head. Hays was greatly frightened, and turned on his heel and began to run, crying as loud as he could yell,— "*Boys in the house,—Boys in the house!—Engens! Engens!--Boys in the house!—Engens!*" He continued to run with all his might, not stopping before entering the house, and in his haste stubbed his foot against the door sill, which threw him, with his whole length on the floor.

The soldiers instead of being pale, through fear, were convulsed with laughter, which continued, peal after peal, without any sign of coming to an end. The *Indians*, too, who had occasioned the alarm, came in directly after, and joined in the sport. Hays perceiving his mistake, appeared exceedingly mortified. But he made no further boast of his bravery.

The company continued on its way, and reaching the

Mahoning, crossed the river, and marched up toward the settlement. They proceeded as far as Roaring Creek, where Van Campen and Salmon proposed again to try and see what they could effect with their Indian dress. They volunteered to go into the settlement, disguised as Indians, and thus test the friendship of the people. They told him of a hunter by the name of Wilkison, who lived not far distant, and proposed to try him first. The Captain though pleased with the idea, apprehended danger in visiting Wilkison, as it was uncertain which party he favored, and as he was known to be a brave man, one or the other of them might be shot. Yet assuring him that they were willing to risk their lives in the attempt, he gave them permission to go, while the main body were to proceed to a certain point and await their return. Arraying themselves in the Indian war-dress, and painting themselves so as to appear like them in color. Van Campen and Salmon started on their undertaking. As they drew near Wilkison's house, they proceeded with great caution, creeping along behind the bushes that hid them from observation. They could perceive from the smoke just beginning to ascend, that he was at home, and probably kindling a fire. The bushes were thick until they came within about a rod of the house and having crept along as far as they could, and remain concealed, they arose and ran across the open space, burst the door open, and raised the tomahawk over Wilkison's head. Supposing they were savages indeed, he dropped on his knees, and begged for his life, assuring them that he was a *king's man and a friend to Indians.* They ceased to manifest further hostility, but appeared sullen, not wishing to be drawn into conversation for fear of being discovered. Wilkison on the other hand appeared at his best, hastened his fire, began to broil venison and show himself an accomplished host. Having prepared a repast he invited his Indian guests to sit by his board, and served to them a bountiful meal. They then assumed a look of greater satisfaction, and their host gaining confidence, began to express his friendship for the royal cause, saying that the settlement which was on their path, *belonged to King's men, and were friendly to the Indians, having often supplied them with provisions.*

Van Campen and Salmon then spoke in broken English, imitating as near as possible, the Indian mode of speaking, and supplying with gestures, the ideas they seemed unable to express. They declared in broken terms their pleasure in meeting with friends,—that they were glad to hear of so many *King's men,* and desired him to go with them and show them *King's men.*

He readily gave his consent and they went together through the settlement. True enough they here met with a very kind reception; the settlers appeared very glad to see them, and were willing to show them any favor. They again resorted to their broken English, and gestures, giving the inhabitants to understand that they belonged to a large party of warriors, not far distant, who were in want of provisions. They were then taken to every house in the neighborhood, at each place receiving additions to their supply, until the three were laden with as much food as they could carry. They then retraced their steps, Wilkison continuing to assist in carrying the provisions to the army. They kept up their march until they came to the point selected as the place of meeting. Captain Robison and his men were lying in ambush, and as the party came trudging along, well nigh wearied out with the burden they were bearing, their hostile friends allowed them to advance until completely within their power, when they arose and fired over their heads, and rushed in upon them with uplifted tomahawk

Wilkison threw down his pack and attempted to escape, but finding it impossible, was willing to surrender. The treatment he received was a little more severe than that shown to his dusky companions. They not being placed under the hatchet, but he threatened with death, if he would not promise to lead the company to every family, from which the provisions had been received.—Choosing the latter alternative he marched back to the settlement, as guide to those by whom he had been taken. He performed his duty faithfully, conducting the party as he had agreed to every house of the neighborhood, thus affording the opportunity of capturing those who had shown themselves so friendly to the cause of the King.

Having thus successfully accomplished the object of the expedition, Captain Robison set out on his return to Northumberland, taking with him the inhabitants against whom he had been sent.—Van Campen and Salmon, though they marched for a time as prisoners, as soon as the opportunity was presented, laid aside their Indian dress and removed the color from their face and hands, and it was quite apparent from the chagrined looks of the settlers that they now understood the strategem laid for their capture.

Arriving at Northumberland their case was laid before the commanding officers, and Col. Hunter disposed to treat them with lenity, gave them their liberty, after having received from them a pledge, to leave the frontier settlements, and not return again until after the war.

Much praise was no doubt due to Van Campen and Salmon for the happy result of this expedition. The officers were saved the trouble of entering into a lengthy examination of the charges against these settlers, who stood before them, self-convicted and self-condemned, it being perfectly evident that the suspicions entertained against them were just.

CHAPTER XVI.

The eye that now glances over the past, sees but partially, the rough storms that assailed the bark of freedom, as she was slowly struggling her way along to her destined harbor, now threatened to be stranded on fearful rocks, now ready herself almost to unjoint, and yield her fragments to the wild fury of the wave, and now scarcely clearing the hidden shoals that promised to her a sudden and awful shipwreck. Distance seems to shed light on the impending cloud, the tumult of clashing elements have lost their rough sounds, ere their notes fall upon the ear, and the calm features of a far removed prospect, seems to spread over it, a mildness, which deceives even the minutest observer. The winter of 1780—'81, cast over the American forest, a gloom, which was relieved by no cheering ray. The army, rent with factions, reduced to starvation, meeting the keen blasts from the north, with tatered garments, there was little in the future to encourage the patriot's heart, and bid him look forward with the least assurance of hope. But honor and fortune had been pledged, the resolution had been taken, and the brave spirits, that had at first encircled the banner of freedom, gathered around it still, and their feeble purpose, aided by Heaven, was yet destined to rise into strength, and triumph in the infancy of its might, By none was a greater spirit of determination shown, than by those who were compelled to bear the chief horrors of the war. The bold woodsman of the frontier, was not disheartened, though he held his life by the most uncertain tenure, and, though he had been most sorely afflicted, in the disasters that had been spread through his territory, he did not shrink from the duties of renewed hostilities. From the activity of the Indians, in the previous year, it was anticipated they would be equally zealous, in the service of the crown, during the coming season, and as a means of defense, the company of Captain **Robison**, was retained on the frontier. In February of this year, Mr. Van Campen was promoted, to the office of Lieutenant, and immediately entered upon active service. For the protection of the settlements, a line of scouts, kept continually traversing the territory usually visited by small parties of Indians, and the route they generally pursued was a circuitous one, leading from the North to the West Branches of the Susquehanna, by the head waters of Little Fishing, Chilisquaka and Muncey Creeks. As Captian Robison was little acquainted with the woods, and not a very good marksman, Lieut. Van Campen usually led these parties upon their several excursions. The service was arduous, yet it was in accordance with his tastes, and the absence of incident, other than that, which is apt to occur in marching through the forests, leads us to give this part of his history, only a few passing remarks.

For the accommodation of his men, and that he might have a convenient place to occupy as head-quarters, he built a fort on the Susquehanna, about one mile above the mouth of Fishing Creek. It was built on the farm of a Mrs. McClure, and from that circumstance was named McClure's Fort. Here he gathered his stores, and from this point proceeded on his excursions through the woods.

In the early part of this year, there occurred a little incident in his history, which brought him into danger, the extent of which he did not learn until some time after its occurrence. It was while he was on his way to Wilksbarre, upon some business connected with the army. The journey he had to perform led him through an uninhabited region, mostly covered with woods. Taking with him a guard of six men, he accomplished most of his journey without observing any thing to excite more than ordinary remark ; but at length as they were pursuing their path, which led along the Susquehanna, at a place called Rocky Island, where the stream could be forded, they saw the marks of a party of Indians, which had apparently but just crossed over, for the water that had dropped from their leggins, was still standing in their footsteps.

Van Campen, who was well acquainted with Indian maneuvers, said to his men, "Here are the marks of quite a large party of Indians ; their tracks wear the appearance of having been just made. Our foes cannot be far off ; they may have their eye upon us now ; we had better press on, with all speed to our journey's end, for they will be apt to send runners ahead and waylay our path."

They did send runners ahead. From a rising point of ground they saw Van Campen on horseback, and, supposing him to be alone they dispatched four of their number to bring his scalp. These ran through the woods, and getting before him, concealed themselves behind a log, which lay near the path, and putting their guns over it, waited for his approach. They cocked their rifles, and were just going to fire, as they saw that he was attended by others, and thinking the company too strong for them, they allowed him to pass without molestation. He was unconscious, while passing, of the danger he was in, but learned the circumstances, while a prisoner in '82. A sprightly Indian after eyeing him closely, then came up to him and said :

"I, seen you before."

"Ah!" said he, "Where?"

"On the Susquehanna," naming the place, "when," (motioning with his hand raised about four feet from the ground,) "corn was about so high. You wore a suit of bottle green turned up with red."

"Yes."

"You wore a large cap with a cockade, part white, part black, and a feather in the top."

"Yes."

"You rode a large bay horse."

"Yes."

"Six men with you."

"Yes."

After telling him of his narrow escape, he said, "We let you go then; but we catch you now."

The company hastened its march to Wilksbarre, and reported what they had seen, that the inhabitants might be on their guard. The Indians contented themselves, however, with surprising one or two families, within the borders, and then fled into their own territory.

Lieut. Van Campen's principal engagements during the year, were at McClure's Fort, whence he directed his movements for the protection of the inhabitants living upon the North Branch of the Susquehanna. While remaining here, news was brought, by a man who had effected his escape from the enemy while his keepers were off their guard, who reported that there were three hundred Indians on the Sinnemahoning, that were hunting and laying in provisions, with the intention of making a descent upon the frontier. He said that they had formed a plan by which they were to divide their number into several small companies, and lay waste all the settlements on the same day. This intelligence was communicated to Colonel Hunter, who selected a party of five, who were to go out in disguise, reconnoiter the ground and ascertain their movements. This company consisted of Capt. Campbell, Peter and Michael Groves, and Lieutenants Cranmer and Van Campen, to the latter of whom was given the command. It was called the Grove Party.

They assumed the Indian dress and color, and taking with them an ample supply of provisions, gave the war-whoop, and started out on their expedition. They soon reached the waters of the Sinnemahoning, yet made no discoveries, save a few half obliterated tracks. They proceeded up the stream some distance, until they were satisfied that there could be no party of the number that had been mentioned, anywhere in that region, and then began to retrace their steps. Upon coming a little below the Sinnemahoning one day, they discovered, near night, as they stood on an elevated piece of ground, a smoke, which struggled up through the trees, in the valley below them, and ascended in spiral and wavy lines, through the thick and heavy atmosphere above. They were certain it must come from a party of Indians. They had no idea of the number, only as they could judge from the appearance of the smoke which indicated only one fire. They determined at all events to wait until the Indians should be laid to rest in the repose of night, and then ascertain their number, and if it was not too formidable, they resolved to hazard an attack. Waiting, therefore, until the time arrived, in which they supposed the savages had all sunk into their first sound slumbers, they advanced cautiously, towards the fire, as they saw it now and then gleaming through the bushes.

As they drew near to where the savages were asleep, Van Campen went on before the others to inspect the ground, with the understanding that they should come immediately after, and be guided by him in making the attack. He crept along with great caution, carrying the tomahawk in one hand, and the rifle in the other. The night was rather warm, and the warriors had rolled to a considerable distance from the fire, and before they were aware, Van Campen and his men began to tread upon them, which awakened them. As they rose up, the Grove party used their tomahawks, but finding that they were rising in such numbers as to overpower them, they fired upon them with their rifles, and then raised a tremendous yell. The savages supposing that they were attacked by a large force, fled with the utmost precipitation, most of them forgetting their guns, and leaving their packs and baggage upon the ground. Van Campen and his men, thus came into possession of a number of rifles, and a considerable quantity of goods that the Indians had plundered. They found several scalps which had been taken from families, that were murdered on the borders of what was called Penn's Creek. There were six Indians killed in this little skirmish, and having scalped these and secured their baggage by secreting whatever they found themselves unable to carry, they directed their march towards Northumberland.

Upon coming near this place they determined to enter it in Indian dress. But as they were obliged to pass by a number of families before reaching the village, they were fearful lest they should occasion unnecessary alarm, and as they were about to abandon the idea, they discovered one of the inhabitants coming toward them on the path that they were traveling. They concealed themselves in some bushes near by, and waited his approach. As soon as he came up they rose upon him, and he supposing himself about to be given up to the tender mercies of the savage, began to plead for his life. His entreaties were not in vain. They assured him he might pass unharmed, if he would go and inform the families on their way to Northumberland, that a scouting party was returning to its head quarters in the Indian dress. Glad to make so fortunate an escape, he joyfully ran forward and prepared the way for their kind reception. As they marched along, their every look wearing the appearance of the savage, bearing in triumph the scalps they had taken from the enemy, which they strung upon poles, as the highest trophy of a warrior, they met on every side a welcome look, and were received with the loud and cheering huzza. They proceeded to the public square, laid their packs upon the ground, and planted around them the poles that were waving the symbols of victory. The citizens gathered around this little company in crowds, and were expressing by their looks, the deepest interest in the scene before them, seemingly waiting for the history of the recent exploits of the party.

A part of their story was told in the spoils that were taken out of the packs, and brought into open view. Among them were found the scalps of women, fathers and children, that had fallen victims to the cruel and relentless foe that had just swept over their borders, leaving in their track the bodies of the slain. As these were brought out and placed under the eager eye of the populace, they were beheld by the women that had gathered around to witness the scene, with the sympathizing tear.

Much of the property that had been taken, belonged to settlers whom the Indians had plundered, and this as far as it could be identified, was returned to its original owners; if these were not living, to their nearest relatives.

As soon as the public curiosity had been sufficiently gratified, Van Campen and his men retired to a public house, near by, where by the aid of a little soap and water, they soon exchanged their swarthy complexions, for their own healthy color, and laying aside the Indian dress, appeared in their own uniform. The same evening they received an invitation from Colonel Hunter, to be in attendance, with their Indian scalps, on the next day at a dinner party, at his own house.

When the appointed hour arrived, they appeared to pay their respects to Col. Hunter and his lady, carrying with them the tokens of blood and strife. Here the *elite* of the town and of the neighboring place, Sunbury, were brought together to meet this brave little company, and show by their looks and words of encouragement, how much they prized the valor and decision of their countrymen, in the midst of the distressing scenes that were every day transpiring around them. Here, too, the smile of beauty met them, as if to pay a grateful acknowledgment, for the security felt when with such defenders, in the very heart of war. The recital of their late adventure called forth, especially from the fair ones, expressions of the utmost surprise. Many of the young ladies appeared very anxious to learn every minute circumstance, and as Van Campen had been the leader of the party he was obliged to answer the various questions that met him on every side.

The Indian scalps were laid in one corner of the drawing room, and many of the ladies who went to view them, taxed their wits severely to find inquiries enough to gratify their curiosity. One especially was so very particular in wishing for a detail of every slight circumstance of the event, that Van Campen became rather impatient of the rigid examination he was compelled to undergo. He was asked, in reference to the Indian camp, "And how many fires had they? and how many Indians did you see? and how were they lying? and whereabouts did you come up to them? and how did you feel?" Finding that the young Miss was beginning to put him to his trumps, he thought that he would take the lead of the conversation a little more into his own hands, and gave an answer, which, from the peculiar circumstances of the lady, was well understood. He said, "Feel!—why, madam, when I found myself among them, and asked myself whether or no I should kill them, my heart went so much as a young lady's often does—pitte-pat, pitte-pat—that I was almost inclined to answer *no*. But again I was so much *in love* with the service of my country, that I was compelled to answer *yes*." The company smiled, and there were no further questions.

Lieut. Van Campen soon after returned to his headquarters at McClure's Fort, and entered again upon the service of conducting scouts around the line of the settlements. But, after the party mentioned, he found no other Indians this year, during his marches through the forest. From the vigilance with which this part of the frontier was guarded, there were very few savages found in this region, during the remainder of the year.

Having been occupied in this service until late in fall, Van Campen was ordered with his company to Lancaster. He descended the river in boats, as far as Middletown,* where the order was countermanded by another, directing him to march to Reading, Berkshire county, where he was joined by a part of the third and fifth Pennsylvania regiments, and a company of the Congress regiment. Their principal duty while here, was to take care of a large body of Hessians, that had been taken pris-

---

*About ten miles below what is at present Harrisburg.

oners with Gen. Burgoyne. These had been under the guard of a company of militia-men whose time had not yet expired.

The march which Van Campen's soldiers had performed, was, on account of lateness of the season and bad roads, extremely fatiguing, and as the time for which the militia were engaged continued them in service a little longer, he allowed them the space which intervened, as a season of rest. This proved grateful to the soldiers, and it no doubt served to invigorate their spirits, for in the approaching Christmas holidays, they were sufficiently recruited to engage in sport. In that company were a number of mad wags and roystering blades, full of fun and frolic, that danger could not terrify, nor hardships sober.

They looked upon the city fellows as milk sops whose cowardly legs would run away with them at the first sign of danger. Some sixteen of these wild frontiers-men stole out of their camp into the woods, put on their war paint, donned their hunting shirts and moccasins and rushed upon the Hessian's camp with terific war-whoops, at the same time discharging their rifles.

On the instant the citizen soldiers threw down their guns without firing a shot and fled, shouting, "Indians! Indians!" The prisoners caught up the cry and bolted also, having a reasonable fear of their savage allies who wanted nothing but scalps, it mattered not whether of friend or foe.

The alarm reached the village and aroused sudden consternation. "*All Niagara is let loose,*" it was said, "*and our camp has been attacked by hundreds of Indians, and we have just escaped with our lives.*"

Van Campen of course was summoned for the defense, and marched at once, with as many of his company as he could muster, to meet as best he could the overwhelming numbers of the greatly dreaded enemy. They had not gone very far, before they were met by some of the soldiers, who assured them that it was a false alarm, and who gave an account of the manner it was occasioned, and of the display the militia men had made of their bravery.

"Captain," said Van Campen to the militia officer by his side, who had heard the story, "I don't think it necessary for me to proceed any further, I suppose most of your prisoners who don't freeze to death, will come back to their camp before morning; Good night. *About face. March.*"

So with roars of laughter, as their truant comrades pantomimically described the panic of the militia men, the Continentals marched back to quarters.

But more than a laugh was to come of it. In a few days Van Campen had orders from Philadelphia to place his sky-larking soldiers under arrest, and to form one of a court-martial convened to try them.

The militia officers refused to look upon the matter as a joke even for Christmastide. They had been exposed to ridicule themselves, put to much trouble in collecting the runaway prisoners, and moreover their men who had left their farms and shops for the irksome and almost unpaid guard duty, demanded redress at their hands.

So the court-martial sat, and the evidence of accusers and accused pointed all in one direction. The militia sheepishly acknowledged that they had run away, without firing a shot, from sixteen Continentals, with guns double charged but empty of ball. The Continentals, no longer mirthful, also sheepishly admitted that they were the sixteen men. The only question now was the degree of punishment.

The militia officers were unanimous that the offenders should be flogged, and so found. Van Campen read the finding over, laid it down, bowed and said gravely: "Very well, gentlemen. This is law, but the finding is incomplete. We must also find, according to the Articles, that the men who ran away from their posts without firing a musket, shall be shot. I won't go so far as to say hanged—only shot."

For three weeks the court-martial wrangled over the Lieutenant's contention, and sought to break down his argument, while the story of the queer dead-lock made post and garrison gossip clear out to the out-posts around Clinton's beleaguered and weakened host on Manhattan Island.

Van Campen would not budge an inch. He said, in fact, the militia had much the best of the bargain. His men would prefer shooting to flogging.

At the end of the third week the remainder of the board persuaded him to find for the breaking of the sergeant in the surprise party. This was done, but strange to say, the sergeant was reduced to the ranks over night, to be restored again the next morning.*

Directly after this Van Campen and his men entered upon the care of the Hessian soldiers, remaining in this service until the next spring, when they were relieved by the militia, who again took them in charge.

---

*As given by my friend, A. J. McAll of Bath, Steuben Co.,

CHAPTER XVII.

In the latter part of March, just at the opening of the campaign of 1782, the companies that had been stationed during the winter at Reading, were ordered back by Congress to their respective stations. Lieut. Van Campen marched at the head of Capt. Robison's company, to Northumberland, where he was joined by Mr. Thomas Chambers, who had recently been commissioned as Ensign of the same company. Here he halted for a few days to allow his men to rest, after which he was directed to march to a place called Muncey, and there rebuild a fort which had been destroyed by the Indians in the year '79. Having reached his station, he threw up a small block house, in which he placed his stores, and immediately commenced rebuilding the fort, being joined shortly after by Capt. Robison, in company with several gentleman, among whom was a Mr. Culbertson, who was anxious to find an escort up the West Branch of the Susquehanna, into the neighborhood of Bald Eagle Creek. Here his brother had been killed by the Indians, and being informed that some of his property had been buried and had thus escaped the violence of the enemy, he was desirous of making search to obtain it.

Arrangements were made, by which Lieut. Van Campen was to go with him, at the head of a small party of men as a guard, and after he had been permitted to examine his brother's premises, the company was directed to take a circuitous route around the settlements, and waylay the Indian paths, since it was about the time when the return of hostilities was expected. In forming this party, Van Campen selected his men according to his usual custom, taking in his hand a small piece of board, on the end of which was a mark of white paper, and standing a few rods in front of his men, who would fire at the mark, as it was held up before them and every man who hit the paper, was permitted to have his name enrolled as one of the scouts. He did not usually go far before he would thus find a sufficient number for his party.

Having selected his men, twenty in number, he took with him a supply of provisions and marched along the bank of the river, while Culbertson and four others advanced up the stream in a boat. Arriving at a place called Big Island, the boat was pulled on shore and all the party proceeded together by land, until they reached Culbertson's farm. They came to this at evening, and encamped for the night. It was now about the middle of April, and the Indian being expected every hour to pay his annual visit to the settlements, they could not observe too much caution in their movements, and having selected their resting place for the night with wisdom, placed their sentinels to give the first alarm of the enemy. They were not disturbed, however, during the night, but early the next morning, were awakened by the appearance of their foes.

While Van Campen with his company was ascending the river, a large party of Indians, not far from eighty-five were on their way down, paddling along in their little bark canoes and were intending when they came into the vicinity of the settlements to separate into small companies, commit their depredations and return home. As they were floating down with the current of the river, they came to where the boat had been drawn on shore. Informed by this of the presence of inhabitants, they secured their canoes, and followed the trail of those who had, but a short time before, left the river.

It is almost impossible to escape the practiced eye of the Indian. So carefully is he trained to all the windings of the chase, that circumstances which elude the inspection of the common observer, are to him the key which unlocks the secret hiding places of his enemy. The bent twig, the bowed grass, or the broken leaf all speak to him, with an unerring voice, of the path his victim has taken, and beckons him onward with the sure hope of success.

Such being the character of the foe that is to follow Van Campen and his men, it was not to be expected that they should elude its pursuit. The Indians crept along the path that had been taken, and by the morning light, concealed by the bushes, approached very near to the sentries, and burst so unexpectedly upon them they had only time to run to the camp, crying, "The Indian, the Indian," before the savages were in their midst, with the tomahawk and scalping knife. Van Campen and his men started upon their feet and in a moment were ready for action. The enemy had a warm reception. The combat was at first, from hand to hand, and so well sustained was the resistance that the Indians were obliged to retire; but they came up on all sides, and one after another Van Campen's men were cut down with the rifle. Perceiving that the party of warriors was so large as to offer them no hope of escape, and beholding their number every moment growing smaller, they determined though reluctantly, to surrender themselves to the enemy, under the belief that their lives would be spared. The Indians were commanded by a Lieut. Nellis, who was in the British service, and often led the savages in their descent upon the frontier settlements. To him they made their surrender; nine of their number had been killed, several were wounded and three in the early part of the action, effected their escape.

The Indians, thus becoming masters of the ground, came up and took possession of the prisoners and their arms, after which they began to dispatch those that had been wounded. Two of Van Campen's men, Wallace and Stewart, were killed with the tomahawk, immediately before him. Another by the name of Craton, was placed on a large stone, and as he sat bending over half unconscious of what was transpiring around him, was made the mark of four or five savages, who took their position a few rods from him, and all aiming their rifles at his head, fired at once, and with their balls tore the top of his skull from his head. Poor Craton fell over, and his brains rolled out and lay smoking upon the ground.

The blood coursed quick through Van Campen's veins as he saw his brave soldiers treated thus, and it was not the least of his suffering, to be obliged to witness the scene, without the means in his power of affording them aid. He was obliged to stand as insensible as a rock, for had he shown the least signs of sympathy or disapproval, it would have been at the peril of his life. Himself, and his men that were not wounded were taken into the custody of Indian warriors, and one of them had tied a cord around his arm, and stood holding it, while the executioners were dispatching those that had been hurt in the battle. Near him, stood one of his men who had received a shot through his arm when raised in the attitude of firing; the ball having entered his elbow, had passed up his arm, and gone out near his shoulder blade. His name was Burwell. Van Campen seeing him, spoke and said, "Burwell, you are losing blood pretty fast, are you not?" "Yes," said he, "I can't hold out much longer." "Stand as long as you can, my brave fellow, your wound is such that if they pass you by now, they may perhaps spare your life."

Just then an executioner saw that one more remained to finish his duty, and he came up towards Burwell, with the tomahawk raised to strike him in the head. Van Campen perceiving this movement, jerked from the warrior who was holding him by the arm, sprang forward with his right hand clenched, and gave the Indian executioner a blow in the breast, which sent him reeling backward, until he fell upon the ground, like one dead. The warriors then turned with their hatchets upon Van Campen. But a part who had witnessed the scene were highly pleased with the bravery that had been shown by their prisoner, and as the tomahawk was gleaming over his head, they leaped forward to rescue him from death. For a few moments, Van Campen could hear nothing but the clashing of tomahawks as the warriors engaged in a fierce struggle for his life. He was pushed about in the scuffle, a part of the time, his body bent over, by those who endeavored to shield him from the threatened blow, expecting every moment to have the hatchet enter his head. But at length the fortune of the contest turned in his favor, the majority being determined to spare his life. When the strife ceased, they gathered around him with looks of exultation and delight, and he could discover, from the pleasure which beamed from their every look, that his life would be protected from any further injury. This well timed blow was the means of sparing Burwell from falling under the hatchet of the executioner, for as they came around Van Campen repeating one after another, "Brave warrior, brave warrior," they seemed by common consent, to yield the life of the one, as a tribute to the noble deed of the other.

This instance of generosity in the savage warrior, is enough to give him some claim to indulgence, ere we pronounce upon him an unqualified censure. The blow that had been given to their executioner in the discharge of his duty might have been construed into an insult. It was so well directed and powerful, that he lay upon the ground a few moments, gasping for breath; but admiring bravery even in an enemy, they would not allow Van Campen to be injured for the protection he had given to one of his soldiers. It is but just to remark that if the Indians deserve rebuke for the excessive cruelty they sometimes practice in war, they at the same time possess other traits of character, which can but win for them the highest admiration. That so many virtues should appear prominent in the midst of a multitude of vices, that a noble generosity should be brought into close alliance with a blood-thirsty spirit of revenge, and that kindness should burst forth from the breast of cruelty, are incongruities so strangely and wonderfully combined in the Indian character, that we are led to view it almost as we would a verdant mead, which breaks upon the eye, in the midst of a barren and desolate soil; the strength of the contrast imparts a beauty to the scene, which is not really its own, and we are willing to excuse the sterility of the surrounding land, because of the surprising beauty that comes in to relieve it from an entire waste.

Immediately after the struggle for Van Campen's life, the prisoners were stripped of all their clothing except pantaloons, and taken a short distance from the battle ground, where they were made to sit down in the form of a circle while the Indians made a larger one around them and bringing up five Indians, who had been killed during the engagement, laid them down near the prisoners. In their movements they observed the stillness and solemnity of death, and as the captives eyed their motions and beheld the dead warriors stretched out before them, they felt that the ceremonies that were in progress, deeply concerned themselves. And though their minds had in a measure become callous to the thoughts of death, by familiarity with the field of strife, still the voice of silence whispered even into their ears, lessons of the tomb which they could not help but regard. Under the present circumstances it was very natural for the prisoners to turn from the slaughtered warriors to themselves, and each one began to reflect upon the destiny which should await him. Van Campen anticipated little short of a cruel and lingering death, especially if he was discovered to be the one who had killed so many Indians, while effecting his escape in the year '80.

When everything was arranged, and the warriors were standing in a large circle around the prisoners and the slain, an Indian chief came forward into the ring, and commenced making a speech. Every eye was turned upon the speaker, and as he advanced, Van Campen watched the countenances of the Indians, and could see them alternately swell with rage, and with the stern and awful looks of revenge, and then melt away with the voice of the orator, into expressions of pity and compassion. He said to his men in a low tone of voice, that their fate would probably be decided by the speech of the warrior, and that they had better prepare themselves for the last extremity. Said he—" If the conclusion is unfavorable, it can be but death at any rate, and we had better part with our lives as dearly as possible. Let us fix upon the weakest point of their line, and if we are condemned to die, let us run upon it with all our might, snatch their weapons from them and engage from hand to hand ; it may be that some of us will be able to effect our escape during the struggle." He kept his eye upon the speaker, and carefully watched the effect of his words until he was through, and happily for them, his conclusion was brightened by a smile, which was the token of mercy. There was left no ill boding cloud behind to warn them of coming evil.

Directly after, the Indians proceeded to bury those

who had fallen in battle, which they did by rolling an old log from its place and laying the body in the hollow thus made, and then heaping upon it a little earth. They then divided the prisoners among them according to the number of their fires, Van Campen being placed with the party which encamped with Lieut. Nellis, who having the first choice of prisoners, chose him because he was an officer. From him he learned the substance of the warrior's speech, who, as he said, had been consulting the Great Spirit as to what should be done with those that had fallen into their hands. He presented arguments on the one hand, to show that the prisoners should be immediately killed, and again he proceeded to remark that they should be treated with lenity. At one time, pointing to the lifeless bodies before him, he exclaimed, "These call for vengeance, the blood of the red man has been spilled, and that of the white man must flow." Yet he represented again that enough blood had been shed, that vengeance had been taken in those of their enemies that had been killed, and that such of their own party as had fallen, met only the common fate of war. He suggested finally, that the lives of the prisoners should be spared, and they adopted into the families of those that had been slain.

In accordance with this recommendation the prisoners were unharmed, and put in readiness to march with the Indians. Packs were prepared for them and having shouldered these, they began to march towards the place where the warriors had first seen the marks which led them in pursuit, and having reached this they entered their little bark canoes, rowed across the river and sent them adrift down the stream.

The Indians then took up their line of march back to Niagara, proceeding up the valley of the Susquehanna and its tributary streams. On the morning of the second day of their march, as Van Campen passed by one of the fires, he saw one of his soldiers named Henderson, seated upon a billet of wood, and two Indians standing by his side. His countenance was sad and pale, indicating the presence of anxious and painful thoughts. He had been wounded in the battle, by a ball which struck his left hand, as it was raised for the purpose of firing, and cut off four of his fingers. Van Campen supposing that the fate of this soldier had been decided, beheld him with mingled pity and concern; yet there was no remedy, and he passed on, bearing his mournful countenance before him. He did not go far before he heard a noise like the sound of a tomahawk entering the head, and in a few moments saw the two Indians, who had been standing by Henderson, run along by bearing a scalp, and carrying a hatchet dripping with blood. The sight filled him with maddening thoughts, yet he did not reveal his emotions, by action or look, but continued to march on reckless of every event that should befall him.

Their march during the day was continued without provisions, till they arrived at Pine Creek, where they halted while the Indian hunters went out in pursuit of game. In a short time they returned, bringing along a noble elk. This was soon dressed and prepared for roasting. The prisoners were allowed the same liberty that was taken by the warriors themselves; they cut from the animal as much fresh meat as they wished, and roasted it on the coals, or held it on the end of a sharpened stick to the fire. This made them an excellent supper, and was quite a relief to their keen appetites.

Burwell whose life had been spared, marched with the Indians as a prisoner; but his wound in a few days became very much inflamed and painful to such a degree that it was with great difficulty he proceeded on his march; and though he promised to give them no trouble, they did not seek to rid themselves of his care in the summary manner in which they generally treated their wounded prisoners, but exercised their skill to restore him to health and soundness. Having collected a parcel of suitable herbs, they boiled them in water thus making a strong decoction, in which they dipped the feather of a quill, and ran it through his wound. Whenever this was done, Van Campen, who had been quartered with a different company, was brought to see the attention which was given to his soldier,—a very simple but flattering token of the respect they paid to his bravery. The operation was exceedingly painful, and as Van Campen stood by, he encouraged him to bear up bravely under his treatment, saying that he must prove himself a man, and that, if he suffered the keenest anguish, he should not manifest it by a single sign. The Indians, who were by, seemed to understand the instructions that were given, and were highly pleased with them as well as the manner in which the soldier endured the pain. In a short time the inflammation was removed, and the wound healed under the harsh but salutary treatment.

Present Appearance of the Site of the old Indian Village of Ga-o-yah-de-o (Caneadea).

[See Page 230.]

Burwell lived to enjoy many a pleasant day after the revolution, yet whenever he has told the story of the blow which Van Campen gave to the Indian executioner whose hatchet was raised to destroy his life, and when he has described the fierce and doubtful struggle that followed, it has always been with tears in his eyes. Several years since, he paid Mr. Van Campen a visit at his residence in Angelica, saying that he was about to remove to one of the Southern States, and that he had come to see, once more, the man who had saved his life at the risk of his own. He paid him an affectionate and grateful farewell, and since then Mr. Van Campen has not heard from him, and in all probability, he is now numbered with the departed sons of the revolution.

Upon starting on their march, the remains of the elk were divided among the warriors and prisoners, each carrying his portion as a supply against further need. Pursuing up the valley, they soon came to the head of Pine Creek, thence striking across the country, they reached in half a day's travel, the head waters of the Genesee river, and, in a journey of two days down this stream, came to a place called Pigeon Woods, where a great number of Indian families, old and young, had come to catch pigeons, which were found here in great abundance, and were important as one of their principal means of living. They here met with about forty warriors, who were on their way to the frontier settlements, and their encampment was not far distant from that of the returning party. Some of the warriors from the advancing party, came from their quarters to hold a consultation with those who had Van Campen in charge, and he soon perceived from the glances that were every now and then bestowed upon him, that he was the subject of their conversation. In this he was not mistaken, for they very soon came up to him, and giving him a tap on the shoulder, said, "*Joggo.*" (*March.*) In obedience to this order, he arose and went with them, and in their path came to a deep ravine, which lay between the two camps. It was crossed by a tree which had been made to fall so that the ends rested upon each side of the gulf, leaving a deep and dangerous chasm beneath. As the Indians came upon this with their prisoner, they began to jostle him and shake the log, at the same time expressing great delight with the ease in which they could dance over the huge rocks that were lying many feet below them. Had Van Campen been a novice in such a situation, he would certainly have fallen into the deep gulf beneath. But he was as well acquainted as they, with a path like this, and as he tripped along over, himself joining in the motion of their slender bridge, the savages were rather pleased than otherwise, with the manifest dexterity of their prisoner.

Upon coming up to the warriors, Van Campen was made to sit upon one side of the fire, where he could be seen by all, who wished to gratify their pride or curiosity in beholding him as a trophy of their artful warfare. But he was no less curious than they, in surveying the forms which met his eye, for he was interested in knowing whether, among those that were before him, there could be found the Indian with whom he had a severe encounter, when making his escape from captivity. Yet he no where saw any thing of the warrior Mohawk, and began to feel a little more at his ease.

On either side of him there was a row of cabins extending about fifty feet, in a line with each other, and were so formed as to present an open front to the fire. They were constructed by driving crotches into the ground and laying poles upon them, which served to support slabs of bark, one end of which rested on these, and the other on the ground, forming at the same time both covering and sides. The two rows faced each other, and a long fire was made between them. While Van Campen was sitting by the side of this, with his eyes directed to the scene around him, the warriors were in earnest consultation, the subject of which he supposed to be concerning himself. They were conversing together in a group not far distant, and presently the crowd opened, and a figure of noble proportions came toward him. He was an Indian in dress and color, but these were all that gave him claim to be a savage warrior. He came to Van Campen and commenced examining him concerning the condition of that part of the frontier, from which he had been taken. He inquired concerning the number and condition of the inhabitants, the manner in which they were defended, and about the number and vigilance of their scouts. To all these questions he gave a correct answer, except to the one respecting the strength of the force by which they were guarded; this he represented as being much greater than it really was, to discourage them if possible, from visiting the frontier. He said that the country about Northumberland, was very strongly garrisoned with troops, and that large scouts were sent in every direction, for the purpose of waylaying and discovering the Indians who might be sent against them. He was next directed to mark out with a coal, upon a bark, the course of the streams emptying into the Susquehanna, the situation of the forts and the path pursued by the scouts. In marking down the course of the streams and the situation of the forts, he observed the accuracy of truth, for the Indians were as well acquainted as himself with these, and his exactness in this, would lead them to give the more credit to that part of his story in which he designed to exaggerate. He executed his work promptly and truly, showing them on his little bark map, the situation of the forts, and the route pursued by the scouting parties, but gave them a very enlarged idea of the number of soldiers and of the preparation of the settlers to receive an attack. This part of his story produced the desired effect; the Indians did not, in this incursion, go into the neighborhood of Northumberland, but invaded another portion of territory which they supposed to be less guarded.

Immediately after this examination, the Indian interpreter by whom he had been questioned, came up to him and said in rather a low tone of voice,—"There is only one besides myself in this company that knows anything about you." Van Campen replied rather sternly, "And what do you know of me, sir?" "Why," said he, "you are the man who killed the Indians." Van Campen's thoughts were then turned to the fire and the tomahawk, supposing that since he was known, he would certainly fall a victim to savage barbarity. He inquired the name of him who was standing by his side, and was answered that it was Jones, and that he might be assured of his friendship, for he too was a prisoner, as well as himself. Van Campen then began to take a little more courage, and as Jones proceeded to give him assurances of secrecy, and promised to exert his utmost influence to have him pass through to Niagara in safety, he began to feel himself in the presence of a friend, in whom he could repose the utmost confidence. Jones said to him, that if he could pass through to Niagara undiscovered, he would then be safe, but if the Indians discovered who he was, they would certainly put him to death in a cruel manner, for they had been informed concerning him, by the Tories, and they need only learn his name, to make his life atone for his activity and success in savage warfare.

The other who was acquainted with the history of Van Campen, was a Dutchman by the name of Houser, and to him Jones immediately repaired to enjoin upon him the utmost secrecy. Upon coming to him, he found him talking aloud to himself in the most ungarded manner, and swearing about, "*Van Camp, vot kilt de Enchens. He's come among us and ve'll all be burnt, every tarn bugger of us; yes ve will, dats vot oney vay.*"

"Tut, tut," said Jones, in a low voice, "what's the matter Houser?"

"*Vy, Van Camp's here, vot kilt de Enchens, un ve'll all be burnt to de stake, so sure as mine gun's a firelock, oney vay.*"

"Stop, stop," continued Jones, "how do you know that he killed the Indians?" To this he answered, that Elisha Hunt, one of Van Campen's men, had just told him. "Well," said Jones, "if any one asks you about this, you must tell them that you know nothing of it—

you must lie like the duce, and *swear to it too.*" By this timely injunction, the report was prevented from being spread farther, and the Indians were kept ignorant of circumstances that would have inevitably resulted in the death of Van Campen.*

---

*Mr. George H. Harris of Rochester, N. Y., who has just spent fifteen years collecting data for a "Life History of Horatio Jones," which will soon be published, has kindly permitted me to excerpt the following from his manuscript.

"Upon the arrival at Pigeon Woods of Nellis' party with Van Campen and his men, Jones who was at a distance, and coming leisurely to camp, ran upon Houser, the weak minded Dutchman, who was talking aloud to himself in an excited and unguarded manner. ' *Vot for dot Van Camp vot kilt de Injuns comes among us? Now ve'll all pe purnt, every darn bugger of us; yes ve vill, dots vot, ony vay!*'

"Stop! Stop!!" said Horatio, looking cautiously around to see if others were near, "How do you know the man who killed the Indians is here?" Houser answered, "that a war party had just come in with prisoners, that he went to see the captives, and recognized one as an old acquaintance named Elisha Hunt. He spoke to 'Lisha, who said he belonged to Van Campen's company, and that that officer was here with the prisoners."

Jones was astonished with the information. He was familiar with the story of Van Campen's marvelous escape, and had by direction of the chiefs, asked questions of prisoners regarding the redoubtable frontiersman, but of late the topic had not been mentioned. As he stood for a moment in deep thought, Houser said, "Dots 'Lisha Hunt vot stands by der dree yonder," at the same time pointing to one of the group of prisoners who were surrounded by men, women and children. all staring at the wretched militiamen.

"See here Houser," said Horatio, with an earnestness that startled the Dutchman, "Don't stir a foot, or speak a loud word, till I come back." Then he walked over to the group, and approached Hunt who was a little apart from his comrades.

"There was nothing in the appearance of Jones to distinguish him from the Indians about him. He was clad in a full suit of native costume, and his bronzed features were as dark as the faces of many of his red associates. Without seeming to notice the soldiers, he addressed the latter in a low voice: "'Lisha Hunt, if you men do not want to be all instantly burned alive, do not tell any one the name of your captain."

Before the surprised militiaman could speak, Jones disappeared in the crowd and returned to Houser. The latter was in great fear, and Horatio purposely increased his distress. " I don't

Mr. Van Campen has ever since regarded this act of kindness, which was shown him by Capt. Jones, as the only means which spared him his life at this period; and so strong was the friendship which they then contracted for each other, and so intimate has been their acquaintance since, that we cannot pass without giving him a short biographical sketch, which we are enabled to do, by a commnnication from a near relative of Mr. Jones.

Capt. Horatio Jones was born in Chester county, Pennsylvania, Nov. 19, 1763. When quite young he removed with his parents to Bedford county of the same State, and, at the early age of sixteen, enlisted as a volunteer, under Capt. John Boyd. It was when the Indians, led on by the notorious Butler, Brant and Nellis, were committing their atrocious massacres among the settlers of the frontier, sparing neither age nor sex, from the tomahawk and scalping knife. While yet in boyhood he was

---

believe the man who killed the Indians is here, Houser," he said, "but if our people once get that idea in their heads, they will surely kill all of us. Now, if any one speaks to you about these men, you must lie like the deuce, and stick to it too, or you will all be burned to death. You keep close to me, where I can see you every minute, and when the Indians ask you any questions, answer, *De-qua*, (I don't know) and do not speak another word." "*Houser*," continued Jones, stepping close to the Dutchman, and speaking in a depressed yet stern tone, that caused the unhappy fellow to start as though struck with a blow, "*if you ever tell a person of this conversation, I will kill you!*"

The look and tone produced the desired effect upon the simple minded man, who promised to strictly obey Jones in every particular. The incident had occupied but a few moments, without attracting the attention of others, and Horatio closely followed by Houser, proceeded hastily to the camp where "the man who killed the Indians" had previously been taken."

(It would appear from the account given by Mr. Harris, that the interview with Houser occurred prior to Jones' examination of Van Campen, and that the interpreter was aware of Van Campen's identity during the examination.—ED.)

an active and brave soldier, and accompanied Capt. Boyd on many important and dangerous expeditions, in which himself and commander had the good fortune to escape unhurt.

At length in the spring of '81 while Capt. Boyd and his men, numbering thirty-two, were in pursuit of Nellis, they were surprised by a large party of Indians, who killed about half of them and took eight prisoners, among whom was Mr. Jones and his commanding officer. They were brought to the Indian towns in the valley of the Genesee, and there made to run the gauntlet, after which, they came very near losing their lives in a savage frolic. The warriors, upon returning from their excursion, gave themselves up to drinking and merriment. Partaking freely of spirits, they became intoxicated and all the hidden ferocity of their natures began to be aroused. They tomahawked one of the prisoners, severed his head from his body, and sticking it upon the end of a pole, carried it around with wild and frantic yells. They next meditated the death of Boyd and Jones, and while they were disputing about the manner in which they would make them suffer, a few squaws conveyed these two prisoners away and secreted them until the passion of the warriors had subsided. Their lives were thus spared, and Jones was subsequently adopted into an Indian family, and was their interpreter when Mr. Van Campen met with him at Pigeon Woods. He was retained as a captive until after the treaty of 1784, when he was appointed by General Washington, interpreter of the Six Nations, the duties of which office he continued to discharge until within a few years of his death, which took place at his residence in Geneseo, on the 18th of August, 1836.

Mr. Jones was of about the ordinary stature, firmly built, and from his nature, fitted to throw energy and decision into every act of his life. By his bravery, physical strength, and the manly traits of his character, he gained great influence over the Indians with whom he was associated, and having their entire confidence, was enabled to render the government an invaluable service in her treaties with the northern and western tribes. He was the favorite interpreter of the celebrated Red Jacket, and his style on all occasions was said to be chaste, graphic and energetic. During the latter part of his life, Mr. Van Campen and he were in the habit of visiting each other once every year, and never did two old patriots enjoy themselves more, at these annual meetings, than they. He descended to the grave full of years, and with the pleasant consciousness of having served well the generation in which he lived.*

---

*Charles Jones, Esq,. of Geneseo, N. Y., a son of Horatio Jones, informs the writer that when a boy, on occasions of his father's and Van Campen's visits, he has often heard the incident at Pigeon Woods talked over. Van Campen said that when in the midst of this throng of Indians, all so curious and inquisitive concerning him, he heard behind him a slight noise, when looking around, he saw them making way for the approach of a man with a white face, who bounding into the ring, came at once to his side. Van Campen who supposed his fate was about to be determined, hastily inquired of Jones, "What are they going to do with me?" Jones replied, "I don't know. I can't tell; *but they don't know you.*" Van Campen would always conclude his account of the incident by saying, "Those were the happiest words I ever heard from human lips."—ED.

CHAPTER XVIII.

We will return to our narrative. After spending two days at Pigeon Woods, the Indians took with them a supply of provisions and continued their march down the Genesee river till they came to a place called Caneadea, which was the first village on their route. Upon coming within two or three miles of this, they began to raise the war-whoop, and as they drew near they made the air ring continually with their shouts. These were heard by the inhabitants of the village, who, warned by this means of the return of a victorious party of warriors, hastened forth, both old and young, to give them a joyful reception. They met each other with shouts of congratulation, and as the inhabitants came up, the warriors halted to give the others an opportunity of learning the result of the campaign. The villagers then went around among them to look after the spoils, but their chief attention was directed in search of those who had been taken prisoners. They were interested in finding these, for the purpose of making them run the gauntlet, a trial which the American aboriginals were in the habit of exacting from the prisoners that were returned by a war party to any of their camps or villages.

This ceremony was well suited to gratify a savage taste, for it often placed the subject in circumstances of extreme danger, as well as pain. It afforded them an opportunity to gratify any private pique or animosity, by inflicting the severest blows upon the prisoner and subjecting him, it might be, to the loss of life. Yet it was not always a scene of cruelty, but was often made the source of high amusement to the Indians, without causing any great suffering to the captive. The prisoner was obliged to run the distance of some thirty or forty robs. to a point fixed upon as the termination of his race, between two parallel lines of people—men, women and children—armed with hatchets, knives, sticks and other offensive weapons, and in passing through, they were at liberty to strike as often and as severely as they pleased, until he arrived at the end of his course, where all their fury was made to cease, and the victim was considered safe from any further injury until his case should receive a final decision.* Much of his success depended upon the manner in which the prisoner conducted himself before the warriors. Should he present a fearless, independent spirit, it might perhaps win for him the admiration of his captors, and they would allow him to pass unharmed. But should he appear cowardly and timid, he would be most surely treated with the utmost severity.

It was to this trying ordeal that Van Campen and the few that were with him had now come; and as the villagers came in among the warriors, they pushed the prisoners around as though they were the most worthless kind of baggage—led them out in front of the warriors, and then prepared to put to the test their nimbleness of foot. The apparent satisfaction with which they

*Stone's life of Brant.

were received, both by old and young, assured Van Campen that the time so much dreaded by the prisoners had now arrived, and that he must be subjected to the trial of a scene which was justly regarded with apprehension. The Indian ladies were furnished with long whips, and as they stood lightly tapping them on the ground, it was certain that they were designing to use them upon other backs than those of their own truant offspring.

Van Campen was placed in front of the other prisoners, all of whom stood a short distance before the warriors. Thus stationed, everything was put in readiness for them to run, whenever the word should be given. The warriors took no active part, but remained spectators of the scene, while the villagers formed themselves on the sides, and their smartest runners in the rear of the prisoners.

While Van Campen was standing in front of his men, he amused himself by observing the movements of those around him. He could see his fellow prisoners straightening their muscles and nerving themselves for a vigorous effort, with their attention directed at one time to the ground that stretched out before them, at another to the forms and limbs of those by whom they were to be pursued. The Indians did not form themselves in lines parallel with the course he was to run, neither were they armed with weapons any more formidable than the cudgel and the whip. Having furnished themselves with these the young Indians and squaws arranged themselves, and awaited with an impatient zeal the time when they should bring them into requisition. Before

[Illustrated by Dennis D. McKibben]

RUNNING THE GAUNTLET AT CANEADEA.

the word was given for them to start, Nellis came to Van Campen, and pointing to the council house,* which was

---

*The Council House, here referred to, it is ascertained upon what is regarded as good authority on such matters, to have been constructed about the year 1780, and in building it the Indians were assisted by a detachment of troops sent out for the purpose, by the commandant at Fort Niagara, by order of Guy Johnson. The nicely hewn logs so neatly dovetailed together at the corners, show the work of artisans of more than ordinary skill.

In size it must have been about 20x50 feet, and so low that a person of ordinary height could easily reach the eaves, and it was covered with "shakes" bound and held in place by long poles which were secured at the ends by withes.

When left by the Indians, and the country came to be settled by the whites, it was found to be on a farm purchased by Joel Seaton. He soon proceeded to take it down and remove it to a position by the roadside, some thirty or forty rods distant from its original location.

In reconstructing it he added three or four logs to its height, as readily appears in the picture. It stood for many years by the roadside, an object of curiosity to passers by, especially to strangers; was used successively as dwelling, barn and stable, the logs in time rotting away at the south end, that part settling considerably as shown, when about 1870, Hon. Wm. P. Letchworth becoming interested in its history, which he had taken considerable pains to learn, purchased it, and removing it to his beautiful country seat at Glen Iris, (Portage Falls) re-erected it under the personal direction and supervision of Dr. John Shanks, an aged Indian, who was well acquainted with the structure in his boyhood, restoring it as nearly as practicable to its original condition.

Oct. 1, 1872, it was re-dedicated with appropriate and imposing ceremonies, which were largely attended, ex-President Fillmore gracing the occasion with his presence, and presiding over the exercises.

Immediately after the ceremony of re-dedication, "The Last Council of the Senecas on the Genesee" was held, and in its deliberations, descendents of Joseph Brant, Red Jacket, Corn Planter, Mary Jemison and others of note took part.

It is indeed from its historic associations a venerable old structure, supposed by those well informed on such matters, to be the only one of its kind and antiquity, now left, and the idea was at one time seriously entertained of (if Mr. Letchworth's consent could be obtained) removing it to Chicago, and there putting it up as a head-quarters for the Indian exhibit for the State of New York at the Columbian Exposition. The project was however for some good reason abandoned.

Much credit is due Mr. Letchworth for his praiseworthy efforts about forty rods distant, said—"Yonder is the place you are to reach in your race, if you can get there without a whipping you will be safe,—look out for your heels and if you ever made them fly put them through now." Just before the word was given, Van Campen saw two young squaws, who appeared to have been left behind, coming along from the village very leisurely, to join the sport. They had their whips in their hands and having come about half way from the council house, to the warriors, stood still with their whips raised, and awaited the coming of the prisoners. Presently the word "joggo" was given, and the captives sprang forward to the race. The Indian whippers started at the same time, with a bound, and made the utmost exertion to reach them with the lash. Van Campen had not yet received a single blow, and was drawing near, in his rapid flight, to the two young squaws who had their whips raised, ready to strike, and he did not expect to pass them without suffering the weight of their descending arms. Just before he reached them, the thought struck him, and as quick as lightning he gave a spring, and raised his feet, which hit them in the breast, and sent them, as if by a whirlwind, in the same direction in which he was running. They all came down together, tumbling heels over head, and Van Campen found himself between the two squaws, who were kicking and squabbling about, endeavoring to gain a more favorable position, yet he did not wait to help the ladies up, but sprang upon his feet, and made good his race.

---

to rescue the "Old Council House" of the Senecas from an early oblivion, and if proper care be exercised in the future, it will survive yet many years. ED.

The warriors who were spectators of this scene, beheld it with the utmost delight. Their eyes had been intently fixed upon the runners, and as they saw Van Campen draw near the two squaws, they were interested with their success in giving him the lash. But when they saw him spring and take them along with him, and as they beheld them all thrown together in a heap, they were filled with merriment and made the air ring with shouts of laughter. Some threw themselves upon the ground, and rolled and laughed, as though they were ready to burst, and long and loud was their enjoyment of this little maneuver. The prisoners by means of this diversion had all of them an easy race, arriving safely at the end of their course. Immediately after, several of the young warriors, who were exceedingly diverted with the manner in which Van Campen had cleared himself, came up to him and patted him on the shoulder saying, "*Shenawana*"—"*Cajena*"—*brave man—good fellow.* The whole party soon came up to the council house and the prisoners were then quartered with the families of the warriors.

Directly after, Van Campen was introduced to the father of young Nellis, by whom he had been taken. He had formerly lived in the valley of the Mohawk, but had joined the British as a refugee and had received the office of Captain in the Indian Department. His son was a Lieutenant in the same service. When young Nellis led Van Campen forward, he addressed his father thus—" I will make you acquainted with one who fought me manfully, and who, if we had been equally manned, would have beaten me, but as my party was the strongest, I overcame him. Since he has been a prisoner he has conducted himself like a gentleman, and I wish him treated as one, so long as he continues with us."

The old Captain bowed and scraped and made a variety of very awkward motions, in attempting to show himself extremely polite, and taking Van Campen by the hand, expressed great satisfaction at the pleasure of seeing him. Van Campen returned the compliment as well as he could, yet if he had made known the true feelings of his heart, he would not probably have said that it was with any great feelings of joy that, as a prisoner, he clasped the hand of a British officer. He was invited to sit, and after conversing for awhile upon the common topics of the day, arose to depart, when the old gentleman requested his presence at the dinner table on the morrow, at twelve. Signifying his assent, Van Campen returned with Lieut. Nellis to their Indian quarters.

The fatigues of the campaign were such that both warriors and prisoners spent the first day and night after their arrival as a season of repose. The relaxation was grateful to their wearied limbs, and with invigorated spirits, Van Campen and Lieut. Nellis repaired to the old Captain's dwelling, to fulfill the engagement they had made on the day before. While on their way Van Campen enquired of Nellis, if his father had a wife; to which he was answered, "Yes." He immediately began to imagine the kind of lady that would soon greet his presence, and concluded that in the wife of a British Captain, he would see a woman of fashion in her satin or silk.

Upon entering the house and paying his respects to

Capt. Nellis, his eyes wandered about in search of his anticipated hostess;—yet he saw no one that could answer his ideal picture. The only female in the room was an old squaw, who was sitting in one corner of the cabin, having a broad face, high cheek bones, and in every respect very ill featured—this certainly could not be the fancied lady, and he dismissed his curiosity for a time, supposing that the Captain's wife would probably make her appearance soon. His attention was next drawn to the dining table. It was one of a truly primitive style, being formed of a plank that had been hewn out of a large log and was supported by the trunks of four young saplings that were cut the proper length and driven into holes that had been bored in the plank. It was relieved by no covering, and the only dishes that appeared upon it were one large wooden bowl and a few plates of the same material. Soon the old squaw served up the dinner in a large bowl, their meal consisting of a goodly supply of pigeons and Indian dumplings. These were smoking on the table, and their host observed —" Come, gentlemen, draw up and we'll take our dinners." They drew up their chairs to the board, leaving the squaw sitting in one corner by the fire, with her back partly turned toward them, and as the old gentleman took his seat he spoke to her and said, " Come, my dear, won't you sit at the table with us ?" The dusky lady obeyed the request of her lord, and drawing up her chair placed it very near his, and sat in motionless silence. Van Campen then began to think seriously that she must be the mistress of the house, and as the dinner was served out to each one, he amused himself very much with his situation.

He thought that the scene before him would make a fine study for a painter, and his highest wish would have been gratified could his friends at home have been apprised of the company in which he was placed. It was as motly an assemblage as was ever, perhaps, brought around one board,—there was a Tory Captain, a Tory Lieutenant, a rebel officer, and an old squaw,—a rare party even for those times that were rich in every variety of incident.

Mr. Van Campen was well pleased with his entertainment, and was afterwards informed that the warriors were going to spend the evening in dancing, and that they expected him to take part, that he might thus become acquainted with some of the Indian customs. But his only articles of dress were a pair of pantaloons that were left on him at the time of his capture, and an old blanket that was given him during his march, to protect his arms and shoulders from the brush and briers through which they were obliged to pass. Nellis had the kindness to add to his wardrobe a calico shirt and blanket, which was rather more respectable in its appearance than the one he wore, and with these he was quite well prepared to take his place among the dancers.

The signal for assembling the warriors, and for commencing the ceremonies, was given at evening. It was the wild and romantic whoop, and as it was heard echoing along the little huts of their village, and penetrating the dark bosom of the surrounding forest, the old and young, the warrior and the prisoner, started out from their places and came together upon a level plot of ground, where a few bright fires were sending up a clear and steady blaze into the still air of night. Around these the dancers paraded with light and airy tread, to make their arrangements for the evening's entertainment, which they determined to open with the wardance. In this, Van Campen took no part; it was performed chiefly by the warriors.

The war-dance is a sort of pantomime, in which the Indians represent all the maneuvers to which they are accustomed in the field of strife. They begin with the song of exultation, and in their movements represent the delight with which they go forth to meet their foes. Their singing and actions for a time illustrate their march to the battle-ground. As they draw near the enemy, the song seems to die away,—they became sly and cautious in their movements, some perhaps will shelter themselves behind trees; others will form an ambuscade under the cover of bushes, while a third party is creeping along, carrying the rifle in trail, or bearing the hatchet, and as they draw near some post or stump, which may represent the object upon which they mean to vent their rage, they rise upon it with all the fury of assailants, and having applied the tomahawk, or discharged the gun, they imagine their victim slain, and perform the ceremony of taking the scalp. The tune and movement are then changed; the song becomes one of triumph mingled with the loud yell and the exulting bound of victory. But should they encounter defeat, or should any of their numbers be slain, their melody would assume a subdued and melancholy tone, and in their cries for the loss of friends, the shout of victory would be changed to the *death-yell*. By this means the young are instructed in their mode of warfare, and as its mimic cruelties are brought into scenes of pleasure, they are suited to make them cherish an early passion for the field of conflict.

This was followed by the turtle dance, so called perhaps from the manner in which the music, by which they timed their movements, was made. Two Indians spread upon the ground a couple of deer skins, on which they seated themselves, each holding in the hands a box made of the turtle shell, which enclosed several kernels of corn. They shook these and made them rattle so as to chime with a tune, which they began to sing in a low voice, as a signal for the dance to commence. It was opened by an aged Indian, who came slowly forward, and as he advanced into the open space, joined in a low hum in the tune that was singing, and began to dance, making the movements principally on his heels. The next one that came forward was an elderly looking squaw, she had her blanket drawn partly over her head, and commenced dancing with a great deal of modesty, her movements being much less violent than those of the Indian who preceded her. Others followed on after them promiscuously, forming themselves into a ring, with their heads most of the time facing the center. Soon the greater part had taken their places in the dance, and as they began to move towards it from the place where Van Campen was sitting, a young warrior who was by him and who could speak English, remarked that it would soon be his turn to take a place with the dancers.

The "Old Council House" to which Van Campen ran the gauntlet, as it stood by the roadside on the "Seaton Place," Caneadea, after its removal from its original site and reconstruction by Seaton.

[See Page 233.]

Van Campen replied that in his country the young men always had girls to dance with them.

"Do you want a girl?" the young warrior replied.

"Yes," said he, "I wish to dance in proper style."

The young Indian then left him, and in a few moments returned, leading forward a beautiful young squaw. Van Campen was somewhat at a loss at first as to what attention he could pay to an Indian lady, yet as she had been brought at his request, he showed her all the politeness in his power, leading her forward to the dance, where they joined with the movements of the rest, who one time observed a very steady motion on their heels, then wheeled around, all the while humming the tune which was sung by the musicians, accompanied by the regular beat of the turtle shells.

Van Campen and his partner continued to dance together for some time, in silence, except as they would now and then join in a low voice, with the notes of their music. At length as they were whirling around he happened to throw his arm around the neck of the Indian lady, and the wind at the same time blowing up, threw his blanket partly over her head and face. The young squaw, unaccustomed to any extra display of politeness, and seemingly frightened, gave a slight scream and darted from him, leaving him to dance alone.

On the next day the warriors, with their prisoners, took up their line of march, following a path which led to some Indian settlements on Buffalo Creek, and after a journey of about two days along this stream, encamped at its mouth. Here they met with a Captain Hilyer and Lieutenant Doxstadter, who had charge of the British stores, sent to this place for the supply of their troops. They hailed the arrival of this body of warriors with demonstrations of joy. Nellis presented Van Campen to them, as an officer whom he had taken, and they, immediately bringing forward wine upon an old oaken table, which was standing in their room, invited him to join them in a social glass. Van Campen declined, saying that they would probably propose toasts which his principles would not allow him to reciprocate, and he therefore begged to be excused. They urged him however to become one of their party, saying that after a fatiguing march through the woods, a little wine could not be otherwise than refreshing, and Doxstadter pledged his honor that no toasts should be given which would be in the least offensive to his feelings. To this the others agreed, and he took a seat with them at the table.

They drank first to each other and next to the health and prosperity of their friends at home, which passed without the slightest objection. Others were given of very much the same character, and every thing seemed to promise the greatest harmony of feeling. But as they continued to drink, their spirits began to rise, and Doxstadter, glowing at length with unusual warmth, proposed a "Health to King George and damnation to his foes." The company drank except Van Campen, who brought down his hand so heavily upon the table as to break his glass.

Nellis immediately accused Doxstadter of forfeiting his honor, upon which many harsh and abusive expressions followed; one accusing the other of taking the rebel's part, and the other replying that the principles of honor were the same whether exercised towards a prisoner, or a fellow officer, and that he felt himself bound to regard the rights of one who had unfortunately been thrown under his protection. They were sitting on different sides of the table, Doxstadter with his back to the fire-place, by the side of which was a little pen filled with ashes. Becoming considerably excited they both rose upon their feet, and Doxstadter giving Nellis the lie, was answered by a blow, which was so well directed and powerful that it threw him backwards, and his feet catching against a bench, tumbled him heels over head into the ash-bed. He came out with his scarlet coat looking as though he had been in a meal chest, and he flew at Nellis more infuriated than ever. The latter warded him off as well as he could, and watching his opportunity, whispered to Van Campen, telling him that he had better withdraw, for, as the Indians were beginning to come up, his antagonist who had great influence with them, might engage one of them to thrust him through. He therefore left the ground and the quarrel ended, as he afterwards learned, with a challenge which was accepted by Nellis, to fight a duel on the following morning.

Morning came, but Doxstadter not appearing to fulfill his engagement, Nellis marched on with his warriors to Fort Niagara, where he arrived in safety and gave up his prisoners into the hands of the British.

CHAPTER XIX.

Upon arriving safely at Fort Niagara, Van Campen could with pleasure reflect that he had passed through the Indian territory, and had not been discovered as the one who had before escaped from captivity. He hoped now to be delivered into the hands of the British, and when once their prisoner, he supposed himself safe, even though the Indians should afterwards learn that he had been within their power. He was conducted into a long council hall, on each side of which were benches extending the whole length, and upon these the warriors with their prisoners, sat down and awaited the arrival of some of the British officers. Soon one of them appeared, and his name passed along the ranks of the Indian warriors —Col. Butler, and as Van Campen was informed that they were about to go through the ceremony of adopting him into the Colonel's family, he began to congratulate himself upon the security he could now feel; for his life would no longer hang upon the slight tenure of Indian caprice or favor, but he would now probably be detained as a prisoner until an exchange should take place between American and British captives. We will relate the ceremony of his adoption.

Col. Butler and his party stood on one side of the council house; the Indian warriors and prisoners on the other, when the chief warrior stepped forward a little in front of his men and made a speech. As this was given in the Indian language, Van Campen did not understand its import, yet there was something in the manner and voice of the warrior, which chained his attention, and led him strictly to observe all of his movements. After speaking awhile he went across the room, took Col. Butler by the hand and made him a short address, then retiring a little, he lighted a pipe and began to smoke. This was so constructed as to serve the double purpose of a pipe and hatchet the bowl being attached to the eye, and the handle being so formed as to admit the smoke to pass through to the end, which was taken into the mouth. After smoking, the warrior made another speech and then conducting Van Campen across the room, placed his hand in Col. Butler's and after briefly addressing him, led Van Campen again to his seat among the warriors. Butler and the Indian chief then took their pipes and smoked again, after which, the chief presented Butler with a large belt, called the *wampum* belt, and returned to his place and continued his harrangue. When he had finished this, Butler conducted Van Campen to his side of the room, where pipes were given them and they smoked together as the Colonel and Indian chief had done before. After smoking, Butler informed him that he had adopted him into his family to make good the loss of his son who had been killed by the rebels on the waters of the Mohawk, and that he would have to be conducted to the British guard-house.

Van Campen immediately replied, "My dear sir, if I have been adopted into your family, I trust you will not disgrace me so much as to place me under a British guard."

The Colonel seemed to be pleased with the reply, and remarked that he would give him a more pleasant situation, and accordingly gave him a very respectable room, that was occupied by a physician, named Stewart, in whom Van Campen found a very agreeable companion. He had not been long, however, at his new quarters before the Indians received the intelligence that he was the very same person who had killed a small party of warriors in the year 1780.

Not long after the party of warriors had left Pigeon Woods, where Van Campen was examined by the Indian interpreter, Jones, Mohawk himself came in and informed the warriors who still remained at that place, that Van Campen from whom he had once but just escaped with his life, had passed through as a prisoner, with the war-party that had gone to Niagara. He then showed them the scar, which he bore on the back of his neck, saying: "This was made by his tomahawk." Their eyes were immediately lighted up with revenge, and they brought forward their interpreter and began to inquire: "Did you not know that it was Van Campen whom you examined?"

Jones with his usual adroitness replied: "How should I know? Here I have been with you going on two years, and how could I tell any better than you, who Van Campen was? But besides, do you want me to lie? If I had known him do you suppose I would now tell you and have you kill me?"

Jones was a universal favorite with the Indians, and

the bold, collected manner in which he spoke, allayed their suspicions and he was suffered to pass without being questioned further.*

The news was soon carried to the Indians at Niagara,

---

*Mr. Harris says in his "Life of Horatio Jones," "Jones remained at the Pigeon Woods with the company from Corn-Planters settlement, and the out-going war party also lingered there, engaged in the sport of catching pigeons. One day an Indian, travel-stained and exhausted with fatigue, arrived in camp. The warriors were hastily summoned to his presence, and recognized the brave chieftain Mohawk.

"He informed them that while on an expedition near Bald Eagle Creek, he had learned of the defeat of Van Campen's company, and the capture of that officer and several of his men.

"Leaving his own party, Mohawk started on the trail of Nellis, and followed the latter to the Pigeon Woods,—hardly stoping for rest or food on the way. Standing up before the astonished warriors, Mohawk related the thrilling story of the massacre of his men, described the terrific struggle between Van Campen and himself, and striding back and forth like a caged tiger, his black eyes glowing with anger, he tore the blanket from his back, and pointed to a deep scar on his left shoulder, saying, 'This was made by Van Campen with my own axe, and this,' holding a tomahawk up to view, 'is the weapon.'

"Mohawk was too exhausted by his forced march from the Susquehanna to the Genesee, to proceed further than the Pigeon Woods, where he remained in camp several days awaiting news from the runners sent out from Niagara.

"Jones talked with the chief regarding his struggle with Van Campen, obtained his version of the affair, and ingratiated himself in Mohawk's good graces. The tomahawk that had borne so fearful a part in the massacre, possessed a peculiar fascination for the interpreter, and as the handle was broken, he finally induced Mohawk to sell it.

"The weapon was of French manufacture, had been obtained by Mohawk in the old French War, and carried through many a bloody fray.

"Unlike the usual form of Indian belt axes, it was of the knife blade pattern. The top was hollow forming the bowl of a pipe, and the handle was bored to serve as a stem. Jones replaced the broken handle with a new one, and thereafter the tomahawk adorned his own belt."

(He preserved the old weapon with care, and left it to his son, Col. William Jones, as an heirloom. From the latter it passed to the youngest and only surviving son of Horatio, Charles Jones, of Genesee, N. Y.—Ed.)

that Van Campen had been their prisoner, and, anxious to avenge the death of their countrymen, went to Col. Butler and informed him of the circumstances which they had heard, and demanded that their prisoner should be surrendered up to them. He put them off for a long time by saying that he would examine the case and let them know in a few days what should be done.

But they were not to be driven from their purpose; they urged their request with renewed ardor, demanding the surrender of Van Campen, and promising in his place fourteen other prisoners. So earnest were their petitions that Col. Butler was induced to send the Adjutant of his regiment to make inquiries of his prisoner in reference to the charges brought against him, and from him Van Campen learned the critical situation in which he was placed. After informing him of the accusations which had been brought against him, and of the desire of the Indians to obtain satisfaction for the number supposed to have been slain by his hand, he asked him whether the reports were true,—whether he was indeed the person who had been taken prisoner, and had effected his escape, by destroying the Indians who had taken him in the year '80.

Van Campen replied that for one placed in his circumstances, this was a very serious question to answer.

The Adjutant enquired further: "Were you brought into Niagara as a prisoner?"

Van Campen said: "No."

"Did you escape and run away from the Indian warriors?"

"No, sir, they *ran away from me.*"

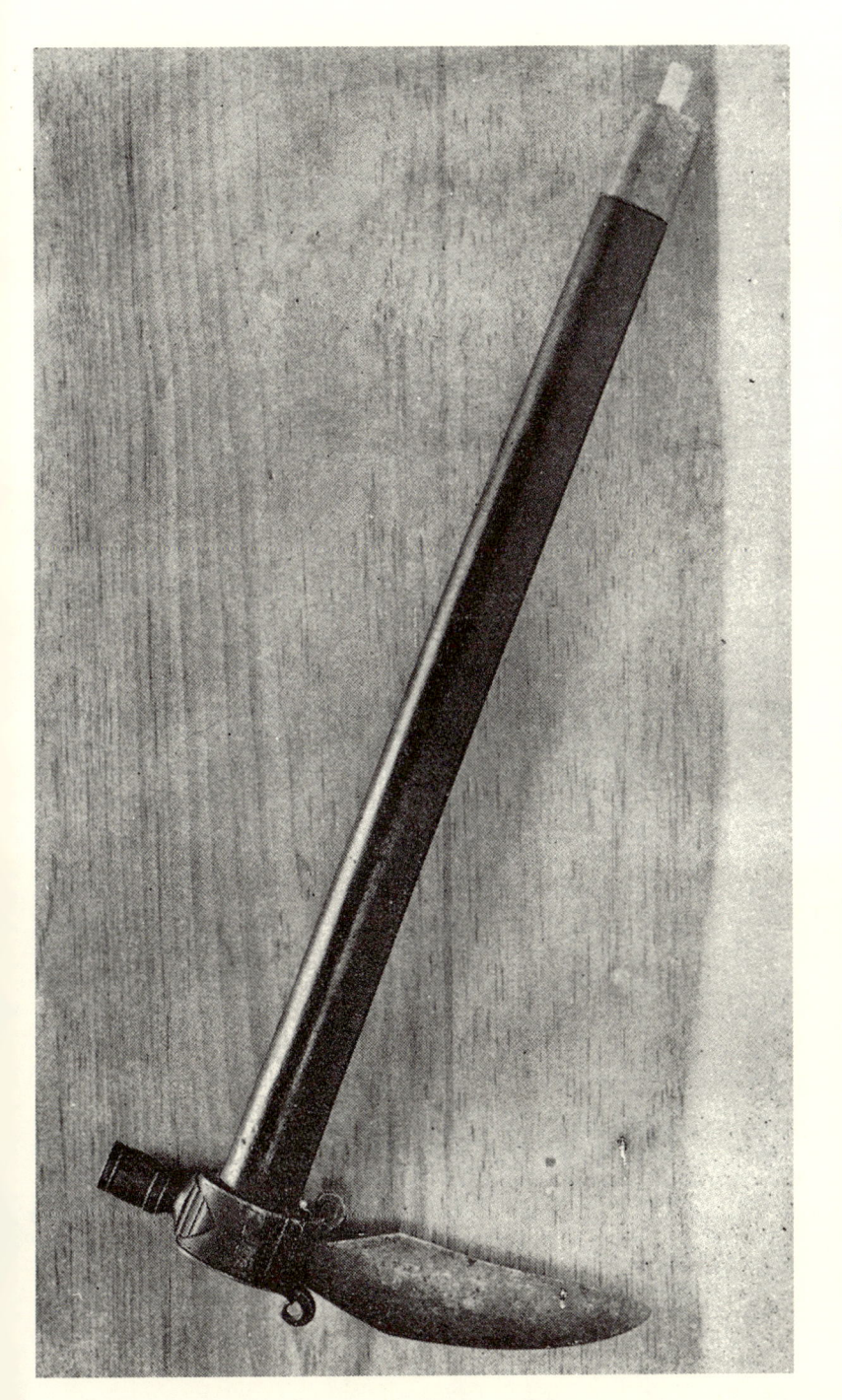

The Hatchet, or Tomahawk, Used by Van Campen in his Encoutner with Mohawk.

Not wishing to equivocate further, Van Campen replied: "Why, sir, I never am accustomed to deny the truth, and if your Colonel is so very anxious to know about this, he can. I was taken prisoner by the Indians, in the year 1780, was in company with two others, who were in the same predicament with myself, and we took advantage of their sleep to dispatch them with the gun and tomahawk. Five of them I killed with my own hand, and wounded another in the neck as he was fleeing from me."

The officer then remarked that he recollected the circumstance of a warrior's coming in, wounded in the manner he described.

Van Campen continued further: "I consider myself a prisoner of war to the British, and I trust they have more honor than to deliver me up, to be tortured to death by the savages. But your Colonel must be aware that, if my life is taken we have it in our power to retaliate; for we have the officers of two of your armies, who have submitted to American valor, and from these it will be easy to repay any indignity which may be paid to her officers by the opposing power."

The officer replied that this was a question which his Colonel would decide, and taking his hat to depart, Van Campen detained him, saying that he had a request to make. "What is it, sir?" he replied.

"I wish you to furnish me with a scalping knife, a scabbard and string."

"What do you mean to do with them?"

"I will hang the string around my neck, and conceal the knife in my bosom, and then if any of your Indian warriors come to pay me a visit I shall know their errand, and if it is to make me the victim of their rage, it will be at the expense of *their* lives or *mine*, for I would rather die the death of a soldier, than be tortured at the stake."

The officer replied that the Indians were his allies and he dared not do it, because should he be discovered he would forfeit his honor and lose his commission. Van Campen rejoined: "If they kill me it will forever remain a secret, and if my life is spared I will pledge my honor that you shall never be exposed." Making no promise he immediately departed.

Van Campen's feelings at this period would be poorly represented by a description. Certain it was that the savages were intent upon taking his life, and *that* by no easy process. Should his hold upon the things of earth be torn from him by piece meal, as in the case of the unfortunate Boyd, how excruciating would be his pangs! His fate hung upon the decision of the British Colonel, and could he have the hardihood to give him up to torture? But for fourteen prisoners in his stead what might he not be tempted to do? Such were some of Van Campen's thoughts as he paced his little apartment revolving in his mind the uncertainty of his present situation.

In a short time, however, the officer returned bringing with him the articles for which Van Campen had made a request, and setting a bottle of wine on the table, invited him to take a glass with him, at the same time remarking that he had brought back a favorable report.

Van Campen expressed his gratification and inquired

what the report was. To which he answered that Col. Butler had directed him to say that there was no alternative for him to save his life, but to abandon the rebel service and join the British. "If you will do so," said he, "the Colonel will give you the same rank in the British army that you hold in the *rebel cause.*"

Van Campen replied indignantly, "No sir, no. Give me the stake, the tomahawk, or the scalping knife, sooner than a British commission."

Their conversation ended here, and Van Campen was left several days in suspense, not knowing at what moment he might be summoned before an Indian tribunal, or how soon he should behold the torch and fagot lighted around him. But discovering that a British guard had been placed at his door, he supposed that it was sent there for his protection, and he began to indulge himself with the hope of greater security.

He next received a visit from the wife of a British officer by the name of Pry. Hearing a rap against the door, he sprang upon his feet, brought his hand to his bosom, and was ready to seize his knife should the occasion demand it; then giving the word, "Come in," awaited the appearance of his guests. As the door opened his eyes rested upon a female very prettily dressed, followed by a British officer. Apprehending no danger from such visitants, he withdrew from the attitude of defense, and as the lady approached him and drew aside her veil, he recognized an old acquaintance and schoolmate. He expressed his pleasure at this unexpected meeting, and she in turn represented her joy in seeing him, but added her regret that it should be under such trying circumstances. She remarked that the Indians had brought very weighty accusations against him, that she had been to her Colonel, to intercede for his life, and that she was permitted to say from him, that his life would be spared, in case of his submission to the terms that had been offered him before.

Van Campen replied that he could not consent to make such a disposal of himself; that his life belonged to his country, and that he would sooner suffer all the cruelties and indignities which the unrelenting savages could inflict upon him, than accept of the terms on which his life had been promised.

The lady regretted his obstinacy in not complying with the liberal terms that had been proposed, and set forth in glowing colors the dignity of the royal army, representing it as being far more honorable to hold a commission in the British service than to be an officer among the rebels.

Van Campen replied that his views and hers were very different, and that with his present feelings—the *knife, the tomahawk, or the stake,* would be far more acceptable than all the honors of a British commission. With this the conversation ceased, and he was left to muse in silence, over the probable course that would be taken in his case, and as he reflected upon the determined spirit of the Indian, and upon the avidity with which he is accustomed to pursue his desire of revenge, he felt that nothing would be left untried, to obtain possession of his person, and their point once gained, he could easily imagine the events that would follow. No punishment would be too severe; no inhumanity too great to be exercised against one who had slain a fellow warrior. He heard indeed, that their preparations of torture were already made, that sharpened fagots had been prepared to drive into his body and then set them on fire, under the expectation that he would be delivered into their hands.

But fortunately he was not delivered over to the tender mercies of the savage. In a few days he was placed on board of a vessel bound for Montreal. A guard accompanied him from his lodgings to the wharf, to prevent his being retaken by the Indians, who began to collect in great numbers around the garrison, as soon as it was rumored that he was to be sent away. Yet he reached the vessel in safety, and among those who treated him with kindness, was Capt. Pry and his lady, by whom he was favored with an introduction to the captain of the boat, recommending him to his attention as one for whom they had an especial regard, and who furnished him with an ample supply of provisions until he should be quartered among the prisoners at Montreal.

On the next morning after entering the vessel, her anchor was weighed, her sails unfurled, and as she gently bowed to the breeze, and began to move down the lake, Van Campen stood upon her deck, and with a joyful heart saw himself wafted from a scene which to him had been one of extreme danger and trial.

Arriving at Montreal he was ushered into the presence of about forty of his countrymen, who were, like himself, prisoners. They were assembled in what was called the guard-house, a large building some seventy or eighty feet in length, and about thirty or forty in width, and was appropriated to the use of the prisoners **and of**

British soldiers, who had them in charge. Within the dark walls of a prison, shut out from the light of day, only as it came struggling through iron grates, Van Campen found a company of men possessing spirits congenial with his own, and he soon formed an acquaintance which from a similarity of fortunes, ripened into the warmest attachment. There were men here from several of the different States, some of whom had been taken, like himself, by the Indians, in their sudden and wary attacks upon the border settlements. Van Campen's coming among them was regarded with no little interest; all gathered around the new prisoner to learn the story of his capture.

They did not, however, surrender themselves to the ill-bodings of despair. The success of their country's arms inspired them with hope, and led them with joy to think of the day as not far distant, when the American banner would wave in triumph over the proud pennon which held in the gale the boasted strength of the British Lion. They began to anticipate the return of peace, and as if to place at defiance the forms existing around them, this little band of prisoners, in the very heart of British authority, proposed the establishment of a Republican Government. They determined to regulate their affairs so long as they remained in prison, according to the pure principles of democracy. They chose from their number seven representatives, who met in a body by themselves to consult for the interests of the whole, and the principal subjects that came before them for their consideration, were such as related to the internal regulations of the prison.

One thing, among others, upon which they brought their skill of legislation to bear, was the enactment of laws concerning the preparation of their diet. This consisted of a given quantity of peas and pork a day for each one of the prisoners, who were obliged to act as their own cooks. It was very gravely presented to the body, which was called to preside over the affairs of this little community, that the preparation of their meals was a subject which demanded an immediate and serious attention. Several plans were proposed, and advocated with all the warmth of eloquence, in the presence of the people; but that which seemed to receive the highest favor was one which corresponded the most perfectly with their ideas of equality. It was that each one should act as cook in turn, beginning with those who held the lowest rank as officers, and ascending to the highest until all had been made to serve. It had been found by experience, that if the peas and pork were put on to boil at the same time, the latter, which required much less time in cooking, would be boiled to pieces before the peas would be in an eatable condition. It was therefore enacted as a solemn law, that the peas should be put over the fire first, and that after they had boiled a given length of time, the pork should also be subjected to the operation of heat. But it was further ascertained that the pork was somewhat rusty, and it was made the duty of the cook to cut this off before boiling. A failure to comply with these laws or any delinquency in the acting cook, subjected the offender to a trial and to such punishment as the people thought proper to pronounce in his case.

Under the operation of these laws their culinary affairs advanced prosperously, and not until it came to be the turn of one who had held the office of Major, was there the least opposition to the regulations that had been made. He began to plead exemption from performing the duties of cook, on account of his being a field officer. In answer to this he was reminded of the fact that he was under a Republican Government, *that all were on an equality and that he could have no excuse for not peforming his duty.*

He therfore complied with the regulations, but it was evidently with great reluctance, and so miserably did he act his part that when that little Democracy assembled around the dinner table, their fare was in such a wretched condition that none of them could eat.

It was found that the Major had not regarded the rule about putting the peas into the kettle first, but had tumbled in peas and pork at the same time. Neither had the rust been removed from the pork, and besides, he had allowed the dinner to get burnt, so that the accusations against the Major were quite numerous, and he was immediately arraigned before the appointed tribunal. The charges were tabled and after hearing the statements on both sides, the evidence appeared to be decidedly against him, the verdict was brought in— "*Guilty*," he was sentenced to be cobbed, and was accordingly laid across a bench with his face downwards, and the magistrate taking hold of one end of his shoe, proceeded to administer the given number of blows.

The Major complained bitterly of his treatment; he was so much dissatisfied that he entertained serious thoughts of rebelling against the government, and as there was no one discontented but himself, he resolved on forming an *aristocracy* in the midst of this nest of republicans. He nailed his blanket up between a couple of joists in the prison, and throwing himself into this, remained most of the time alone, not mingling with the common herd, and being emphatically above the majesty of the sovereign people.

While the Major was occupying his chosen quarters in his suspended blanket, removed from the bustle and turmoil of the little world below, yet not so far as to be unacquainted with what was transpiring around him, there was a plan formed by the prisoners to effect their escape by rising upon the British guard. They matured their purpose, so far as to engage some of the Canadians, who were favorable to the American cause, to furnish them with boats to conduct them across the river St. Lawrence, intending after they had gained the opposite shore, to enter the State of Vermont by the way of Lake Champlain, and thence to proceed to their several homes.

The day and hour were appointed, and the parties for attack selected—one to fall upon the sentries, another to dispatch or secure the guard. Just as they were about to put their designs into execution, the courage of one who was to act a conspicuous part, failed him, and receiving the signal to withdraw, instead of the one for attack, Van Campen and a few others with him, who were appointed to take care of the sentries, returned with chagrin to inquire into the cause of this change in their anticipated movements. They were told by a Capt. White, who had been appointed to lead the other party, "that it was too hazardous and it had better be abandoned."

This scheme was followed by another, somewhat different in its character, but more intimately connected with the Major, who still swung in his blanket. The political birthday of American freedom was drawing near, and the prisoners determined to celebrate the anniversary of their National Independence. But they were destitute of the means of observing it according to their ideas of propriety. This difficulty was removed by one of the number, who informed them that if they would provide him with some quicksilver and a few old coppers, he would give them a coin that would pass for an English shilling. A Canadian friend supplied these, and whenever their market boy went to purchase provisions, he took of the new coin to buy a small quantity of vegetables and receiving change in return, expended it for brandy, which he brought into the prison by concealing it in his basket. In this way the prisoners had collected a good sized keg full of liquor, and kept it in readiness for their anticipated holiday.

Only ten of them, Van Campen among the number, dared enter upon the plan of celebration, and these determined to carry it through, even though their imprisonment should, on this account, be attended with ten-fold rigor. The others feared the consequences of the undertaking, and declined having any part in the festivities which had been prepared for the occasion.

The Fourth of July at length came, and it was never, perhaps, hailed with more heart-felt expressions of joy, than by that small party, who, within the dark walls of a Canadian prison, hailed the feeble light that came streaming in through the iron casements as the herald of a brighter day, whispering the mild accents of hope.

This small company of avowed patriots brought forward their entertainment at an early hour, and it was not long before their joy began to expend itself in the loud and merry laugh, and the Hessian soldiers, who were that day on guard, very often sent some of their number into the upper room where the prisoners were assembled to command order. These commands becoming at length rather too frequent and troublesome, one of their number was stationed at the trap door by which their apartment was entered, with the direction to shut it upon the first man who attempted to come with order of "*Silence.*" Beginning soon to grow noisy, one or two soldiers came running up, and as they began to rise above the floor, the keeper slammed the door upon their heads and knocked them down the stairs. The next order that came was from the mouth of the Hessian guns, several of which were discharged up through the floor, but fortunately without injury to the prisoners.

Splinters from the fractured floor were thrown about the room at so lively a rate that the unruly prisoners began to think seriously of observing greater silence. They were therefore, for a time, quite orderly, and as night began to draw near, Van Campen proposed that they should invite the suspended Major down to their evening's entertainment. The suggestion was approved by the others, and the inquiry was made, "How shall it be done?" "In military style, of course," replied

Van Campen. Directing two of them, therefore, to sharpen their knives, and being prepared, he gave the order—" MAKE READY,—TAKE AIM,—FIRE !" As the last word was pronounced, the two who were holding their knives, applied them to the sides of the blanket, and out came the Major, head first, to join the party at the table. The Major was received with loud shouts of applause ; the prison rang with acclamations, and merry cheers resounded from every quarter. But to the poor Major it proved a more serious disaster than they had anticipated. Falling upon a bench in the room one or two of his ribs were somewhat fractured, and he was taken away to the hospital to receive medical attention. It was not, however, without leaving a threat to expose all who had been the actors in this scene.

He was true to his word ; on the next morning an officer came into the prison with a list of names upon a piece of paper, the first of which was Van Campen's. As the ten who had been engaged in celebrating the Fourth were called out together, the others began to congratulate themselves that they were not of the party, and as they were led out of the prison, they followed them with an anxious look, anticipating the most serious consequences. They were brought into a Court Martial of British officers, and Van Campen, being requested by the others to represent their case for them, determined if their conspiracy should have been revealed to deny it, unequivocally, since it would at once decide their fate.

When paraded before the officers, Van Campen's name was called, and upon answering, he was told that he and his party had been arraigned for misconduct in prison, and that the first charge against them was for a conspiracy to destroy the British guard.

Van Campen, believing that the crisis demanded a denial of the fact, answered firmly, "It's a *lie, there is not a word of truth in it.*"

The British officer then proceeded to enumerate the charges consequent upon the celebration of the Fourth of July. He replied there was a little more truth in this, that himself and some of his comrades had thought it proper not to pass over their National Holiday without giving it some little attention, and they had accordingly done all that, under the circumstances, they could to keep it in remembrance. He then related the story of their celebration, the regulations they had made in their Republican Government, the manner in which the Major had been punished for not conforming to the laws, the offence he had taken, described his abode in the blanket, and in short, gave such a comic history of the whole affair, that all of the officers were thrown from their gravity as judges, and began to laugh, regarding it as a subject of the utmost merriment.

While he was engaged in the narration, a young Hessian officer, who seemed to take a deep interest in the story, came around and stood close by Van Campen, that he might hear every word that was uttered, and when he had ended, Van Campen turned to him and inquired if he was acquainted with any of the Hessian officers taken with the army of Burgoyne, who had been stationed in Berks County, Pennsylvania. To which he answered in the affirmative. Van Campen then informed him that while an officer there, he had often invited them to dine with him, that others had paid the same attention, they being allowed the honor of a parole, and that he thought the same privilege should be allowed to the American officers.

The young officer then represented the case to his General and was informed that it would be taken into consideration, and an answer given on the next day. Without giving them any censure, therefore, the prisoners were told that they might appear before them again, and they would then be informed whether they could be allowed the privilege of a parole. Upon returning to the prison they resolved not to inform their fellows of the result of this summons, but to keep it as a secret among themselves, revealing only this—that their case would be decided on the morrow.

On the next day, when the officer came to conduct Van Campen and his comrades from the prison, they assumed the appearance of concern, and bade their companions farewell, as though they never expected to meet them again in this world. The others sympathized deeply with their fate, at the same time feeling that they had themselves happily escaped a sentence, which they supposed would be death. Upon coming before the British officers, Van Campen and his comrades were informed that they would have the privilege of the streets of Montreal during the day, if they would consider themselves in honor bound to return to the guardhouse for lodgings at night. To this they readily agreed, and were happy in the thoughts of again breathing the open air of heaven, without receiving it through the iron grates of a prison. Thus ended this tragic affair, but it was not without chagrin that those who through fear of punishment, refused to participate in the honors paid to the hallowed day of freedom, beheld their companions who had the hardihood to commit so great an offence, permitted on this very account, to enjoy a liberty denied to themselves.

Soon after this, Van Campen and the nine who were with him on parole, were sent to the island of Orleans, five miles below Quebec, and remaining here until November, were placed on board of a vessel bound for New York, and after a dangerous voyage of five weeks, arrived in safety at their place of destination. Here a British commissary came on board of their vessel and began to inquire of the prisoners concerning the treatment they had received. All of them told in turn a very doleful story, finding much fault with their treatment and making a great variety of complaints, until he came to Van Campen, the last whom he examined. As he came up to him he said rather impatiently, " Well, sir, have YOU *any complaints to make ?*"

Supposing it to be altogether useless to offer any, even though he had been treated ever so ill, he replied, " Not at present, sir; but I soon may have."

" Ah, upon what grounds will you make your complaint ?"

" Why, sir, if you don't send us on board, ten gallons of wine, a quarter of fresh beef, and a good supply of fresh bread, *I shall complain of you.*"

The officer took him by the hand, and shaking it heartily, replied, "If this is all, you shall *have* it, sir— you shall have it;" and, true to his word, he soon sent him the articles he had named. As long as the wine and beef lasted, the prisoners found no fault with their fare.

Gen. Carleton then proposed to let them go to their own country on parole, they pledging themselves not to take up arms against His Majesty, the King, and that they would repair to whatever point or place his Generals should call them, and placing them on board of a cartel-ship, sent them up the North river to the American lines. The officer of this vessel, perceiving that they had a good supply of wine with them, began to treat them very civilly, inviting them into his own cabin, and becoming a guest with them. They here enjoyed themselves exceedingly, and having permission to sing some of their songs, they sung several which were replete with burlesque upon the British arms, and as these drew forth the loud and merry laugh, the Captain would join in with the rest, and before he placed his passengers on shore, he was so much pleased with the company of the prisoners, that he was willing himself almost to be called a rebel.

Upon coming on shore and into the society of their own countrymen, Van Campen and his fellow prisoners found themselves at some distance from their immediate friends, with scarcely a penny in their pockets to bear the expenses of a journey. They each had a blanket, however, and disposing of these, raised a little money, and with this began to proceed on foot towards their homes. In passing through New Jersey they staid over night at a public house, where the landlord requested them to leave their names before starting in the morning, stating that inquiries were often made concerning prisoners who were returning home, and that he wished to have it in his power to gratify any friend who might desire information about them.

They had been gone but about an hour, when one of the inhabitants came in, and began to inquire of the landlord, if there was any news. "None," said he, "but the passing by of a few prisoners, who staid with me the last night."

"Can you give me their names?"

He presented him with a list of these, and upon beholding Van Campen's, declared that he must see him, "For," said he, "I was at Northumberland soon after one by that name was taken prisoner, and every man, woman and child was lamenting his loss, and this must be the same person; if I can be of any assistance to him, I will." Learning that they had been gone but a short time, he mounted his horse and pursued on after them.

Upon coming in sight of the prisoners, he called to them, requesting them to halt, and as he drew near, inquired for Van Campen. Answering to his name, Van Campen stepped forward and demanded his wish.

Upon receiving from him the name of the place where he had been taken captive, the stranger informed him of his having heard of him before, and inquired if he had with him what money he wanted to bear his expenses on his way home. Van Campen replied that money was at that time a very scarce article with him, and thereupon the stranger handed him half a joe (about eight dollars), saying that it was all he had with him, and that as he had a family to support, and was expecting to remove into the vicinity of Northumberland, he might have the privilege of returning it to him again if he chose. Van Campen thanked him for his kindness, and promised to do so with interest, as he afterwards did. With this addition to their funds, the prisoners proceeded on their way with **lighter hearts,** and upon arriving at Princeton, the Free Masons learning their history and apprised of the fact that one or two of them belonged to their fraternity, called a meeting at which they raised funds sufficient to hire a carriage, in which they were conveyed to Philadelphia. They were a rare looking company for the elegant vehicle in which they rode and were amazed by the curiosity excited on the way by their singular appearance.

At Philadelphia Lieut. Van Campen received his quarter's pay, procured a suit of uniform for which he exchanged his Canadian dress, and returning to Northumberland, was received by his friends with demonstrations of joy.

CHAPTER XX.

From the time of Lieut. Van Campen's return home, which was in the month of January, 1783, until early in the spring, he was mostly occupied in visits, which this season allowed him to make among his friends. While journeying in the upper part of Pennsylvania for this purpose, he received a letter from Capt. Robison informing him that an exchange had been made between prisoners, so that he could enter into service, and that he must now return to duty. Making his preparations therefore he immediately directed his course towards Northumberland, and upon arriving there was sent with a company of men to take charge of Wilksbarre Fort.

He was stationed here to protect the inhabitants from the continued depredations of the Indians, who, though peace had been established between America and Britain, still continued to infest the region of the border settlements, that they might plunder whatever objects came within their reach. But the mere presence of a military force was not sufficient to prevent the mischief of these troublesome neighbors, who crept cautiously up to the quiet farm-house, and watching their opportunity, drove away cattle and horses.

Soon after Van Campen had taken charge of Wilksbarre Fort, Capt. Robison arrived to receive the command himself, while he directed the former to proceed up the Susquehanna as far as Queen Esther's Flatts, with a company of men and there lay in wait, that he might intercept parties of Indians who were infesting the country for the purpose of plunder. Selecting his men, he proceeded up the river in a boat, with provisions and the equipages of the camp and soon pitched his tent at the appointed place. Remaining here a few days without making any discoveries, curiosity led him one day to go and examine his old battle-ground, at Hogback Hill, which was but a few miles above, on the river. He was accompanied by none of his party and had gone about five miles when he heard, at a short distance from him, the tramping of a horse. Supposing an enemy to be near, he threw himself under the cover of a thick growth of bushes and awaited his approach. Just then there hove in sight a beautiful horse, mounted by one of elegant appearance, in the British dress. The first notice he had of the presence of Van Campen, was as he saw him in the path before him, aiming his rifle at his head, giving the order, "*Halt!*" He checked his horse and his hand dropped immediately upon a holster pistol. "*Draw a pistol*," said Van Campen, "*and you are a dead man!*" He then received the order, "*Dismount, sir!*"

The rifle was still pointing towards him and he obeyed. "*Tie your horse!*"

The horse was tied. "*Right about face, march!*" He wheeled and marched. "*Halt!*" He halted.

Van Campen then went to his horse, untied him and with his rifle in one hand and the reins in the other, mounted. He then took one of the pistols from its place, and finding it loaded, cocked it and directed his prisoner to march in front. As he passed, he gave a wishful look at the bridle, as though he would seize the reins. Van Campen said : " *Touch the reins, sir, and I will blow your brains out !*" Submitting quietly, he began to march on before Van Campen, and the latter inquiring his name and business, the other replied—Allan, and that he was on his way to Congress, from the Six Nations, for the purpose of making a treaty of peace.

Upon coming to the Flatts, Van Campen's soldiers discovered him riding an elegant grey horse, marching his man before him. The Sergeant paraded his soldiers immediately in front of the tents, and as he came up gave him the military salute and inquired—" Where did you get that bird ?" Van Campen replied that he caught him on the waters of the Chemung, a little below their old battle-ground. Dismounting, he gave the horse into the care of one of his soldiers, and found that he had given a true account of his business. He then remarked to him—" Allan, your name is regarded with so much infamy by the inhabitants of the country through which you are to pass, on account of your more than savage cruelty, exercised among the defenseless families of the frontiers, that when once they hear of your presence, they will certainly put you to death; and that you may go on your business in safety, I will break up my camp and conduct you beyond Wilksbarre."

He therefore made his arrangements in accordance with this determination, descended the river to Fort Wilksbarre and conducted Allan into the Fort. He had not been here long however, before the intelligence was spread among the inhabitants that Allan had been captured and was in the Fort; and coming up in a mass they demanded that he should be surrendered. So determined were they upon getting possession of Allan, that though Van Campen used his utmost influence to dissuade them from their purpose, showing them the importance of an Indian treaty, and that until one was formed they could not expect to occupy their farms in safety, it was with the greatest reluctance that they withdrew from the Fort.

On the next day Van Campen accompanied Allan with a guard until he was beyond the probable reach of danger, and proceeding on his way, he arrived safely at Congress, and made arrangements by which a treaty was concluded with the Indians, during the succeeding summer.

Lieutenant Van Campen returned to Fort Wilksbarre, where he continued in command until the month of November, when upon receiving news that the terms of peace had been ratified, the army was disbanded and he retired from military life to engage in the duties of a private citizen.*

---

*As there are only six or seven pages more of Mr. Hubbard's text, which are devoted chiefly to a brief survey of his life, and deal somewhat with matters introduced in my part of the work, I have thought best for this reason, and also to avoid any unnecessary repetitions, to suppress them, and continue as nearly unbroken as may be, the story of Van Campen's life and adventures to the end.—ED.

CHAPTER XXI.

Very soon after his retirement from the service, Lieut. Van Campen married Margaret, the daughter of Mr. James McClure, a wealthy farmer who formerly resided in the vicinity of Northumberland, and had recently died.

Van Campen at once undertook the management of the estate, and "carried on" the farm for several years. The writer has not been able to learn of any important or unusual occurrence with which he was in any way connected, during that period, which is considered worthy of note.

Left to the quiet and peaceful occupation of the "broad acres" of the McClure place, it is safe to presume that he prosecuted farming operations, as he did every thing else he undertook, with zeal and energy, and, as his marital relations were most pleasant, and three daughters were born to him during his stay on the place, it is also safe to conclude, that he was for the times, a "model husband."

Mary, who afterwards became the wife of George Leckhart, and the mother of Alfred, James, Joseph and Mary Leckhart, was born on the 10th of October, 1784. Anna, who married Alvin Burr, and was the mother of Moses Burr, was born October 29, 1786, and Priscilla, afterwards Mrs. Samuel Mulholland, was born September 15, 1789.

About this time (1789) he purchased a large tract of land in the neighborhood of Briar's Creek, to which he soon after removed, and resided there for about five years, when a good opportunity offering, he sold out, reserving however, a lot of sixty acres, which he promised to an evangelical society, upon the condition that they should build a church, which they afterwards did, when the terms being complied with, he executed a conveyance of the land as he had proposed.

It was during the residence of the family in the "Briar Creek" neighborhood, that their two last children were born; Elizabeth, who married Rev. Robert Hubbard, and became the mother of Rev. J. N. Hubbard, the author of the preceding part of this book, on April 3, 1792, and Lavina, who became Mrs. Dr. Samuel Southworth, on March 3, 1794.

In 1795 or 1796, more likely however in 1796, although he might in 1795 have made a preliminary reconnoissance, and felled some trees and girdled others preparatory to further improvements, he left the "Briar Creek" neighborhood, and settled in what was soon afterwards, and is now known, as "McHenry Valley," in what is now Almond, Allegany Co., N. Y.

The journey from Briar Creek to Almond must of necessity have been attended with many interesting, and quite likely some exciting incidents, involving as it did, the poling up the Chemung and Canisteo rivers of flat bottomed boats or arks,* laden with their household

---

*Guy H. McMaster, in his interesting history of Steuben county, page 75, refers to a meeting between Van Campen and Mohawk, which, without doubt, occurred during the progress of this journey, thus: "Major Moses Van Campen, well known to the

effects, and other property which they needed to make a start with in the "new country" to which they were going.

Of a necessity it must have been laborious, annoying, and attended with more or less danger; and the five little girls, the eldest eleven years of age, and the youngest a babe in its mother's arms, certainly afforded sufficient objects for maternal concern and anxiety.

It seems to be a conceded historical fact, that in McHenry Valley in 1796, were built three log houses, one on the "old Sanders farm," by Major Moses Van Campen,[*] one by Henry McHenry, and one by William Gray.

They were of course, of the most primitive style, quite likely for awhile, with blankets hung in the door openings, and "factory" cloth or oiled paper stretched

---

Six Nations, as a powerful, daring and sagacious ranger in the border wars of Pennsylvania, moved up the river with a colony destined for Allegany county, and offered to land at the settlement on Canisteo Flats. Van Campen was especially obnoxious to the Indians for the part he had taken, as a leader of a bold and destructive attack made in the night by himself and two others. * * * The savages recognized Van Campen on his arrival at Canisteo, as 'the man that lent John Mohawk the hatchet.' Captain Mohawk himself was there, and had a special cause of grievance to exhibit, in a neck set slightly awry from a blow of the tomahawk. The settlers rallied for the defence of Van Campen. There was every prospect of a bloody fight; but after much wrangling it was agreed that the two parties should divide, while Van Campen and Mohawk advanced between them to hold a 'talk.'

"This was done, and in a conference of considerable length between the two old antagonists, the causes of difficulty were discussed, and it was finally decided that each was doing his duty *then*, but that now, war being ended, they ought to forget past injuries, Mohawk offered his hand. The threatened fight became a feast."

---

[*] This farm is now owned by **Abizor Phillips.**

across the window openings, and they managed through the warm weather to get along without chimneys, as, " in the fall they all united, and in one week built three chimneys,* and killed thirty-six deer," so stated Major Van Campen to John McNitt, who as late as 1879 was living at Almond.

The knowledge which Van Campen had acquired of the surveyor's art, and his skill with the compass, which he attained by his practice in the Northumberland and Briar Creek regions, soon became known in this new neighborhood, and new settlers coming in, and frequent purchases being made, his services in laying out land and setting up boundaries were soon in frequent demand.

It was not long before his fame had spread beyond the limits of his immediate " settlement," and became known to Col. Williamson, the accomplished agent of the Pulteney Estate, who gave him considerable employment, and justly appreciated his ability and judgment.

Soon Philip Church, then quite a young man, made his appearance in these western wilds. He had just made a purchase of 100,000 acres, not very far distant from this new settlement, and desiring to place it on the market, was soon in need of a surveyor.

Col. Williamson, who had become acquainted with Mr. Church and was aware of his requirements, took occasion to recommend Van Campen as the man he wanted. Accordingly Church determined to visit him,

---

*It is said a part of the old Van Campen chimney is still standing.

and made the journey through the woods to McHenry Valley, and the two men met for the first time.*

The impressions made by this first meeting were mutually favorable; the acquaintance thus formed soon ripened into the strongest friendship, and except by death, was never for a moment, even, interrupted.

Van Campen's stay in McHenry Valley was short. His acquaintance with Church and employment in his service, which required the greater part of his time, and the scene of his operations being so far distant from his habitation, all conspired to make his location quite inconvenient. So it was soon deemed necessary to make another remove, which was soon after accomplished, locating this time, on what afterwards turned out to be the eastern limits of the village of Angelica, a site selected with rare good judgment.

In August, 1801, he was employed by Mr. Church to make a thorough exploration of his whole tract. In company with Evart Van Wickle, John Lewis, John Gibson, and Stephen Price, Mr. Church met him at Almond, then the settlement nearest the Church Tract, and from thence proceeded directly to a point near the south-east corner of the tract, following very nearly the route afterwards adopted for the Erie Rail Road.

Before me lies a letter from Miss Mary Leckhart, a granddaughter of Major Van Campen, in which speaking of this visit she says: " * * Philip Church came to secure his services to survey his large tract of land. * * * It was in the latter part of summer, and the family observed a person in the corn field, very vigorously shaking his clothing, which they learned afterwards, was to divest himself of fleas, as he had been much exposed to them while in the woods. It was but an hour or so afterwards when he came to the house, and introducing himself, stated the object of his visit."

Just here it may be well, for a brief moment, to pause and study the character and make-up of this party.

Van Campen at that time was in the full meridian of life, in possession to the fullest extent of all his powers and faculties, physical and mental, not one in the least impaired, all at their best ; his varied experiences during the eventful years of the war had given him such a knowledge of life in the woods, such a familiarity with nature in her grand old solitudes, as was well calculated to render his service of great practical value in such an undertaking ; Church, a young man of twenty-three, alert, resolute, courageous, and inspired with a zeal born of the enterprise he was engaged in, having of course a personal interest which no one else could have, and the other members of the party stout, athletic, daring fellows, and dressed, of course, in such plain, convenient garb, as was suited for the enterprise ; taken all in all they must have made a group which we of today would fain look upon, a party in fact, just suited to the business in hand.

The work was at once begun, prorecuted with diligence, and continued until they became thoroughly acquainted with the whole tract; with its streams, its hills and valleys, its peculiarities of soil, its timber and herbage, the facilities its streams afforded for dams and mill privileges, and possible sites for villages; in short, they made such a study of the territory, as became of great value in prosecuting the work of subdivision, which was soon afterwards commenced.

Terminating their reconnoissance near the north-west corner of the tract, Church and Van Campen made up their minds to take a *pleasure trip to Niagara Falls.* Dismissing the other members of the party, who departed in an opposite direction for their homes, they took an Indian trail that bore off in the desired direction. This they pursued for two days, when they arrived at the Seneca Indian village. Proceeding on their way they soon made their appearance in the little white settlement of "New Amsterdam" (Buffalo), in a very sorry plight; with clothes badly torn, beards unshaven, features tanned and camp smoked.

They visited the falls, returned to Buffalo and took the "white man's trail"* on their return to Bath. As no such a tramp had been contemplated, soon after leaving Buffalo, money and provisions were exhausted, with the exception of a surplus of chocolate, which they managed to exchange with the settlers for meals. Mr. Ellicott had just got his land office built at Batavia. At Ganson's there was a militia training, the first ever had west of the Genesee river. One of the officers, Richard W. Stoddard, supplied Mr. Church with money, and they resumed their journey improved in purse and spirits, halting at Geneseo for a brief visit with Mr. Wadsworth, with whom Mr. Church had become acquainted in New York, and finally arriving at Bath much fatigued in body, well pleased however with their adventurous "trip to Niagara Falls."

It is safe to say that this expedition involved as much

---

*The early settlers were wont to call the first track made through the forest, which by any means could be followed, with the rudest conveyance even, "the white man's trail," to distinguish it from the "Indian trail," and such a road had been cut through to Batavia.

personal discomfort and peril as were encountered later in Sherman's famous "march to the sea."

Van Campen's foresight in selecting the location for his home, was afterward proven by the location of the Bath and Olean turnpike, which passed the place just in front of his house.

Clearing off a small piece of groumd, and the erection of some rude tenements in which to live during the time to be devoted to the construction of the large brick house he soon after put up, was the first work which engaged his attention. Making an excavation at the base of the hill a few rods in the rear of the site selected for his dwelling, he discovered material of the proper consistency to make a good article of brick. Stone well adapted for building purposes, were found in abundance conveniently near, and soon in the midst of that forest of pine and oak prevailing, arose as it were by magic, in grand proportions, a house whose walls at this writing (1892), after the lapse of eighty-four years, are still intact, whose foundations show no signs of settling, a house indeed whose salient features typify the substantial character of the man who reared it.

It was during the erection of this house that a thrilling incident occurred. The Major was at the time called away on business, which detained him for several days. He had in his employ a colored man, whom he held in servitude under the then existing laws of the State. One night as Mrs. Van Campen and a domestic were about to retire, they, with true feminine instinct, looked under the bed, when lo! and behold! there laid the brute of a negro, with a butcher knife in his hand.

THE VAN CAMPEN PLACE, ANGELICA, ALLEGANY CO., N. Y.

Screams of the most violent kind of course were in order, which quickly aroused the laborers, who slept in a small structure conveniently near. They immediately made their appearance upon the scene, and secured the ugly creature. Upon the Major's return he at once sold him to Gen. Cruger, of Bath, and never after owned such property.

CHAPTER XXII.

In the search for material for the proper treatment of Van Campen as surveyor, the author has not, in some respects, been rewarded with results commensurate with his expectations.

For instance, nothing can be learned of the Churches as to the terms upon which he prosecuted the work, whether by the day, acre or mile, for length of lines run; all who constituted his party of assistants have long since been numbered with "the great majority," and it is not learned that any one has been sufficiently interested in the matter, to gather up any data or details and preserve them for possible future use.

His "Field Notes" have, however, been carefully preserved by the Churches and Burrs, and an act has been passed by the Legislature which is now a law, under which they may be authenticated, for use in Court, when lines are in dispute on the Church Tract, and copies of them have at different times been made by surveyors for use in their immediate practice upon the lands which he subdivided, and a careful inspection of them affords good facilities to the practical surveyor for a reasonably fair estimate of his ability in that line of work, and inferentially, of certain peculiarities in the prosecution of his surveys.

Consulting the "Book of Surveys" of the Church

Tract, and his "Field Notes," one is at once struck with the neatness of his chirography, the care with which he made all his figures, and the excellence of his plots; he is in fact drawn irresistibly and rapidly to the conclusion that he is inspecting the work of a man of a good deal more than ordinary ability.

His method of describing and perpetuating "corners," was of uniform application, as well as the way in which he caused his lines to be "marked" or "blazed." An instrument was carried along by some member of the party with which to mark the "corner posts" and "corner trees" with the numbers of the adjacent lots, and the course and distance of the "corner trees" from the "corner posts" were carefully noted in his "Field Book." "Corner posts," in his surveys subsequent to the subdivision, were invariably referred to as being marked with a "blaze and three notches, two above and one below."

His party of assistants must have numbered five at least, and possibly six, and it is known that a pack-horse laden with camp equipage and commissary stores accompanied them; so, wherever night overtook them, they would make their camp, selecting of course a place conveniently accessible to water. It is a matter of tradition that his chief axeman for most of the time, was a half-breed Indian, whose name cannot be given, who was remarkably expert with the "wondrous instrument." Of more than ordinary height, his striding abilities were first-class, and his stout arms and hands cleared away with remarkable celerity the obstructions to sight which came in their way. Quick of perception, he knew just what, and how much, to cut, which greatly facilitated their progress.

The extreme low prices of the lands which he subdivided, precluded the taking of as much pains as are now taken in laying out and dividing land; the lines he ran in the prosecution of these original subdivisions were "needle lines," and about six miles per day was the average of work done.

Taking all these things into consideration, the author is, from the observations which he has of necessity been called to make upon his work, in a practice of nearly forty years, during which time he has had frequent occasion to retrace his lines, in some instances where roads have been laid, extending nearly across a township, led to the conclusion that his work as a whole was *well done*, indeed *so* well done as to justly excite surprise that it *was* so well done, and admiration for the ability displayed in its prosecution.

In support of this conclusion, I am pleased to quote the following from so good an authority as Leander Gorton, the veteran and accomplished surveyor of Belmont, N. Y.

" Of all the early surveyors I have followed in this region, I long ago learned to know and like his work the best, and have cherished a feeling of acquaintance and comradeship with him, derived from my knowledge of his work."

One of the objects incidental to the subdivision of a tract of wild land, is to obtain the data from which to make a reasonable estimate of the amount, character, and variety of timber on the several lots, obtain information as to soil, herbage, surface configuration, streams, springs, ponds, swamps, etc., so as to make an intelligent appraisal of the land upon the different lots, preparatory to sales.

For this business Van Campen, from his habits of close observation, and long experience in border warfare, which of necessity made him familiar with the primitive woods which covered this country, was eminently qualified. So with mind and eye intent upon the business in hand, equipped with compass and Jacob-staff, Field Book and pencil, he carefully directed the course, and with the progress of his chain-bearers, noted the distances at which brooks, creeks and rivers crossed his lines, made mention of their width and directions, ascents and descents, the exact distance at which they attained the summit of some hill or ridge, the base of some steep bank, and the character of soil, whether "open flats," "1st qual. uplands," "2nd qual. uplands," "highlands," etc., etc.*

The extent of his subdivisional work was considerable. In addition to the 100,000 acres embraced in the "Church Tract," which he surveyed in 1810–11 he subdivided T. 1., R. 7, of the Pulteny Estate (Phelps and Gorham), which is now the town of Independence, in 1815. In 1817 he surveyed the "Patterson Tract," in Tps. 1, & 2, R. 2, and in 1818, the "Cazenovia Tract," now West Almond. Besides all this work which covered about

---

*In many of his reports to Judge Church, the term "*strict measure*" is introduced after giving the number of acres, and the names of the chain-bearers and other persons present. It is supposed that in those instances more than ordinary importance was attached to the work.

150,000 acres, he did a great deal of work for Judge Church in measuring off land for settlers, as appears by the voluminous " Book of Surveys," so long kept in the land office at the Church Manor House.

He was also called in various instances to act as Commissioner and surveyor of roads laid and opened by the State.

April 10, 1810, by act of the Legislature, he was appointed surveyor, and with Valentine Brother of Canandaigua and George Hornell (afterward Judge Hornell), of Hornellsville, Commissioners, to lay out and open a road, "from Canandaigua, by the head of Conesus Lake, by the most eligible route to the mouth of Olean river."

In 1813 he was placed at the head of a commission of which Christopher Hurlbut, of Arkport, and Jedadiah Strong, of Olean, were the other members, to lay out a road "from the termination of the 'Pine Creek Road,' at Crestown, Pa., to Hamilton (Olean), and thence to the outlet of Chautauqua Lake."

With Joseph Ellicott, Robert Troup, Charles Carroll, Philip Church, Dugald Cameron, Seymour Bouton, Sylvanus Russell and William Higgins, he was appointed in 1819 to lay out a road from Angelica by way of Van Campen's Creek, to the village of Olean (Hamilton).

When the "turnpike," from Bath to Olean came to be located and constructed, Van Campen was a leading spirit, and helpful from the inception of the project, to the completion of the work. Judge Church was an interested co-adjutor in the turnpike enterprise. With this brief recapitulation of his services as surveyor, to which of course must be added the surveys of various roads for his own and other towns, which work he continued to do even after his removal to Dansville (1831), and the original survey of the plat of Angelica and other villages, the reader will readily conclude that his life during the years mainly devoted to this work, must have been one of unusual activity, and required a degree of endurance seldom equalled, and very rarely excelled.

Whether Major Van Campen held any civil office in Pennsylvania, is not known to the author, nor is it important. It is known that he was Assessor during his brief sojourn in what is now Almond, and Excise Commissioner in Angelica in 1805. As these offices were of minor importance, it will be assumed for the purpose of this resume that the years covered by Major Van Campen's incumbency of civil office, began with 1807, and ended probably in 1831.

Aug. 12, 1807, he was appointed Judge of the Court of Common Pleas, along with Philip Church as first Judge, and Evart Van Wickle and Thaddeus Bennett as associates. From the records in the Allegany County Clerk's Office, it appears that he was appointed " Judge and Justice of the Peace," June 13, 1810, and was successively " sworn in " as such officer, in 1811-13-14-15-19 and 21. He was County Treasurer " from 1814 to 1826 inclusive of both years;" so says our present incumbent, the veteran and venerable Daniel D. Gardiner. From the records it therefore appears that during some of the time he must have held two offices at the same time, and next to Mr. Gardiner, he held the office of County Treasurer longer than any other man.

June 25, 1828, he was " sworn in " as Deputy County

Clerk; just how long he filled that place is not now precisely known. November 12, 1830, he "qualified" as Commissioner of Deeds, an office corresponding very nearly to our present Notary Public, and held that office until his removal to Dansville the next year, and it was quite likely the last public office he ever held.

Assuming his first civil office in 1807, at the mature age of fifty years, possessed of a naturally vigorous mind, enriched by such varied experiences as very seldom fall to the lot of one individual, a knowledge of affairs drawn from large intercourse with the world, in almost every phase conceivable, rare perceptive faculties, and strict integrity, combined with sound judgment, he brought to the discharge of official duties, a competency of qualifications which eminently fitted him for their intelligent discharge and administration.

NOTE.—He was also for several years Commissioner of Highways of the town of Angelica, and records of surveys of roads by him made, are found in the Angelica Town Clerk's Office, as early as 1805.

CHAPTER XXIII.

It had for years, previous to his removal from Angelica in 1831, been the custom, on public occasions which failed to command the attendance of Major Van Campen, to form in procession in the public square, and keeping step to the inspiring music of fife and drum, with the dear old colors flying, march to his residence nearly a mile distant, pay their respects, and receive his cordial greeting, accompanied with words of cheer, and sometimes of kind advice and encouragement. His presence alone was a benediction.

Horatio Jones, the long ago captive with the Indians, whose strategic maneuvors at the Pigeon Woods, in the spring of 1782, saved Van Campen's life, afterwards for many years the renowned interpreter, possessing and wielding great influence over the Indians, highly respected also by the whites, and better known in his time throughout the whole Genesee river country than any other man, was yet spared to spend the evening of his days at "Sweet Briar," on his extensive farm near Genesee.

These two old patriots had for years been in the habit of each paying the other a visit at least once a year, and these occasions had come to be regarded as important in the calendar of yearly events. They were greatly enjoyed by themselves, and others would somehow time their work or business so as to listen to their legends, hear them recount their exploits, their hair-breadth escapes, their varied experiences with the Indians, and other reminiscenses of the Revolutionary period, and feel that they were richly rewarded for the time thus spent.

These visits were continued, and with more frequency after the Major's removal to Dansville, as the distance between them was made considerably less.

In 1836, Capt. Jones died. It was a hard blow for Van Campen, who felt his loss very keenly. Mr. Sanburn and Capt. Elnathan Perry were still left. His acquaintance with them since the Revolutionary war was not however so intimate as with Capt. Jones, and he was deeply impressed with his loneliness.

In the summer of 1841, the people of Rochester, which place had just merged into city proportions, moved thereto by feelings of patriotism, inspired quite likely by some recent utterances in regard to one of the most cruel episodes of the Revolution, conceived the idea that it would be a very proper thing, indeed *the* proper thing, to remove the remains of Lieut. Boyd and his companion Parker, and their comrades, who were so cruelly slain by the merciless savages when Sulivan's army invaded the Seneca country in 1779, from Livingston County, where they had so long lain, "unwept, unhonored, and unsung," give them appropriate funeral services, and with imposing ceremonies, elaborate eulogy, and labored panegyric, consign them to proper and respectful interment, in a certain elevated section of the then newly opened and beautiful cemetery of Mt. Hope, which should be set apart forever for the interment of soldiers of the Revolution, dignify the sacred place with the name of "Revolutionary Hill," or "Patriot Hill," and mark it with an appropriate monument; and with promises of such a nature, obtained not only the consent, but the approval and co-operation of the people of Livingston County in the enterprise.

Accordingly meetings were held, not only at Rochester and Genesee, but at other places as well, along the beautiful Genesee Valley, for the purpose of preparing to take part in the imposing demonstration with which it was thought best to accompany the patriotic undertaking, and committees were appointed to whom were confided the arrangement of all the details of the funeral pageant.

Gov. Seward accepted an invitation to attend and grace the ceremonies with his presence, and prominent citizens from different parts of the State signified their intention to be present. Promising to be an occasion to be made memorable in the history of the Lower Genesee, not only on account of its nature, but also from the character and position of those who were to participate in the exercises, and appealing as it did to the patriotic element so dominant at the time, great care was taken by the committee having the matter in charge, to make a proper selection of a person to preside at the ceremonies.

With remarkable unanimity the minds of the committeemen met upon one man. All eyes were turned to the venerable patriot, the brave soldier, the eminent civilian, Major Moses Van Campen, then residing at Dansville, N. Y. He was appealed to, and kindly consented to preside at the exercises to be held at Cuylerville, but was in too feeble a condition to think of accompanying the cortege to Rochester.

Judge Hosmer, of Avon, in consideration of his years, prominence as a citizen, and known ability, was selected to deliver the oration at Cuylerville, and accepted the invitation, but about a week before the event, he informed the committee that he could not comply with their wishes.

In this extremity, a promising young man, of conceded ability and good attainments, who has since for many years worn with honor, and shed lustre on the judicial ermine in St. Louis, then principal of the Temple Hill school at Geneseo, and who had at the recent Fourth of July celebration at Geneseo, delivered a very acceptable oration, was appealed to, and at a late hour pressed into service.

On the afternoon of August 19th, a flotilla of five canal boats, upon which embarked as many military companies, invited guests and members of the General Committee of Arrangements, left Rochester, while the Mayor and several members of the Common Council took carriages, all arriving at Mt. Morris early the next morning. After partaking of a bountiful breakfast, prepared by the citizens of Mt. Morris; and a parade of the troops through the principal streets, they returned to Cuylerville, where great crowds had already assembled.

Geneseo was awake. A long procession of carriages was formed. Dirges were played by bands of music. A new brass field piece,* upon which was appropriately

---

*On a visit to Geneseo in September, 1892, Judge Abbott (who

engraved its name, "*Major Moses Van Campen*," was brought out, a salute fired, and the long line moved in solemn procession for the grove at Col. Cuyler's, bearing with them in a beautiful sarcophagus, the remains of the comrades exhumed at Groveland.

Arriving at the mound from whence had been taken the relics of Boyd and Parker, they were placed in an urn, and from thence appropriately surmounted the sarcophagus; and soon was reached the place selected for the exercises.

On the platform, seated beside Major Van Campen, who was then eighty-five years of age, were Capt. Elnathan Perry, aged eighty-one, and Mr. Sanburn, seventy-nine, all three actively engaged in, and the only known survivors at that time of, Sullivan's historic army.

After appropriate religious services, Mr. Treat was introduced, and addressed the assemblage in strains of eloquence eminently fitting to the occasion, and highly creditable to him as a scholar and historian.

After specially addressing the military companies present, he turned to the venerable Van Campen, and thus concluded his remarks. "* * * * Yours has been an eventful life, but you have been kindly spared to receive the grateful tributes of your admiring countrymen, and to witness the unparalleled growth of your country, and the success of her free institutions."

---

by the way is a staunch Democrat) kindly conducted the author to the Park to see the old gun, where it was found on the ground, wrong side up, the carriage in a terribly shattered condition, in fact mostly "broken to pieces." Said the Judge "The Republicans took the old gun out to ratify the renomination of Harrison, loaded it to the muzzle, and touched it off—result—carriage all in pieces, and gun 'tother side up.' The old fellow was indignant and kicked the whole business over, you see!"

Then again turning to the military he said, "Soldiers! One of the few surviving officers, Major Moses Van Campen, our presiding officer, and the old schoolmate and companion in arms of the gallant Boyd, is now standing before you, to perform in behalf of himself and his venerable comrades, and in the name of Livingston County, the sacred duty of committing to you these honored relics.

"Listen to his words, and call to mind his own matchless heroism and virtues,—those of one worthy of this high duty,—the brave soldier and patriot, surrendering to the soldiers of another age, the precious remains of his own patriotic and lion-hearted comrades, that they may receive at the hands of a grateful posterity, the honors which are ever the just due of heroism and virtue."

Impressed with a deep sense of the solemnity of the occasion, in a voice which betrayed the emotions which required an effort to suppress, Major Van Campen, as President of the day, then addressed the vast concourse of people by whom he was surrounded. Said he: "Fellow Citizens,—We no longer hear the war-whoop of the savages. We are no longer alarmed by the martial drum calling us to arms. We no longer hear the roar of canon, nor the din of small arms. We are no longer shocked by the cries of the wounded, nor the groans of the dying. We no longer see the fertile fields of our country stained with the blood of your fathers, and of my companions in arms. But we see the relics of those patriotic youths, who shed their blood for the rights of man, deposited in that sacred urn before you.

"Gentlemen of the Committees! Citizens and soldiers of the counties of Monroe and Livingston! You have conferred upon me the honor of presiding upon this day on this important and interesting occasion.

"I confess I want ability to discharge the duties connected with the deep interest felt on this occasion; yet I feel happy in doing what I can to commemorate the scenes which are this day brought before us. It will not be necessary for me to say much after the interesting address which we have just heard. Yet I must say that I little expected to see the time when the remains of some of my companions in arms, whose blood was shed in the glorious struggle for the liberty and independence of our country, and shed on the soil of Livingston County, and whose patriotic remains for sixty-two years have been mouldering in her dust, should here this day be presented to the view of this great assembly.

"How different do they appear to me now, from what they did sixty-two years ago, when I saw them in the vigor of life, and in the bloom of youth.

"Aye! my noble Boyd! could your immortal spirit witness the scenes of this day, methinks it would rejoice to see your old friend and companion making a surrender of your mortal remains and those of your brave men, who fell a sacrifice to the tomahawk and scalping knife of the savage, surrendering you to the honorable committee and associations from Rochester, who have prepared for you a resting place, till you are called from the slumbering dust by the voice of your God.

"And you, gentlemen, who have taken so honorable a part in the scenes of this day, your names are worthy of a page in the history of our country, for this act of patriotism.

"Gentlemen, I now with these my worthy companions and the only two surviving members present, of the army of Gen. Sullivan, and in the name of the Committee of the County of Livingston, surrender to you these sacred relics for an honorable interment at Mt. Hope, where you will pay to them the highest tribute of respect. Gentlemen, they are yours."

Hon. E. F. Smith, Mayor of the city of Rochester, then appropriately responded, saying among other things, that "he was confident the citizens of Rochester would sacredly discharge the duty of rendering their last resting place in Mt. Hope Cemetery, an appropriate mausoleum for those whose services in the cause of freedom entitled them to honor in death as in life."

The imposing cortege re-embarked and returned to the city of Rochester, where they arrived on the 21st in the morning, when a grand procession being formed, Gov. Seward and many others joining them, they proceeded to Mt. Hope, where with appropriate exercises and patriotic speeches of the Governor and others, the sarcophagus and urn containing the sacred relics, were left on "Revolutionary Hill," and thus ended the most imposing pageant, the really most patriotic demonstration, thus far happening in the history of the young city of Rochester.

CHAPTER XXIV.

As had been well attested in many a bloody fray, Van Campen's conduct during the war of the Revolution was well calculated to inspire terror among the Indians, and yet his relations with them in subsequent years were generally of a pleasant nature.

Up to the time of his removal to Dansville (1831), and for some time after, even, the Indians from the Caneadea, Tonawanda, and Buffalo Reservations, used frequently to visit him. Some of these visits, no doubt, were prompted by mere curiosity to see the man; some to renew old acquaintanceship, some to barter baskets, needlework, ladles, etc., for articles which they wanted, and had good reason to suppose he might have, and it is known that some came to him for advice and counsel in matters of importance.

John Mohawk, then an aged chief, formerly a warrior of renown, was still living on the Caneadea Reservation, about twenty miles below Angelica. (This must have been along in the twenties.) His famous encounter with Van Campen was known "far and wide," and he had frequent occasion to exhibit the scar which he bore, as a sort of *souvenir* of that interesting event.

Meeting Capt. Horatio Jones one day, (it is hardly known where, though his son Charles Jones thinks it must have been at "Sweet Briar," Jones' home, near Geneseo;

the fact is Capt. Jones was in those days quite a ubiquitous character; he was here, he was there, he was everywhere, and anywhere, and all pretty much at the same time, and more extensively known than any other man in the Genesee country,) Jones told him he ought to go and see Van Campen. Mohawk said, " Van Campen would not want to see me." Jones said, " Van Campen is a warrior. It is peace now;—he will be glad to see you."

Mohawk finally yielded to his persuasions, and soon after went to see him. Some one accompanied him to Van Campen's house. The Major was sick and confined to his room and bed. It was warm weather, and just at dusk. Their errand was made known. A daughter of Van Campen, who answered the call, went and told her father there was an Indian there, whom she thought, from his appearance, was John Mohawk, who wanted to see him. Said the Major, " Tell him to come in." Said she, " Are you not afraid ?" He said, " No, tell him to come in." Mohawk then came in. Van Campen then said, "Are you John Mohawk ?" Mohawk said, " Yes." Then Van Campen said, " Come here." The Indian came up to the bed. Van Campen placed his hand on his neck, and running it down under the clothing, very plainly felt the scar made by the hatchet, and said, " Yes, you *are* John Mohawk, *that's my mark.*"

Some time after, Mohawk came to Van Campen's for some corn. Geo. Lockhart, who had recently married one of the Van Campen girls, was present. He knew all about the hatchet affair, but from curiosity to know

Relics of Van Campen, now in Possession of Moses Burr, of Angelica, N. Y. Rifle, Compass, Jacob's Staff, Chain, &c., &c. (See Page 298.)

how Mohawk would take it, upon observing the scar, innocently (?) asked him how he came by it. When Mohawk answered, "Yankee done it, Yankee done it. Peace now!" and said no more about it.

Mr. N. A. Pettee, of Wiscoy, New York, says his father, the late Ebenezer Pettee, of Pike, N. Y., used frequently to tell of witnessing a meeting between Van Campen and Mohawk, which occurred at a public house, at Cold Creek (Hume), very likely the one kept by the late "Uncle Chauncey G. Ingham," when they talked over "war times." The famous encounter was gone over with, when Mohawk asked Van Campen to drink with him, remarking, "*White man too much for Indian that time!*"

The good feeling existing between Mohawk and Van Campen, during those later years, was feelingly attested by Mohawk's carving a very fine ladle and giving it to a daughter of Van Campen, Mrs. George Lockhart, as a pledge or token of friendship.

This ladle was for many years used in the dairy operations of the Lockhart family, and is now carefully preserved by a daughter, Miss Mary Lockhart, of Almond, N. Y., though the real custodian of this interesting old relic at this writing, is Hon. Wm. P. Letchworth, who is deeply interested in everything pertaining to Mohawk and Van Campen.*

---

*John Mohawk, *alias* "Old Wayne Washington," by which name many of the early settlers in this vicinity knew him, was buried on what came afterward to be known as Lot Twenty-six, of Joseph Jones' subdivision of the Caneadea Indian Reservation, (Town of Hume, Allegany Co., N. Y.,) a few rods to the rear of the present farm house of Delos Benjamin, Esq. He must have died late in the twenties.

Moses Burr, of Angelica, N. Y., a grandson of Van Campen, still has the favorite rifle of the Major, a beautlful piece of workmanship, made to order, and elaborately embellished with silver—and it is said, a remarkable good shooter in its day, in the hands of its owner—his compass, Jacob-staff, chain, drafting instruments and various other things he left, most of which are shown in the picture, " Relics of Van Campen."

Hon. Wm. P. Letchworth, at his beautiful country seat, Glen Iris (Genesee Falls), last summer showed the author an old traveling trunk, which Major Van Campen once, and probably for long years, owned and used. Compared with some of our modern "Saratogas," it is of quite diminutive proportions. Its material is leather, over a steel or iron frame, lined with bed ticking, and it is now quite badly " demoralized."

On the inside is still to be seen the business card, or advertisement of the house from which it was obtained, which reads:

"McKenzie,
Corner Broadway and Wall St.,
Traveling Trunks of Every Description."

And on the outside is an oval brass plate upon which is neatly engraved the name,

Moses Van Campen.

CHAPTER XXV.

After removing to Dansville (1831), Major Van Campen did some work in the line of surveying, and continued to be quite active for some years. He lived on Ossian St., in a house which is still standing, but has been removed to Seward St., and is now owned by Miss Anna Adams. The place on Ossian St. is now occupied by a furniture establishment.

In a recent interview with Mrs. Dr. Branch, a daughter of the late Gen. Mills, of Mt. Morris, she informed me that he used frequently, while living in Dansville, to visit her father, and they would return the visits. She was quite young at the time, and her recollections of the Major are remarkably distinct. She speaks especially of his methodical habits. At precisely eight o'clock every evening he would wind up the clock, then read a portion of Scripture and have family worship, after which anyone was at liberty to retire or remain up longer for reading or conversation, as they might elect.

He was of a cheerful nature, somewhat of a humorist, enjoyed greatly the jokes, anecdotes and stories of others, and could, as occasion seemed to require, contribute his full share toward making pleasant a social gathering. Many came, some from long distances, to gaze upon his features and listen to his conversation, which, for their gratification, was largely made up of stories, anecdotes, incidents and reminescences of Revolutionary days. He could accommodate himself to any society, whether learned or illiterate; was equally at home in the drawing-room of the rich, or the humble cabin of the "settler," and his character and attainments were such as to command universal respect, and even admiration.

In February, 1845, he was stricken with paralysis—a severe shock—and during the next month his wife died. Afflicted in body and bereaved in spirit, his fourth daughter, Mrs. Hubbard, then a widow, came and kept his house, affectionately caring for him, ministering to his necessities, and relieving, as much as possible, his distress. Faithfully attended to, he made partial recovery, became so much improved in 1847 that he enjoyed a reasonable degree of health for one of his years, in fact, his body was so much restored and faculties so recovered as to enable him, in the exuberancy of his spirits, and with a kind of old man's pride, to execute those examples of computation of areas, of which is so neatly given a reduced *fac simile*, in such a style and manner as would do credit to a much younger man.

In May, 1848, he removed to Almond, and took up his abode with Joseph Lockhart, a son of his daughter Mary, Mrs. Geo. Lockhart. As the debility of age and increasing infirmities became more and more apparent, he frequently expressed a desire to get back to the "old place" to die.*

---

*The "old place" had many years before been sold on a judgment obtained against him on paper he had endorsed, and obligations he had incurred for others, and the well earned accumulation of years of hard labor was thus swept away. His son-in-law, Alvin Burr, was the purchaser, and so for a long time it was kept in the family.

This wish was gratified, as in June, 1849, he made his last remove, this time, indeed, to the "old place," to live with his daughter Anna, wife of Alvin Burr, who now owned it. He was feeble, his constitution broken, his body suffering with pain, so distressing at times as to throw dark shadows over his naturally cheerful spirits.

Slowly moving around as best he could on crutches, he passed the remainder of his days mostly indoors, and when October came, with "meadows brown and sere," when the rich autumnal tints fell upon the forest foliage, giving hint that the season was ended and the harvest had come, it became painfully apparent that his end was near, that this golden sheaf was soon to be garnered in.

So, slowly the candle of life burned down in its socket. The tongue lost its cunning, the eye its luster, the faintly flickering light went out on the 15th inst., and his spirit departed to be forever at rest with his Maker.

Previous to his death he had expressed a wish that the Rev. Thomas Aitken, of Sparta, might preach his funeral sermon. A messenger was dispatched for his friend, and he came.

After the burial, which was on Sunday, the 17th, the services were conducted in the Presbyterian church. "I have fought a good fight," was the text used as the foundation of an able discourse, which was listened to by a large concourse of people, notwithstanding the weather, which was very rainy.

In the beautiful village cemetery at Angelica, not far back from the street, and at a distance of only about twenty feet from where now repose the remains of his lifelong friend and early patron, Judge Philip Church, can be seen a plain marble slab, bearing this inscription:

IN MEMORY OF
MOSES VAN CAMPEN,
A BRAVE OFFICER OF THE REVOLUTIONARY WAR,
AN EMINENT CITIZEN AND AN ENLIGHTENED CHRISTIAN.
DIED OCTOBER 15, 1849,
AGED 92 YEARS AND 9 MONTHS.

"The notes of war are hushed,
   The rage of battle o'er,
The warrior is at rest,
   He hears our praise no more."

"The soldier nobly fought
   For all we dearly love,
He fought to gain a heavenly crown,
   And now he reigns above."

In religious faith and convictions Major Van Campen was a devoted Presbyterian. He was one of the six who united in organizing the Presbyterian church at Angelica, in 1812, and was the first, and for many years the only, ruling elder.

In the language of his obituary, written by Rev. Mr. Aitken, who also prepared the inscription for his tombstone, "His Christianity was pure, his views of religion sound and scriptural, and his fidelity and integrity of character were like his own well aimed rifle, true to the mark."

APPENDIX.

NOTE A.

Pearce, in his "Annals of Luzerne County," speaking of this transaction, as related by Rogers, a boy at that time, and taken prisoner with the others, says (using Rogers' language), "Pike proposed to kill the Indians. The prisoners were all pinioned but myself, and it was agreed that I should procure a knife, which I did. Pike cut himself loose, and while the Indians were sleeping he took away their guns, and then cut the other men loose. One Indian awakened and immediately Pence fired at him. Major Van Campen took a hatchet and killed two Indians before they arose; the rest ran. The prisoners all escaped and arrived safely at Wilkesbarre."

"Jonah Rogers was thirteen years of age, and was known as a person of truth. His statement conflicts materially with that of Van Campen, who says the Indians were killed chiefly by his own hand, and that Pike was an arrant coward. We have also found Van Campen's stories of other matters to be erroneous, and we are disposed to receive the account of Rogers as unqualifiedly true."

Col. John G. Freeze in his "History of Columbia County" says:

"Mr. Pearce says that Capt. Walker erected Fort Jenkins, and charges that Van Campen claims that honor.

Certainly no such claim is made in the "Life of Van Campen," and I cannot account for this inadvertance.

"Mr. Pearce asserts that Fort Muncey was built by Capt. Walker. It was so built in 1778, under Col. Hartley, but it was also as certainly abandoned, and substantially destroyed, and remained so in December, 1779. Major Van Campen says that "in March, 1782, at the head of Capt. Robison's company, he was ordered to march to a place called Muncey, and there rebuild a fort, which had been destroyed by the Indians in the year 1779."

"I see no reason to question Major Van Campen's veracity in this matter. He was certainly with Capt. Robison in June, 1781, and in September, 1781; and in April, 1782, Col. Hunter writes to Vice President Potter that Capt. Robison is then at Muncey, and is repairing the fort. Besides Van Campen's narrative was written and published at a time when, if false, it could and would have been contradicted by many living witnesses.

"I am furnished the following letter by a gentleman who shows himself competent to speak on the subject: "You are no doubt aware that certain sapient historians have endeavored to make Abraham Pike the hero of the killing of the Indian captors, instead of the hated and despised Pennamite, Van Campen. Abraham Pike was a rather worthless fellow, doing but little good for himself and still less for others; wandering around from house to house, retailing his Munchausen tales, thereby securing his whisky, bread, and a warm place by the fire, on the strength of his wonderful exploits as related by himself. I have heard of an incident related of him, for

REDUCED FAC-SIMILE OF TABLES OF COMPUTATION OF AREAS, MADE BY MOSES VAN CAMPEN, IN THE 91ST YEAR OF HIS AGE.

Courses	Dist	A	S	E	N	M. D	Ch. a	S c
East	57.06			57.06		57.00 / 114.00		
N 23 E	4.67	4.11		1.74		115.74 / 117.48	475.69.14	
N 66°30′ E	5.00	1.99		4.59		122.07 / 126.66	2.62.51.93	
North	4.06	4.06				126.66	506.66.00	
N 50°26′ W	6.44	2.82			3.42	123.84 / 119.91	347.53.68	
N 2°15′ E	2.68	2.68		0.09		119.91 / 126.00	249.41.28	
West	66.00				66.00	60.00 / 00.00		
South	15.00							
		15.00	15.00	63.42	63.42	/.3 18.2.2.2 0.13		

Area 91 11/100

The above Table is the Calculation of a Lot of Land Surveyed for John Bennit May 11th 1803 Church Tract Allegany County Surveyed by (See page 5)   Moses VanCampen
Dansville March 1st 1847

Courses	Dist	A	S	E	N	M. D	Ch. Area	S area
West	48.00				48.00	48.00 / 96.00		
North	19.00	12.00				96.00	1152.00.00	
East	36.50			36.50		59.50 / 23.50		
S 46° E	16.68		12.00	11.50		2.00		138.00.00
		12.00	12.00	48.00			1152.00.00	
							138.00.00	

Area 50 70/100

/.3 1014.00.60 / 597 0 0/100

The above Table is the Calculation of a Lot of Land Surveyed for Saomme Ashley November 1st 1803 Church Tract Allegany County
See page 106 Surveyed by   Moses VanCampen
Dansville July 2d 1847

which at this distant day I cannot vouch. He had procured the services of some one of the many historians of the Wyoming Valley to write his "Memoirs;" the ready writer proceeded until he came to a case of sheep stealing in which Pike had been engaged. The writer, as an honest man, insisted on inserting the transaction, while Pike swore roundly that it should not be put down, which cut the "Memoirs" of this wonderful man short, and deprived the world at large of a full knowledge of his heroic deeds.

"My father was well acquainted with the boy Rogers, who Van Campen relates was captured from the Wyoming settlements, and was present at the killing of the Indians. He told the same story that Van Campen did, and, furthermore, said he did not contradict Pike, unless specially appealed to, as the poor old fellow's whisky and living depended in a great measure upon his self-glorification. Pike died as he lived, a pauper. The absurdity of Pike's claim to killing the Indians, in ordinary times would have been hooted at, but at that time the passions of Yankee and Pennamite ran so high, that almost any tale reflecting to the discredit of the Pennamite, was received without question." (By those, of course, of Yankee proclivities or antecedents. ED.) THE AUTHOR.

In a recent letter from an eminent historian who has spent much time in investigating this interesting matter, as well as occurrences and incidents bearing more or less directly upon it, he says :

"Regarding the Pike story, I have not a shade of doubt that Van Campen told the truth. Horatio Jones often confirmed the story. Stone's Life of Brant reports the main facts. The Pennsylvania Historical Collections confirm it in a dozen ways. * * * Pence was one of the noted historical characters of the Pennsylvania border, a fearless, reckless, backwoodsman, a fit comrade for Van Campen in such a frightful enterprise, while Pike passes out of history with the ending of his existence.

"If Van Campen's story was false, why should the Indians place a price on *his* head and utterly ignore Pike? for in all references to the affair in that day, Van Campen was regarded as the leader of the party. There is every probability that Van Campen spoke truly regarding Pike."

The meetings of Van Campen and Mohawk, as well as the interesting episode attending the meeting of Chief Shongo with Van Campen, elsewhere related, and which was witnessed by quite a number of reputable men, give the best of reasons for crediting Van Campen's story.

It has always been claimed that "Mohawk was the Indian to whom Van Campen lent his hatchet," and it is the editor's opinion, that he in some way got away with the hatchet, and that it was in fact his, having been stolen away the same as the guns were. Mr. Hubbard's text does not state that Van Campen found it. Carefully read Mr. Harris' note, found in its proper place.

ED.

JUDGE PHILIP CHURCH
AT 81.

[Half Tone from Miniature by Fagnani.]

SKETCH OF JUDGE PHILIP CHURCH.

CHAPTER I.

Philip Church was born in Boston, April 14, 1778. His mother was Angelica, the eldest daughter of Gen. Philip Schuyler; his father, John Barker Church, an English gentleman of considerable means, and liberal education. Mr. Church, entertaining a profound sympathy for the people of the colonies, resolved to espouse their cause, and made his way to America.

Under the assumed name of Carter,* he was Commis-

---

*This change of name has always to the author, and presumably to others, been enshrouded in mystery. Two different versions of the cause or reason for assuming this *alias* are given by his descendants, in substance that although his sympathies for the colonists were ardent from the outset, it is now by his descendants considered reasonably well settled, that the immediate cause of his leaving England at the particular time he did, was that " he had fought a duel with a man of rank, and supposing he had killed him he fled to this country to avoid the consequences, assuming the name of John Carter. * * * Some time during the war of the Revolution he met an old friend from England, who informed him that his supposed victim was not dead, and he then assumed, or rather resumed, his right name." Others think another explanation more entitled to credit, which is this: John Barker, who married his father's sister, was a very prominent merchant, and noted for his kindness to the poor. He was a man of large wealth, and John Barker Church was named after him, and would, if he had remained in England and adhered to the crown, have inherited it, as his uncle had no children, and was disposed to bequeath it to him. John Barker Church had, however, expressed his opinion as to the on-coming struggle with the American colonies

sary to the French army during the Revolution, aud under this *nom de guerre*, he made the acquaintance of many of the officers of the American army, prominent among whom were Alexander Hamilton and Philip Schuyler. With the Schuyler family he became socially intimate, and with Angelica, the eldest daughter, he was deeply impressed, and a friendship resulted, which, in becoming time, ripened into love, and the twain were made one on the 23d of July, 1777.

It is supposed that "John B. Church must have brought quite a handsome sum into this country, which was largely increased by his business partnership with Col. Jeremiah Wadsworth, of Hartford, Conn., they having charge of the subsistence of the French army."

His duties made it necessary for him to be in Boston, New York, Philadelphia, Albany, and other places. To show the esteem in which his amiable wife was held by those whose sympathies were with the crown, in other words, "Loyalists," and their estimation also of him, the following quotation from a book entitled, "Men and Manners in America, One Hundred Years Ago," edited by H. E. Scudder, is introduced. The article from

---

too emphatically to retract it, nor did he desire to, so coming to America where he could have opportunity to express his sympathies in a practical way, he assumed the name John Carter, thinking that perhaps his uncle, who was very much displeased with his political utterances, might not discover it, and he thereby might still inherit the fortune. His uncle, however, found it out, and directly bestowed his wealth in other ways, cutting him off entirely. The nephew becoming apprised of this, immediately resumed his own name, by which he was ever afterward known. While these two versions of this matter may not effectually clear up whatever of mystery there may be connected with it, it is thought best after maturely considering the matter to introduce them.

which this quotation is made, was written by the Baroness Riedesel, and the reader should keep in mind the excited state of feeling which then existed, which should go far toward excusing extravagant expressions.

Says the Baroness: "Curiosity and desire urged me to pay a visit to Madame Carter, the daughter of Gen. Schuyler, and I dined at her house several times. The city throughout is pretty, but inhabited by violent patriots, and full of wicked people. The women, especially, were so shameless that they regarded me with repugnance, and even spit at me when I passed by them. Madame Carter was as gentle and good as her parents, but her husband was wicked and treacherous. She came often to visit us, and also dined at our house with the other generals. We sought to show them by every means our gratitude. They seemed, also, to have much friendship for us, and yet, at the same time, this miserable Carter, when the English general Howe, had burned many hamlets and small towns, made the horrible proposition to the Americans, to chop off the heads of our generals, salt them down in small barrels, and send over to the English, one of these barrels for every hamlet or little town burned down; but this barbarous suggestion fortunately was not adopted."

Philip, while yet an infant, was present during a visit of his mother at her father's, when the memorable attempt was made by John Waltemeyer, a tory refugee, at the head of a party of tories, Canadians, and Indians, to capture Gen. Schuyler, and remove the powerful influence he was exerting against the success of the banded tories and Indians.

Gen. Schuyler, looking out of a window, saw that his house was surrounded by armed men. Immediately posting himself with his servants at the foot of the stairs with the best weapons they could lay their hands on, he resolved at least to protect the family.

The banditti soon forced an entrance into the house. At this juncture Margaret Schuyler (afterwards the wife of Gen. Stephen Van Rensselaer), discovered that her sister's infant had been left asleep in the cradle upon the ground floor. Rushing down stairs and passing her father against his remonstrances, she seized the child, and was passing the besiegers, when John Waltemeyer, mistaking her for a servant maid, demanded of her "*Wench, where is your master?*" "Gone to call the guard," she replied, with remarkable presence of mind, and made a safe retreat with the child, not however, without receiving some disagreeable attention from an Indian, who hurled his tomahawk at them, which fortunately did no further harm than to tear Miss Schuyler's dress, slightly graze the infant's forehead, and finally spend its futile force in making a cut in the stair casing or railing. Judge Church, in later life, used to exhibit the scar, and the mark of the tomahawk on the casing, for ought the author knows, may be seen today; it could at least only a few years ago.

The rare presence of mind exhibited by the daughter, was only equalled by the ruse resorted to by the father, who suddenly raising a window, as if a host had come to his rescue, called out at the top of his voice, which no friends were there to hear: "My friends, my friends, quickly surround the house, and let not one of the rascals escape!" The banditti were panic striken, ran down stairs, sweeping the silver from the sideboard as they passed out, hurrying off with them in their retreat to the woods as captives, two slaves,—the first armed rescue perhaps of "persons held to service," that ever occurred in this State.

Soon after the close of the Revolution, John B. Church and his partner, Col. Wadsworth, went to Paris, where they remained for about eighteen months, a good share of the time being devoted to settling up matters pertaining to the Commissary business.

Mr. Church's family accompanied him, and while residing in Paris, the celebrated American artist, Col. Trumball, was employed to paint a portrait of the boy Philip, which picture has always been regarded by the family as a treasure of inestimable value.

In Paris Mr. Church renewed his old time close relations with La Fayette, and made the acquaintance of Tallyrand and many other eminent statesmen of France.

Leaving Paris, he took up his residence in London, and at "Down Place," his country residence, on the Thames, about four miles from Windsor Castle. The house of Mr. Church in London was the frequent resort of Fox and Pitt; of prominent Americans who visited that city; and, on the breaking out of the French Revolution, when the refugees fled to London, he had as guests, Tallyrand and many of his companions, with most of whom he had become acquainted in America and Paris.*

---

*The family coat of arms impressed in wax lies before the author, who confesses to not being familiar with heraldic emblems and devices, and therefore is unable to decipher or explain the peculiar significance of the three open hands (sinister) shown

On his return to England, John B. Church, having been a decided partisan in the Revolution, and moreover having connected himself by marriage with so notorious a "rebel" family as the Schuylers, found himself not in good repute with the high tory party, and had especially the disfavor of his patron uncle. Fortunately, however, the American adventurer was as independent in his purse as in his politics, and soon grew in favor with Fox and Pitt and their party. He was elected a member of the British Parliament from Wendover, warmly espoused the liberal party, and adhered to Mr. Fox, when it was said in derision that "his party could go to the House of Commons in a hackney coach."

Mr. Church's family physician was the physician of George the Third, and long before it transpired publicly, the physician informed Mr. and Mrs. Church of the king's abberration of mind, and did not hesitate, confidentially, to attribute the development of hereditary tendency, to the loss of the American Colonies.

As is well known, Robert Morris, the "financier of the Revolution," soon after the termination of the war for independence, engaged largely in land speculations, and soon became the largest individual land holder in the States; and as sometimes occurs, he did not realize so rapidly, nor so much, as he anticipated from his investments.

This, together with his liberal advances to support

---

on the upper part of the shield; but the mailed arm, the hand grasping a truncheon of command, would certainly imply, to a novice at least, the idea of a good degree of importance, and assign to the family a position of prominence, and commanding influence or power.

the Continental army, which were not promptly restored, caused him serious embarrassment, and he was compelled to borrow money from different individuals, giving for security mortgages on his property. John B. Church loaned him a considerable sum of money, taking security in the name of Alexander Hamilton, a brother-in-law, as trustee, on property in the city of Philadelphia, being the square between 8th and 9th Sts. and Chestnut and Sansom Sts., on a part of which square the Continental Hotel now stands.

Some time in the latter part of 1795, or early in 1796, Mr. Morris having determined to erect a palatial residence on ground encumbered by this mortgage, proposed to Gen. Hamilton, to change the security to 100,000 acres of his land in the Genesee Country. Gen. H. wrote to John B. Church, who was then in London, stating the proposition, and advising him to accede to his request, stating that he thought the security good, and if not good, Mr. Morris' bond was good for the amount.

In accordance with this advice, the mortgage on the Philadelphia property was discharged and another executed, bearing date May 31st, 1796, for the sum of $81,679.44, which amount was quite likely inclusive of some interest, taken on the 100,000 acres. Mr. Church still being an alien, this was also given, running to Gen. Hamilton. (More of this mortgage further on.)

At the proper age Philip was sent to Eton, where he pursued his studies for six consecutive years. It is a proverbial saying that "Harrow makes Scholars, Westminster, Blackguards, and Eton, Gentlemen," and Mr. Church was no exception to the truth last mentioned.

All his manners proclaimed the dignified and polished gentleman, and in this respect he was a worthy representative of that justly celebrated school, one of the glorious institutions of Old England.

At Eton he formed intimacies with many who became eminent in English history. During vacations he returned to his father's house in London, and there met many prominent statesmen of the day. On one occasion he met the Prince of Wales, afterward George IV. The Prince was always friendly, but George III could never forget the part his father had taken during the Revolution, and as the King rode by "Down Place," he would sneeringly point to it as the residence of the "American Commissary."

Philip, as the eldest son of a member, was entitled to the privilege of attending the Parliamentary debates, and often listened to Sheridan, and that wonderful trio of illustrious English statesmen, Pitt, Fox, and Burke, the most brilliant galaxy of orators that ever convened at any one period in the world's history, and though quite young at the time, he ever remembered the tinsel of Sheridan's eloquence, the impetuosity of Fox, and the grandeur of Burke.

The latter he seldom mentioned without speaking of the empty benches when the great orator was delivering his stately sentences to the business-like House of Commons, and usually concluded by quoting Goldsmith's well-known lines:

> "Here lies our good Edmund, whose genius was such
> We scarcely can praise it, or blame it too much;
> Who for the universe narrowed his mind,
> And to party gave up what was meant for mankind.

SKETCH OF JUDGE PHILIP CHURCH. 315

> Who too deep for his hearers still went on refining,
> And thought of convincing while they thought of dining;
> Though equal to all things, for all things unfit,
> Too nice for a statesman, too proud for a wit;
> In short, 'twas his fate, unemployed or in place, sir,
> To eat mutton cold, and cut blocks with a razor."

In 1797 John Barker Church removed with his family from England, and resumed his residence in New York. At that time, he was considered as one of the richest men in the country. Philip accompanied the family, resumed his law studies* in the office of Nathaniel Pendleton, Esq., and was admitted to the Bar, receiving his license from Morgan Lewis, Justice of the Supreme Court, dated July 14, 1804.

During his law studies, in 1801, he acted as second to Philip Hamilton in his duel with E. Eckhard, in which young Hamilton fell mortally wounded on the same ground where his father subsequently met his melancholy fate.

Previous to his admission to the Bar, the prospect of serious difficulty with France made necessary the organization of the provisional army, under the administration of John Adams. Washington was appointed Commander-in-Chief, and on the 28th day of July, 1798, Alexander Hamilton was appointed Major General and Inspector General of the army.

On the very day of his appointment, Hamilton addressed the following to James McHenry, the then Secretary of War:

---

*After leaving Eton, Philip entered the Middle Temple and commenced the study of law.

"January 25th, 1798.

"Allow me to remind you of my nephew, Philip Church, whom I warmly recommend for a Captaincy in the infantry. He is the eldest son of his father, has a good education, is a young man of sense, of genuine spirit and worth, and of considerable expectations in point of fortune. I shall esteem his appointment to this grade a personal favor, while I believe it will consist with every rule of propriety. A. HAMILTON."

Washington at first declined to approve the appointment, owing to his youth, but afterwards, in deference to the wishes of Gens. Schuyler and Hamilton, and being favorably impressed by the efficiency and promptitude of young Church, who had been frequently employed as a medium of communication between himself and Gen. Hamilton, he gave his approbation, and the appointment was made.

Immediately thereafter he received from Hamilton the appointment as his Aide-de-camp, as appears by the following commission, the original still in possession of Major Church :

"To Philip Church, Esq., Captain in the regiment of Infantry, whereof William Smith, Esq., is Lieut. Colonel Commanding :

"In virtue of the privilege and authority to me given by law, I do hereby appoint you to be my Aide-de-camp, to have and to hold all the compensations, rights and authorities to the said office annexed or appertaining, so long as you shall continue therein, and I do hereby require all persons to whom it may concern, to obey and respect you accordingly. Given under my hand at the

City of New York, the 12th day of January, in the year of our Lord 1799. ALEXANDER. HAMILTON."

To show the progress that Mr. Church was making in the esteem of Washington, while the application for the appointment to the Captaincy was pending, the following copy of a letter is introduced. It is copied direct from the original in the hand writing of Washington, which has been carefully preserved. Mr. Church had just delivered despatches to Washington, and the enclosures referred to were letters addressed to Mr. Church's father and grandfather, Gen. Schuyler:

"Sir: I beg leave to commit the enclosed letters to your care. If business, duty, or inclination, should ever call you into the State of Virginia, I shall be very happy to see you at Mt. Vernon, the place of my retreat. Being with esteem, sir,

Your most o'bt. and h'ble servant,
GO. WASHINGTON.
Philadelphia, 4th December, 1798."

Precisely one year and ten days after the date of the foregoing, viz., Dec. 14th, 1799, the immortal spirit of Washington passed from the stirring scenes of earth to his glorious reward. Capt. Church (as it is now proper to call him), as Chief of the Staff, accompanied Hamilton to Philadelphia to take part in the solemn obsequies, and to pay the last tribute of respect to the great departed.*

---

*Capt. Church also acted as Hamilton's private secretary, and held the situation through the year 1800. He remembered having filed away during this period, among the papers of Gen. Hamilton, the original of the Farewell Address of Washington.

CHAPTER II.

In 1799, Capt. Church visited Canandaigua to attend the sale under foreclosure of the 100,000 acres, previously spoken of, Mr. Morris having become unable to pay off the mortgage. He bid in the property and took a deed in his own name, dated May 6th, 1800. The property, however, was really purchased on joint account with his father, who offered him a half interest if he would assume the management, and conduct the subdivision and sales of the tract.

Capt. Church having enlisted in this land enterprise, and public attention being attracted to it, he at once became very much interested in it. Absorbing his attention almost entirely to the exclusion of other pursuits, he soon abandoned a brief practice of his profession, in order to give personal attention to bringing it into market, conducting the sales and business generally.

So in 1801, he left the city on an exploring expedition, stopping for a day or two at Geneva for the purpose of obtaining the necessary camp equipage and provisions, and plunged into the wilderness which then, almost unbroken, covered all of Western New York. By previous arrangement he had engaged the services of Major Moses Van Campen as surveyor, and John Gibson, John Lewis, and Stephen Price. They all met by appointment at Almond, which was the settlement nearest the tract.

This point was eighteen miles distant from the property, and had not as yet been dignified with a name.

The company at once applied themselves to the business in hand. Proceeding along the route which was designated partly by the course of an Indian trail, and part of the way by blazed trees, with now and then a log removed to admit the passage of a pack-horse,— they made their advent upon the tract at a point about one-half a mile north of the present village of Wellsville, substantially at the south-east corner, and pursued a route from Almond, nearly identical with the subsequent location of the Erie Railroad. They at once commenced an active and thorough exploration of the entire tract.

They encountered fatigue, hunger, hardships and privations. This opened a new and startling chapter of adventures to Capt. Church. And indeed it was a great transformation, from the City of New York to this primeval forest, peopled with bears, deer, wolves, and other wild animals, and certainly called into requisition courage, energy and endurance of a high order to execute the undertaking, and in after life he frequently related an exciting incident which occured, and with which he was strongly impressed.

Capt. Church had cut his foot, and was confined to the camp. The rest of the party had been out all day, and in making their way back became bewildered. He heard their shouts afar off. They were evidently going in the wrong direction. He endeavored to get their attention. He called into service a good pair of lungs, and shouted at the top of his voice, but all to no purpose ; they heard him not, and finally their shoutings died away in the distance, and as the sombre shades of evening came spreading over the grand old woods, with strangely impressive stillness, he described the sensation of loneliness as almost intolerable. The night at length wore away, and with the arrival of morning the lost party returned.

The reconnoissance was soon after completed, not however until their stock of provisions was well nigh exhausted.

This exploration afterward proved of great value to Major Van Campen in the subdivision of the tract, which he made a few years later. Nothing daunted by these rough experiences, Capt. Church determined to visit Niagara before his return. So selecting Van Campen to accompany him, the two started on their journey, pursuing an Indian trail westward, their companions taking an opposite direction for their homes.

Major Van Campen was a remarkably athletic man, with a vigorous constitution and indomitable spirit, distinguished alike for his daring feats in Indian warfare and his skillful forest strategy, and from this time on he became an important co-adjutor to Capt. Church, and continued in his service more or less for the remainder of his active life.

After a tramp of three days through the forest, the last forty-eight hours without food, other than was afforded by primitive woods, they reached the village of New Amsterdam, now Buffalo, with torn garments, nearly shoeless, and almost famished.

They visited the falls and gazed in rapture upon the stupendous cataract, surrounded as it then was by an almost unbroken forest, returned to Buffalo, and after a brief rest resumed their trip by the "White Man's Trail," a road having been opened to Batavia, shoeless and moneyless, but with renewed physical powers and full of youthful vigor, for the village of Bath, about one hundred miles distant.

They passed through Batavia, where the Holland Land Company had just built their office. Here Capt. Church borrowed some money from a Mr. Stoddard, and with replenished finances, well shod and comfortably, if not fashionably clad, they proceeded cheerfully on their way. At Geneseo they visited Mr. Wadsworth, a friend of Capt. Church, and finally reached Bath in safety.

Capt. Church soon after returned to New York, and set himself earnestly at work to commence the settlement of his lands. In 1802 he sent as his agent Evart Van Wickle, to select the site for the village. It was accordingly done, and he named the place Angelica, after his mother.

As one of the means employed in advertising these lands, a map was published showing the relative situation of the tract, in the margin of which appears an announcement, from which the following extracts are made.

"This tract of land contains 100,000 acres, and is situated on the Genesee River, twenty-two miles south of Williamsburgh, one hundred east of Presque Isle, eight north of the Pennsylvania line, and sixteen west of the navigable waters of the Susquehannah. The land is of an excellent quality, and there is every reason to believe, from the purity and abundance of the streams with which it is watered, as well as from the healthiness of the inhabitants in the adjoining settlements, that the country is remakably healthy.

"A town called Angelica is laid out near the center of the tract, with four lots in the middle of it, upon which churches and schools are to be erected; for the building and supporting of which, 200 acres are reserved near the town, and as the settlement advances, 200 acres on the north and 200 acres on the south part of the tract will be appropriated for a like purpose.

The proposed State Road from Catskill to Presque Isle and New Connecticut, is now opened as far as this tract, upon which a settlement was made in October 1802, since when a store has been established near the center of the tract, and a grist and saw-mill erected.

"The lands will be sold at a moderate price on the following terms, which are calculated *particularly* to accommodate *actual settlers.*

Those purchasing 100 acres and under, to pay 1-5 cash, 1-5 in two years without any interest, and the remainder in three equal annual payments, with interest.

" " from 100 to 200 acres, 1-5 cash, and the remainder in four equal annual payments, with interest.

" " from 200 to 300 acres, 1-4 cash, and the remainder in four equal annual payments, with interest,

" " from 300 to 400 acres, 1-3 cash, and the remainder in two equal annual payments, with interest.

"As an assistance to settlers building good houses, boards will be sold to them at a low price for their notes, payable in nine months, and should the proprietor, on visiting the lands, be satisfied with their houses, he will, to those who may wish it, extend the payment of their notes nine months longer."

"For further particulars, apply to the subscriber, residing at Angelica Town, who is the real agent for selling and disposing of the said lands.

EVART VAN WICKLE."

In the same year he made another personal visit to the country, and selected the lands for his farm, and the site of his future residence, on the banks of the beautiful Genesee. In making this selection he exercised sound judgment and a high order of taste. Indeed, were one to make the selection now, with an open cleared up country spread out before him, he could not in any particular improve upon the choice then made.

The 2,000 acres set apart is the finest land in the whole tract, and the situation of the house is incomparably the finest in the whole country. The wonder is that he should so readily have made such a strikingly favorable selection, so encompassed as he was with the interminable woods, when the sight was so circumscribed, and he could only form his judgment from a knowledge obtained from personal explorations.

This place he very properly named Belvidere.

In 1804 he built his temporary residence at Belvidere, called "The White House" by early explorers, from its being the only *painted* structure in western New York.

This building is still standing (1892), and in a tolerably good state of preservation.

During this year Capt. Church received a severe shock, by the arrival of a messenger from Canandaigua, bringing him the intelligence of the meeting between his uncle, Alexander Hamilton, and Col Burr.

He immediately started for New York, not knowing whether the wound would prove fatal or not. He soon, however, learned the melancholy result, and on his arrival home found that the remains were taken to his father's house, and thence carried to their last resting place in Trinity church-yard. His father was appointed one of Hamilton's executors.

Two letters from William Stewart to Capt. Church, the first announcing the meeting and probable fatal effect on Gen. Hamilton, the second penned the following day, communicating the particulars of the "affair" and his death, are still preserved by Major Richard Church. They are directed to "Philip Church, Esq., Angelica, near Bath;" Bath as then being the nearest post-office.

Although slightly foreign to the subject of this sketch, it is thought, in view of its connection, and as an item of historic interest, that the following digression is permissable.

Col. Burr had previously, in the summer of 1799, fought a duel with John B. Church on the same ground where Hamilton fell. At a dinner given by Chancellor Livingston, Mr. Church, after the cloth had been removed, remarked that he had heard that the Holland Land Company had cancelled a bond for $20,000 against Burr for services rendered in the Legislature. This reached the ears of Col. Burr, and he demanded an apology. Mr. Church declined, further than to say that perhaps he had been indiscreet in repeating the accusation without fuller authority. This was not accepted. A challenge was sent, accepted, and they met, exchanging shots without effect, the ball from Mr. Church's pistol striking a button from Col. Burr's coat, and passing through his vest. Col. Burr then received the explanation which Mr. Church had previously made, remarking that "an explanation might be received as satisfactory after shots had been exchanged, that would not have been admissible before."

The pistols used in this duel are now in the possession of Major Church, notwithstanding, every now and then, the public is regaled with an account of the pistols with which they fought, sometimes located in Illinois and sometimes elsewhere, with every detail in particular.

The pistols were the property of John B. Church, and were the same used by himself and Burr, and by Philip Hamilton and Eckhard. They were of London make, the barrels about twelve inches long, hair trigger with flint, set locks, the vents bushed with gold, of fine workmanship, in a fine wood case lined with soft green flannel. From John B. Church they came into the hands of Philip Church, and thence into the hands of Major Richard Church.

On the 4th of February, 1805, Capt. Church was united in marriage with Anna Matilda, eldest daughter of Gen. Walter Stewart, of Philadelphia, and the next June the youthful pair started for the home prepared for them in the wilderness.

The "White House" was ready for their reception, and they reached it by riding from Bath to Belvidere, a distance of forty-four miles, on horse-back, most of the way following a bridle path cut through the woods.

Gen. Stewart was an intimate friend of Washington, and when in Philadelphia, as he frequently was, he was much of the times a guest at Gen. Stewart's. A desk at which Washington was in the habit of writing, while there, is now in possession of Major Church. Another valued treasure, highly prized by Major Church and other members of the family, is a miniature of Washington, accompanied by the following note written by himself.

" Wednesday, 16th March, 1796.

"Not for the representation or the value, but because it is the production of a fair lady, the President takes the liberty of presenting the enclosed, with his best regards, to Mrs. Stewart, praying her acceptance of it."

Capt. Church lived in the "White House" until 1810, when the stone mansion now standing on the banks of the Genesee, was ready for their reception. They were soon established in their new residence, and there spent the remainder of their days.

On the 8th of June, 1807, he was appointed by Gov. Morgan Lewis, First Judge of the Court of Common Pleas for Allegany County, the county having been organized the year before. This office he retained until 1821, and it was the only office he ever held. For the remainder of this sketch he will therefore be spoken of as Judge.

CHAPTER III.

In April, 1811, Judge Church visited England. Arriving in London at a season when most of his old friends and acquaintances were in the country, he, in company with Mr. Russell, the American Minister to the Court of St. James, visited Norfolk. At Yarmouth, a public dinner was tendered him by the old friends of his father. He also visited Mr. Coke, afterwards the Earl of Leicester, at Holkam Hall, and was present at the annual "Sheep Shearing."

Here he met with four or five hundred of the landed gentry from every part of England and Ireland. He used frequently to speak of the pleasure of this visit. He remained two days after the guests had departed, and Mr. Coke rode with him about his beautiful and highly cultivated estate, and explained to him his improved methods of cultivation.

By invitation of the Duke of Bedford, the father of Lord John Russel, he visited Woburn Abbey, the Duke's mansion. This visit also happened at the time of the Duke's annual "Sheep Shearing" and cattle show.

He staid at the Abbey with about twenty noblemen and gentlemen. On the last day of the fair, the Duke reserved a seat for him next to himself at the table, in consideration of his being from America. Sir Philip Francis, the reputed author of the letters of "Junius," addressed a letter to him, containing an invitation to pay him a visit at Tunbridge Wells, where he was going to stay for a few days.

This letter of one of the most distinguished literary men of his age, amusing and characteristic, is carefully preserved by Major Church. It was for many years mislaid and supposed to have been lost.

On his return to London, he had the honor of receiving a kind invitation to visit the distinguished statesman, Lord Grenville. Judge Church was much pleased with his visit and enjoyed, with high relish, the kind hospitalities of his distinguished friend. He was enraptured with the beauty of the country part of England, yet it did not in any degree lessen his love for his own country, as is manifest from the following extract from one of his letters while there : " Although I am delighted with the beauties of England, my visit has a contrary effect from what I expected; it has increased my attachment to Angelica."

Upon one occasion during the Judge's absence, Mrs. Church attended one of the annual festivals of the Indians at Caneadea, contributing to its feast out of her stores, and enjoyed very much their rude sports and pagan rites and dances.

They received her very kindly and were much pleased with her visit, which was also evinced by the fact of their giving her a name, " *Ye-nun-ke-a-wa*," which signified that she was "the first white woman that has come."

The Judge being in England at the breaking out of the war of 1812, a party of Caneadea Indians went to Belvidere, and in gratitude to Mrs. Church for her kindness to their people, offered to place a guard around her house to protect her from the British Indians, but regarding herself as secure from invasion in the woods of Allegany, she thanked them kindly, and declined their proffered gallantry.

Judge Church returned from England in 1813. The following spring he received a letter, which is here introduced for the purpose of showing the interest he took and the deep concern he felt in the improvements then being inaugurated in this new country.

"New York, April 19, 1814.

Sir: I had the honor of presenting, in your name, to the Common Council of this city, at their meeting on the 18th inst., the drawings of the sewers of London, together with the explanatory documents on that subject, which you had the goodness to procure on your late visit to Europe. I am instructed, sir, by the Common Council, to present to you their thanks for your zealous attention to the interests of this city, in procuring these documents, so interesting and important to its future regulations.

I am, sir, with great personal regard,
Your humble servant,
Philip Church, Esq.   J. Morton, C. C. C."

This system was adopted, and for thirty years or more his grandson, Benjamin S. Church, was chief engineer of the Croton Water Works, and was also Chief Engineer of the new aqueduct.

One of the principal objects of his visit to England

was to learn from personal observation the system of English agriculture. He devoted himself to a careful study of the most improved methods of husbandry employed by the most intelligent and enterprising practical agriculturists of that country, and collected a number of works on the subject, which he studied on his return.

It is however questionable whether these studies, owing to the largely differing circumstances of soil and climate of the two countries, contributed very much to his success as a farmer ; yet the country is placed under a lasting debt of gratitude to him for the introduction of a very superior stock of cattle and sheep.

The difficulties encountered in the enterprise of introducing improved stock into what was at that early day an isolated frontier settlement, are forcibly portrayed by the expedient resorted to for the purpose of transporting a Merino buck from Albany.

The services of a wagon maker were engaged and an ingenius arrangement whereby a crate was suspended beneath the Judges gig, or sulky, which of course was of the style peculiar to those days, the most striking feature of which was the extremely large wheels, was adopted, and so the father of future generations of sheep in Allegany was carried thus suspended from Albany to Belvidere.

This buck was purchased of Chancellor Livingston, who imported it from Spain, and the price paid was eighty dollars.

This novel method of transportation of course brought into exercise a good degree of care and patience, and when we consider the condition of the roads at that time, we are constrained to concede that it was quite a formidable, as well as commendable enterprise, and award him the credit he so richly deserves, for the interest he took in such matters so clearly conducive to the comfort, convenience and material prosperity of the people of this country.*

As previously stated, John B. Church married Angelica Schuyler. A distinguishing characteristic of Gen. Schuyler's descendants is the more or less strongly marked family resemblance, which appeared in some members of Judge Church's family. This incident in proof.

In 1824 La Fayette visited this country, and as is well known, his progress through the States was marked by a continuous series of ovations. His visit to Rochester was no exception. Judge Church and some of his family were there, and when a daughter (Angelica, no doubt), was presented, before her name could be spoken, La Fayette exclaimed, "There comes a Schuyler," or "there is Schuyler blood in her veins." So well was he acquainted with the general, and so strong was the family resemblance, though two generations intervened.†

---

*In 1805 Judge Church purchased and drove to Belvidere twenty-four sheep. Arriving late in the evening, they were folded close by the house. In the morning, a brother-in-law from New York being his guest, he invited him out early to see them. To their surprise they found nineteen out of the number lying dead. The wolves had tracked them in and made the havoc. Such were some of the hardships and discouragements attending the introduction of sheep into Allegany.

†In a letter to Judge Church, dated at LaGrange in 1826, La-Fayette thus alludes to this incident: "Happy I am in the opportunity to remind you of the old friend of your beloved parents, to present my respects to Mrs. Church, doubly dear to my most precious recollections, and to your amiable daughter, whom

The greatest advantage derived from Judge Church's visit to England, and which proved to be one of the initial forces which started the wheels of progress and development in Western New York, is found in the light obtained, and the impulse given to his mind by the study of the subject of internal improvements, especially that of the Railroad system, which was just then beginning to attract the attention of speculative and enterprising minds.

By common consent he has been accredited with first conceiving the idea of the Genesee Valley Canal, and afterwards exerted no slight influence in formulating that conception and hastening its completion. It may be proper to remark, however, that it was his opinion freely expressed at the time, that a railroad would better subserve the purpose to be achieved. In this preference he was overruled, but in the light of recent developments the wisdom of his opinion is clearly established.

But the great work to which, for a number of years, over and above all other things, he devoted his time and applied his energies, and where he met and finally overcame the most formidable obstacles, was the New York and Erie Railroad. Few knew how long, and with what heavy odds to contend with, he fought for this project, which he himself had originated, and which he was determined to carry through. Step by step he obtained the necessary appropriations for surveys, and

---

a friendly image engraved on my heart, made me recognize before she was named to me. Your affectionate friend,
La Fayette."

finally the charter, with the requisite powers and restrictions to carry out the stupendous project. Two points he watched with utmost vigilance, one that the route should be confined to the southern tier of counties, and the other that the work should not stop short of, nor be diverted from, the two extremes.

He left in his office, letters, notices, petitions, memorials, papers and memoranda, proving that he was one of the chief and earliest of the originators and advocates of that immense undertaking.

His life was spared to see it completed and witness the marvelous transformation of this vast region of desert solitudes to a wonderful landscape of varied beauty, dotted with cities, villages and hamlets, and teeming with a population of industrious, thrifty and patriotic inhabitants.

Doubtless it was a consoling thought, and a source of pure satisfaction to him, to observe the many and pleasing evidences of the prosperity of his immediate neighborhood, and to reflect that he had done well his whole part in hastening the day-dawn of a prosperity so plainly visible on every hand.

Judge Church was blessed with a vigorous constitution, which he retained in a remarkable degree until he reached more than fourscore years. He was accustomed to athletic sports, excelled in fleetness, and has been known to outrun some of the swiftest of the Indians with whom he had several contests. He was passionately fond of cricket, and, in advanced years, frequently engaged in the game, at which he was quite expert.

He was a good marksman. Major Church relates a

trial of his skill with the rifle, with Major Van Campen. It was on the occasion of a "General Training," when one of them, fastening a little piece of white paper on a tree with a pin, paced off a reasonable distance, and turning, took deliberate aim and fired, driving the pin into the tree, the paper still adhering; handing the gun to the other, he requested him to beat it, which, of course, was impossible. It was, however, taken, loaded and fired, when, upon examination, no new ball hole could be found. It was claimed by some of the bystanders that he did not even hit the tree. He claimed that he did, and it was only settled by chopping into the tree, when it was found that both balls had entered the same hole.

The villa Belvidere was, for many years, the seat of the kindest hospitality, and many distinguished men have visited the place and been royally treated and sumptuously entertained. From its stately southern porch, the beautiful valley of the Genesee could, for a long distance, be seen; only a few rods distant the river bank was gently laved by its waters on their "winding way to the sea," while to the southwest reclined the pleasant valley of Van Campen Creek, gently reposing in the receding distance, the grand old hills on either side of creek and river presented a beautiful background, their summits crowned, as they were, with much of this primitive forest, everything considered made a picture, one of the most beautiful and attractive to be seen in Western New York.

The scene from this historic old porch, when the foliage is colored with autumnal tints, is, indeed, almost entrancing.

The eastern part of this stately mansion was devoted to the purposes of an office, a genuine land office, equipped with desks, drafting tables, and other furniture proper for the business, and has been preserved intact as it was first opened for use in 1810.

It was the writer's privilege to meet Major Church in this old room, one day in the winter of 1891-2. The country was covered with a depth of fifteen inches of snow. A cheerful fire blazed upon the old hearth, as of yore. Over the mantle hung the portrait of the Judge, by the celebrated artist, Fagnani, and those historic pistols before spoken of. The walls were hung with pictures of various kinds, including some illustrating English sports and pastimes, fine sheep and blooded cattle, and the shelves were loaded with venerable old law books, books of surveys, and records of land sales, covered with the accumulating dust of antiquity; and there were letters from Washington, La Fayette, Gen. Greene, the English statesman Fox, and official papers bearing the signature of Jefferson, Hamilton, Adams, and others.

Shades of the dead past seemed to fold him in their loving embrace, and he fancied, as it were, he could see the ghosts, and hear the tread of those bronzed faced, horny handed pioneers, who were wont to come to that old office to get their "articles," see to having their boundaries adjusted, make their payments, and so forth.

Lengthy as this sketch already is, many more interesting facts and incidents might have been recorded relating to his long and varied life. Limited space, however, will prevent further amplification, yet it is hoped that enough has been set forth to challenge the attention, and even the special interest and admiration of our younger people, while to the older ones, who were more nearly cotemporaneous with Judge Church, it will certainly revive the memory of old time associations and events, and cause their minds to revert more frequently to the happenings and incidents connected with the most interesting period of our history.

At the close of 1859, the Judge laid aside as much as possible all business cares and sought ease and comfort, devoting much of his time to reading the general news of the day, in which he was deeply interested.

Books of a religious character also received a good share of his attention.

In the summer of 1860, an attack of disease much enfeebled him, and though confined to his house during the fall and winter, he retained all of his faculties and enjoyed the many comforts of his cheerful and happy home.

His last illness was brief. He dressed himself as usual on Monday morning, but about noon he was suddenly seized with severe pain. His devoted friend and faithful physician, Dr. Charles, of Angelica, who had attended the family for more than thirty years, was hastily summoned. The doctor came at once. His case, however, defied his skill and the efficacy of medicine.

On Tuesday morning his pain was relieved, but he continued to fail until Thursday, when at a little past two, in the most perfect consciousness, he departed this life without a struggle, in the faith and hope of the Christian religion.

On Saturday a public meeting of the citizens of Angelica was held, at which resolutions of respect, briefly setting forth his virtues and expressing their high esteem and sorrow for his loss, were reported and adopted by his fellow townsmen. On Sunday, the 10th of January, 186[1], his funreal was very largely attended at St. Paul's Church, Angelica, and his remains deposited in the village cemetery.

The public journals made honorable and becoming mention of his death, and recounted his public services.

Nine children were born unto Philip Church and Anna Matilda Stewart, and Mrs. Church was almost the ideal mother. Her kindness to the poor was such as to excite comment, and her benevolent deeds are remembered with pleasure by elderly, long resident people of the neighborhood. Her benefactions were many and judiciously bestowed.

The children were Angelica, who married John Warren, now living in New York; John Barker, who married Maria Trumball Silliman, and died in 1875; Sophia Harrison, who married N. P. Hoosack, and died in 1891; Walter Stewart, who died in 1890; Philip, who died in 1874; Mary, who died in 1822; Elizabeth, who married Rev. Robert Horwood, and is now living near London, England, Richard, still living at Belvidere, N. Y.; and Wm. Henry, who died in 1860.